The
CAGE

Must, Should, and *Ought* from *Is*

DAVID WEISSMAN

State University of New York Press

Published by
State University of New York Press, Albany

For information, address State University of New York Press,
194 Washington Avenue, Suite 305, Albany, NY 12210-2384

Production by Marilyn P. Semerad
Marketing by Susan M. Petrie

Library of Congress Cataloging in Publication Data

Weissman, David, 1936–
  The cage : must, should, and ought from is / David Weissman.
    p. cm.
  Includes bibliographical references (p.   ) and index.
  ISBN-13: 978-0-7914-6879-1 (hardcover : alk. paper)
  ISBN-10: 0-7914-6879-8 (hardcover : alk. paper) 1. Normativity (Ethics) I. Title.

BJ1458.3.W45 2006
117—dc22

                                                      2005031414

10 9 8 7 6 5 4 3 2 1

To Kathy, Michael, Sarah, and Eli

Contents

Introduction   1

Chapter One. Categorial Form   9
  1. Evidence of Categorial Form   10
  2. The Method for Discovering Categorial Form   11
  3. Kantian Objections   12
  4. Some Possible Categorial Forms   14
  5. Antecedent Formulations   19
  6. Practical Applications   19
  7. Which Is the Better Hypothesis?   21

Chapter Two. Nature   25
  1. Logic   26
  2. Possible and Actual Worlds   31
  3. The Actual World: Nature   34
     A. Spacetime   35
     B. Causality and Natural Laws   35
     C. Dispositions   41
     D. Systems   50
     E. The Whole   55
  4. Testability   55
  5. Humean Objections   57
  6. Natural Norms   60

Chapter Three. Practical Norms   **61**
  1. How are Systems Formed and Stabilized?   61
  2. Practical Imperatives   63
  3. Ends and Aims   67
  4. Consequential and Instrumental Values versus
    Intrinsic Values   70
  5. From *Is* to *Must, Should,* or *Ought*   72

Chapter Four. Moral Norms   **73**
  1. Semantic Preliminaries   74
  2. The Context of Morality   77
  3. Ontological Assumptions   80
  4. Signature Values   89
  5. Moral Psychology   94
  6. Thick Moral Concepts: The Cognitive and Emotive Aspects
    of Moral Norms   99
  7. Duties to Systems, Their Members, and Others   105
  8. Moral Flashpoints   126
  9. From Facts to Norms   139
  10. Opposed Perspectives: Norms Founded in Material Systems
     or Rational Ideals   150
  11. Norms of Several Kinds   161
  12. Rights   165
  13. Layered Publics   166
  14. Truth and Error   171
  15. *Should* and *Ought* from *Is*   174
  16. Support from Principal Moral Theorists   186
  17. Resolving the Diversity of Moral Theories   190

Chapter Five. Aesthetic Norms   **201**
  1. The Conditions for Aesthetic Value in Created Works   202
  2. Objections   209
  3. Natural Beauty   213
  4. Virtual Form   215
  5. *Must, Should,* and *Ought* in the Context of *Is*   217

Chapter Six. Cultural Variation 221
  1. Generic Needs and Their Determinate Expressions 221
  2. Aristotelian and Nietzschean Problems 226
  3. Change 228

Chapter Seven. Freedom 231
  1. Positive and Negative Freedom 231
  2. Alternative Ontologies 233
  3. Free Will 236
  4. Positive Freedom: Character and Opportunity 240
  5. Pathologies of Freedom 245
  6. Is Freedom Good-in-Itself? 263

Conclusion 265

Notes 269

Index 287

Introduction

Natural order is everywhere apparent. There are kinds, processes, sequences, and cycles. Yet, many thinkers regard nature as a collage, its elements bound by spatial and temporal relations only. *Must*, *should*, and *ought* cannot derive from *is* if this is so, because no thing constrains another if each might be joined to any other. This has material and practical consequences. There should be no roles in systems having corporate identity—no pitchers and catchers, for example—if no team is more than the sum of its members. Ecology cannot be a description of the complementarities and constraints intrinsic to nature, if nature is an array of self-sufficient atoms or events. It follows that environmentalism—respect for nature's alleged constraints—is merely an ideology, one that competes with many others to organize thought and practice. The appropriate response to ecological arguments is, therefore, political, not scientific: oppose this ideology with another, usually one that celebrates our biblical right to Earth and its wealth. But ecology is a hypothesis about the character of systems and their relations, not an ideology. The complementarities and mutual dependencies it describes locate each species within a niche where its freedom is constrained. The system of niches, dependencies, and material norms tolerates gradual change and adjusts to catastrophic change, but it punishes reckless abuse.

The prudence ecologists commend is resisted for practical reasons: poor people want more than subsistence; the rich want comfort. But intellectual vanity is complicit. Philosophers justified our oblivion to natural norms before Western societies were transformed by the industrial revolution. They argued that nature has no intrinsic form: nothing

1

within it does, can, or should resist us. The differentiations and organization we ascribe to things express our ways of thinking about them, not the character and structure of things themselves. Let will and clever thinking transform our circumstances in whatever ways satisfy us.

Each step in the argument having this conclusion seems innocuous, though we see it in retrospect as the slippery slope to an error. Descartes is our point of reference. He sought ideas that exhibit their structure, as the clear and distinct ideas of triangles or circles do. Certain features are essential to such ideas: they are necessary in the respect that changing them introduces contradictions, or content is altered so that the idea of a circle becomes the idea of an ellipse. And equally, there is necessity in the deductive relations of ideas, as theorems derive necessarily from premises or axioms.[1] Necessities of these two sorts—the essential structures of ideas and demonstrative arguments—track necessities that God inscribes in the material world. For he would not mislead us by making necessities essential to ideas and inferences if they were not intrinsic to the affairs about which we think.[2] But why would God be excessive? Why double the effort by making a material world that parallels the domain of thought and its clear and distinct ideas? God could have stopped when he had created thought and thinkers. The coherence of our thinking is guaranteed if we think of the world as structured by necessities; it isn't required, as Malebranche observed,[3] that there be a material world corresponding to our clear and distinct ideas. Berkeley agreed: ideas have no external referent, except for ideas or structures they intimate in God's mind.[4] Hume dispensed with God, arguing that no idea has an extra-mental referent or ground. *Dog* and *cat* signify congeries of sensory data, not extra-mental entities. Modalities that Descartes ascribed to the contents or relations of ideas—necessities ascribed to the essences of geometrical figures or to the relations of causes and effects—were treated in a similar way: they were credited with logical or psychological content, but no reference beyond our thinking; the necessity that causes have effects is merely our expectation that we shall perceive one of two regularly joined impressions when the other is perceived.[5] Kant feared that Hume's psychologized notions of *must* and *ought* imply that experience might turn chaotic or immoral, with only expectation or inclination to hold the place where necessity and obligation once stood. Yet, Kant, too, denied that either necessity or obligation is a feature of nature itself. For we know nothing of things-in-themselves. The only necessity Kant emphasized is the "transcendental"—but still psychological—requirement that mind must apply certain rules when creating a thinkable experience.[6] *Ought*, too, is extracted from actual human relations and displaced to mind: it should will only those maxims that all could will without contradiction.[7] Accordingly, we arrive at the current impasse in philosophic thinking about nature, morals, and aesthetics. *Must, should,* and *ought* are thought's distinctive ways of thinking about material or moral states of affairs. There is no place for them in nature itself.

Philosophers who stress the subjectivity of norms provide for them in either of two ways. One side invokes Hume's dictum: circumstances are value-free; *ought* is not derivable from *is.*[8] Normativity originates in the rules or laws—stipulations—sanctioned by interest or emotion. Responsibility for the other side falls to Kant. Rules for differentiating and organizing sensory data—empirical schemas—give determinate expression to the Categories of understanding (quality, quantity, and relation). Their application synthesizes "objects" of the sort apparent within every thinkable experience (of cats or dogs, for example). Why choose one empirical schema rather than another? Because a particular desire or inclination would be satisfied by the things thereby created.[9] Objects and relationships qualified by *must, should,* and *ought* are the shadows cast by values.

The views of Hume and Kant are, from this perspective, mutually exclusive: facts and values are categorially different (Hume), or there are no facts without the values that motivate their creation (Kant). Yet, this difference disguises principal points of accord. Both Hume and Kant believed that mind is passive to the reception of sensory data and that there is nothing of value in the data received. We emphasize Kant's divergence from Hume, because they disagreed about the accessibility of unschematized sensory data: are we aware of the data before thought differentiates and organizes it? Hume said yes, implying that mind can differentiate neutral data from the values ascribed to it. Kant said no: data cannot be experienced prior to schematization. We perceive what we want or dread. Data presented to awareness exhibit the differentiations and order prescribed by data-organizing schemas. But there are many ways to organize experience. We choose schemas that satisfy our aims or express our fears. This difference doesn't compromise their point of accord: value has its inception when mind attends to the data (whether to inspect or schematize it), selecting and prescribing as interest dictates. Things considered valuable—ships, stamps, or shoes—are distinguished and ranked. But these discriminations seem arbitrary, until we ground them by perceiving or inferring mind's value-bestowing intentions.

The hypothesis proposed here differs four-square from the one of Hume and Kant. We can't live without selecting and prescribing, but norms are discovered as often as made. Traffic laws are conventional; but we learn the range of viable variations for metabolism and heartbeat. With Heraclitus, we distinguish sameness from change, process from its inherent *logoi*.[10] For there are no constraints without the material constrained, no phenomena without intrinsic limits that restrict their expression (laws of logic or nature, for example). *Must, should,* and *ought* everywhere inhere in the circumstances that constrain us.

This hypothesis provokes questions that are often suppressed or ignored. What is the material foundation for constraints on motion and change? How far does natural normativity penetrate domains that distinguish human life? Is morality conventional only, or is it permeated with constraints—duties—we acknowledge but do not make? The experience of beauty is often a response to things enjoyed. Is it also the acknowledgment of norms intrinsic to things perceived as beautiful? Is culture a tissue of contingent practices smoothed into coherence by time and habit? Or is it true that most practices—child rearing and education, for example—exhibit one or another of the transcultural universals that constrain human activity? I shall be saying that the natural world is pervaded by normativity, including natural necessities (laws of nature), causal norms vital to practical life, regulative principles immanent in human social life, ideals expressed by aesthetic objects, and the universal but determinable norms of culture. Every such domain has its norms; every such norm is a *must, should,* or *ought* immanent within something that *is.*

Natural normativity is often perceived as an obstacle to positive freedom (freedom to). The more norms inhibit us, the less we are free to choose. This affronts the romantic demand that we be exempt from all norms. Let no one impede me as I decide what to do or be; let no one frustrate initiative by promoting the belief that current norms are fixed. For why suppose that any limit can ultimately deter us? Most are apparent and temporary: they retreat under the assault of plans that are well calculated and persistently applied. The implications for negative freedom (freedom from) are equally pernicious. Natural norms would be an oppressive cage, one from which there is no escape. Poverty, gender, race, class, religion, ethnicity, and nationality are layered constraints that have justified centuries of abuse. Call them natural, and we oblige people to endorse the abuses they suffer.

These are reasonable considerations, but they overstate the risk of acknowledging that some norms are natural. Which is the more accurate perception of our situation? Never be deterred by apparent limits, because they are only as firm as our reluctance to challenge them. Or limits are real. Many obstruct us, but some are salutary. Having bound-aries defines our tasks and possibilities. We may cross a line or tear down a wall, but then there are other boundaries in which to locate ourselves. We sometimes misconstrue temporary arrangements as unalterable limits; but there is the offsetting risk that we may take no limit seriously though some are fixed. Attitudes and behaviors are different as we con-strue our circumstances in one or the other of these two ways: Expecting that we shall breach any boundary that annoys us, we give only grudging acknowledgment to any we confront, including personal duties and artistic rules. Or we acknowledge—because we must—that we live within overlapping or nested contexts, including a climate, culture, and economy. We challenge some, but defer to others. We know where we are and realize that our psychic identity—our information, attitudes, and skills—are a function of our place within these circumstances. Different norms would require that we be different, as we cannot be and may not want to be.

Should we challenge the standing norms, altering, for example, our biological nature? Do we know the difference this would make? We are edgy and anxious, poised between opportunity and fear. One side embar-rasses us: it says that the firmness of every natural norm is the inverse of our courage and imagination. The other urges caution: don't challenge the norms, either because we shall certainly fail—we won't change the laws of motion—or because we don't know and might not like the conse-quences of successfully altering particular norms. Would life be better if natural birth were eliminated—freeing women of pregnancy—because humans can be hatched in vats of amniotic fluid? The technology is avail-able: should we use it? Do we hesitate merely because the practice is unfa-miliar, or because we realize that human identity is founded in the nurture and associations that come with being a member of a family? How much social stability is the effect of carrying this experience into successively more complicated social roles: friendship, marriage, school, and work, for example? There may be reasons to remove a child from the family of his or her parents, but they would have to be carefully considered.

Not every norm is the contingent effect of history or power. Others are intrinsic to reality at large (chapter 1), nature (chapter 2), practical life (chapter 3), morals (chapter 4), aesthetics (chapter 5), and culture (chapter 6). Ignoring these inherent norms makes us ineffectual and foolish, not free. What are the domains in which natural norms constrain us? Where is the balance of necessity and contingency within or among these norms? These six chapters are an answer.

Chapter 7 considers the implications for freedom. Modern philosophy has given its imprimatur to the biblical claim that man inherits the Earth. But philosophers have misconstrued the relevant facts: nature tolerates us; it isn't a projection of human desire, a warehouse of unlimited goods, or a playground we can endlessly exploit. The message to prudence is familiar: freedom is power and opportunity within a context. Freedom without constraint is a fantasy. Violate the constraints, strip contexts of pertinent detail, and we are less free. This chapter implies a puzzle we never solve: the limits of initiative in a world laced with norms.

These issues are formulated against the backdrop of three ontological theories: atomism/individualism, holism, and the systems theory known in its humanist applications as communitarianism. I shall be saying that atomism and holism are falsified by the same empirical data that confirm communitarianism. Each of these ontological theories has distinct implications for the status of norms. The communitarian claim is the one I shall be defending: it affirms that many norms are intrinsic to the systems they regulate.

Hilary Putnam's recent book, *Ethics without Ontology*, challenges assertions like mine on Kantian grounds. Ethics doesn't need an ontology—one of Putnam's chapters is titled "'Ontology': An Obituary"—because there is nothing "behind" our reportorial uses of language,[11] and because much of our ethical language is regulative, not descriptive.[12] Ethical principles are "conceptual truths" such that it is "impossible to make (relevant) sense of the assertion of [their] negation."[13] Putnam is more comfortable with examples drawn from logic or mathematics—he cites none that are ethical—but his point generalizes: mind lays down regulative principles for thinking about ethics, logic, or science, then formulates its theories or claims within the compass these rubrics prescribe.

Putnam's conceptual truths are near cousins to Kant's synthetic a priori truths. This is the implication of his two ways of characterizing them: we make no relevant sense of their negations (close to saying that their negations are contradictory), and "conceptual truth and empirical description interpenetrate."[14] Putnam believes that much of thought's work is accomplished by using regulative principles, his conceptual truths: so, no objects are conjured by listing things alphabetically or by invoking the rules of a game. But nothing in this reasonable claim justifies Putnam's belief that he has purged ontology's "stinking corpse."[15] Ontology is the science of what is, not the inventory of what we say or think there is. Ontology would be defunct only if there were nothing, for example, no thinker-speakers who use synthetic a priori rubrics to think about nature or morals. But is it plausible that there are no extra-mental objects and specifically none pertinent to practical life, art, science, or ethics? Surely, people and their associations—families, businesses, and states—are objects no moral ontology should ignore.

Putnam is ambivalent:

> About all this, there are at least two things to be said. First, the sheer hubris of supposing that a few philosophical arguments, be they good or bad, of the kind that I have described can really overthrow the very idea that thought has reference to objects outside of thought and language . . . the very idea that all of this can be and has been overthrown by a handful of philosophical arguments seems to me an example of breathtaking arrogance.[16]

This passage is anomalous in the context of *Ethics without Ontology*, but the generous sympathy it expresses is my point of departure: what are the material bases for normativity in nature, practical experience, morals, art, and culture?

CHAPTER ONE

Categorial Form

Philosophic inquiry was once dominated by two linked questions: What are the categorial features of reality? What moral difference do they make? Plato, Aristotle, Spinoza, Hobbes, Marx, and social Darwinists believed that answering the second question presupposes an answer to the first: human character, actions, laws, and virtues are properly sensitive to our nature and circumstances.

Skeptics challenged this link: what do we know of the external world and its constraining effects? Idealists (the skeptics' heirs) shrink the ambient world to the luminous space where individual minds create thinkable experiences by schematizing words or sensory data: we assemble words that tell a story about us and our circumstances, or—like filmmakers—we use words or rules to differentiate and organize sensory data. Experience is our product, though paradoxically the experience is autonomous. Like a dream, it may have little or nothing to do with anything external to the mind that creates it. For as skeptics forever remind us: how could we know that it does? Like the reel of a film playing in a theatre for one, the experience is autonomous. All its references signify other moments or episodes in the film: none is the effect or sign of the extra-mental states of affairs we see or otherwise encounter.

This chapter reprinted from "Categorial Form" by David Weissman in "Categories" edited by Michael Gorman. Used with permission: The Catholic University of America Press, Washington, DC.

Behavior is a part of the experience thereby created—I perceive myself to be reading what I type—but this action, like every other, has no application beyond the experience I schematize. This is consequential, for it implies that my freedom of action is unconstrained by rules other than those I use to organize my experience. This response—implied by Descartes, embellished by Kant, and favored by contemporary "pragmatists"[1]—is familiar but indefensible, if mind is the activity of body. For mind's materiality entails that we humans are everywhere constrained by physical laws or social rules we do not make. The rules are sometimes changeable, the laws are not. Either way, rules inherent in our circumstances make a considerable difference to the things we do or cannot resist doing.

This chapter invokes categorial form to reaffirm that physics and metaphysics have consequences for practical life, morals, and art. It argues that what and where we are constrains what we ought to do or be. If categories are the generic features of being, categorial form is its design. Think of the architect's plan realized in a building. Discount the designer, and suppose that reality too embodies a plan. This plan—the system of categories—is categorial form. There are seven points to consider: i. the evidence of categorial form; ii. the method for discovering it; iii. Kantian objections to the realist, essentialist implications of categorial form; iv. a sketch of plausible candidates; v. antecedent formulations; vi. practical implications; and vii. a question: which hypothesis about categorial form is best?

1. Evidence of Categorial Form

No one lives through a waking day without engaging some or all of the principal features of categorial form. These experiences are practical and parochial: our understanding of bodies, space, time, and motion is calibrated to the scale of middle-sized things moving at relatively low velocities. Hypotheses about categorial form would be crippled were we to stop with these first approximations. We elaborate, revise, and sometimes replace them with the hypotheses of empirical science: they have the scope, economy, and depth appropriate to our inquiry. Yet, science is not the last word about categorial form. Aristotle's remark—that sciences invoke causality without explaining it—is still pertinent. Scientists are careful to explicate some features of categorial form—mass and spacetime, for example—but casual about others. The status of laws may be the signature example of our time: scientists discover and cite them without specifying their place in nature. Philosophers of science gloss the issue by identifying natural laws with sentences or equations, but laws have a regulative force that is unexplained by any feature of these inscriptions.[2]

Who worries about the ontological status of laws? Who formulates and tests notions of categorial form when science and practical reflection decline the responsibility? Only philosophers, and especially metaphysicians. This is our defining task, though we often disqualify ourselves in three ways: we ignore the work for the good reason that it is difficult; we are too often apriorists who don't know how to use the empirical information supplied by practical life and science; and we have devoted ourselves, for 2500 years, to two, sterile projects, one theological, the other mentalistic. Rational theology proposes that God is the capstone, necessary ground, or container for all Being. It usually ignores the natural world, while adducing no evidence or compelling argument to justify its claims about God's character or existence. The other failed project is mentalism. Making nous or the cogito the ground for Being, it says that nothing is better known to mind than mind itself, including mind's structure and ideas. Nature is ignored, because apriorists suppose that natural phenomena derive all their character from ideas they instantiate. Thinkers since Democritus have objected to this claim, but it was engineers and physiologists—not philosophers—who confirmed that being cannot be located altogether in thought, because mind is the activity of a physical system.

Theological and mentalist metaphors have been squeezed for every useful nuance. Metaphysicians who reject them look for categorial form in the material world. Our evidentiary bases are the two just mentioned: practical experience and empirical science. Both expose us to things that embody categorial form, and both provoke inferences that specify additional categorial features—universals and modalities, for example. Our aim is a theory—an integrated inventory—of categorial form.

2. The Method for Discovering Categorial Form

We learn the shape of things by engaging them. Like people moving without light in a strange house, we go slowly at first, learning as much from mistakes as successes. Evolution averts egregious errors by supplying a good if partial map of our world's categorial form. But the map is generic, not particular: it prefigures an unbounded space, not the chair that trips us in the dark. Our information about categorial form is appropriate to the scale of our activities but warped by perspective. Inherited instincts are calibrated to the aims of middle-sized creatures who survive by engaging things of similar scale. Our assumptions about the world's categorial features need revision in the light of inferences that generalize, analogize, and extrapolate from findings germane to this scale and perspective.

The inferences that power inquiry are, principally, inductive and abductive. Induction generalizes: we infer from the bits we know to generalities about a domain or the whole. Abduction is conceptual exploration. Starting from an effect, we infer its possible condition or conditions. Sometimes these conditions are necessary, as space and time are necessary conditions for motion. More often, the inferences are probabilistic: we infer from an effect to one or more alternative sufficient conditions, each contrary to the others (different explanations for global warming, for example).

The possibility that the same effect may have either of two or more mutually exclusive conditions is an obstacle to theories about categorial form, because a preference for one contrary or the other is provisional and fallible. It is also troubling that suspected aspects of categorial form may be integrated in either of several ways. Is mass distinguishable from spacetime or only the effect of its intrinsic quantum fluctuations? (There was, presumably, no mass previous to the formation of particles after the Big Bang.) Even the target is speculative: the idea of categorial form—the integrated assembly of categorial features—signifies a possibility that may not obtain. These difficulties guarantee that the inquiry is piecemeal and dialectical, not linear and sure. Still, this idea dominates metaphysical thinking. Discovering any particular categorial feature, we locate it, however tacitly, within the hypothesized network of categorial factors.

3. Kantian Objections

Should we agree that categorial form is a regulative idea (a schema used to organize experience or thoughts of it), not the immanent design of things whose existence and character are independent of ways we think about them? Is the dialectic of categorial hypotheses a political struggle, one whose winner prescribes the idea used to organize our understanding of the "world"? These Kantian or postmodernist objections scorn the realist, essentialist bias of my suggestion that reality has a particular categorial form, one having normative effect on every feature of being, irrespective of what we think of it. Here are some realist answers to three Kantian questions:

i. Kant argued that character and relations are projected into experience by rules used to make it thinkable. Is this so? Is every candidate for categorial form merely a schema used to organize experience?

Suppose a circle, a square, and a triangle are set before us on a flat plane. Could we perceive all the figures in each of the three ways? Remember the Whorf hypothesis: a tribe's language determines the character and relations of phenomena perceived, varieties of snow or sand for example.[3] Empirical studies—of the sort my example invites—refute Whorf's claim. People see many differences not anticipated in their languages: we distinguish shapes—faces, for example—while having no words for them. A culture or language might emphasize two of the figures while saying nothing of the third. Or we might see one as an oddly distorted version of the other two. Still, we would see it as different from them.

ii. Is categorial form merely a regulative idea? It may be. There is likely to be no a priori proof that the categorial features of things are integrated as a single categorial design. This is a question for empirical inquiry: can we establish that one or another integrative design does obtain? Doing this requires two steps: formulate a theory that specifies the categorial features of things; then adduce evidence the theory applies. We may fail to confirm that candidate theories do apply, but this would not prove that reality has no categorial form: not finding what we look for doesn't prove it isn't there. Kant would demur. We are chasing our tails: experience—the only reality we know—must shadow the conceptualization used to think it. Its coherence is an effect of the integrated conceptual system used to schematize sensory data; or experience is fragmentary because the schematizing conceptual system is unintegrated.[4]

What is the point of inquiry—implying theories revised under the press of experiment—if this is so? Why not contrive whatever consistent theories we can, showing that each may be used throughout experience? Let fiction and fantasies of every sort replace empirically testable hypotheses. We demur, because the experiments of practical life and science confirm that most conceptual systems are false: reality has a character and edge we discover but do not make. Let Chicago's street plan be our example. State and Madison are point zero in a Cartesian coordinate system. Numbers in the four quadrants progress from there. Do I impose order on otherwise chaotic data when I go to a particular address; or have I navigated within an order, one that limits and directs me?

The paradoxes of quantum theory challenge this surmise, without refuting it. Phenomena that sometimes look like waves, other times like particles, are not concurrently (at the same time and place, in the same respect) waves and particles. This perplexity is sometimes construed as evidence of an equivocation in nature, though the history of thought, practice, and experiment suggests that our inability to comprehend quantum effects under a single rubric—one that may differ from any currently available—is evidence that we don't fully understand them. It is too early to affirm that nature does not have a single, decided, categorial form.

iii. Is the dialectic of alternative categorial forms a struggle for the power to impose society's organizing theory or myth? We fear truths that would restrict our freedom to do or be as we choose. We resent the idea of categorial form because it implies restriction. Never mind that we are already confined by layers of restraint, including age, gender, size, intelligence, wealth, custom, citizenship, gravity, the shape of space, and the laws of motion. Categorial form is one more insult to our freedom. Anyone proposing it must have hegemonic aims. But I do not. Categorial form is merely the last step in a hierarchy of limits. It obtains or not, irrespective of our fears. Discerning this form would illumine our situation, better enabling us to master it and ourselves.

4. Some Possible Categorial Forms

Here are three hypotheses about categorial form: individualism, communitarianism, and holism. Each exhibits the generality and explanatory power required of such hypotheses, though each is the schema of a more detailed theory. The three may be represented graphically as shown in figure 1.1.

Individualism—atomism—affirms that reality comprises self-sufficient particulars. There is, presumably, a medium in which the particulars are distributed: spacetime or God's sensorium, for example. Some variations suppose that particulars are self-activating; others say that things do not move unless pushed or pulled. All agree that relations, whether

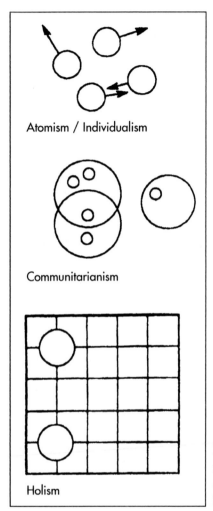

Atomism / Individualism

Communitarianism

Holism

Figure 1.1. Three theories of
reality: atomism/individualism,
communitarianism/systems theory,
holism

dynamic or static, are incidental to the character of the things related.
Individualist theories have illustrious support and an ancient history.
Democritean atomism and Aristotelian primary substances are materialist
formulations.[5] Luther's souls, Cartesian minds, and the free citizens of
democratic theory are its spiritualist, mentalist, and political versions.[6]
Holism affirms that there is a single particular—the whole—and that
every "thing" is its aspect or part. It acknowledges that parts are distinguishable within the whole but denies they are separable. Its preferred

metaphors are organic, or political and social: separating body parts kills them or the body, people separated from states or societies suffer civic or cultural death.[7]

Communitarianism is the humanistic name for systems theory. It shares some of its claims with individualism and holism, but this is the third point of a triangle, not an eclectic stew. It alleges that "things" are systems, each created by the causal reciprocity of its proper parts.[8] Let molecules be our example. Their proper parts are ions, meaning atoms that have more or less than the standard complement of electrons. Ions join when one gives and the other receives one or more electrons. The molecule thereby formed is stabilized by the balance of forces—the reciprocities—that bind the atoms: each constituent binds the other to itself.

Systems are modules. Each is somewhat autonomous because of the integration of its parts, not (as in Aristotle) because of the portion of matter that supports its properties. Systems also behave holistically: each is sustained by the complementary roles of its proper parts. There is, however, no single totalizing system (with one exception). For systems relate to one another in either of four ways. They are mutually independent, reciprocally bound, overlapping, or nested.[9] Reality is an array of systems, some that are more or less densely nested or overlapping, others that are mutually independent. The one, totalizing exception is spacetime. Every system falls within the backward light cone of its successors, either directly or by way of intermediaries, and each is affected gravitationally by everything in its backward light cone. Communitarianism is not otherwise holistic.

How do these hypotheses fare when compared to one another in respect to a feature or features for which each must provide? Let the modalities, possibility and necessity (the *must* of this book's subtitle), be our example. Certain features of both are common to all three theories. Each acknowledges that the laws of logic—identity and non-contradiction, especially—apply necessarily in all possible worlds. There is controversy about the universality of the law of excluded middle and about the domain of logical laws: do they apply to every thing and relation, or only to thoughts, sentences, or words? Modern thinking sometimes restricts their application to thought or language. But this is odd when these are the only domains where they are regularly violated. All agree that the laws of motion apply necessarily in our world. But this is parochial necessity. It lacks the universal applicability of logical laws: laws of motion are different in other possible worlds. Possibilities, too, are acknowledged by all three theories: each acknowledges possible changes of position, quality, or organization.

These affinities are a backdrop to emphases that differentiate the theories. Atomism stresses possibility, hence the freedom it ascribes to every individual, be it a material particular, soul, or mind. Necessity is minimized but not eliminated, because spacetime is a necessary condition for the freedom of material particulars: their motion is a trajectory through spacetime. Souls exhibit possibility in their freedom to will good or evil and symmetrically in the necessity that they be rewarded in kind. Minds are free to reflect upon ideas of their choice, with the proviso that possibilities for thought are subject to necessities of three sorts: mind is necessarily conscious of itself whatever ideas it entertains; necessities are discerned in the invariant structures of its ideas (of circles or squares, for example), and in the deductive relations of thoughts or sentences. Each of a democracy's citizens may freely choose among several possible courses of action, though every choice is subject to the practical necessity that no one be harmed by the actions it directs.

Holism emphasizes necessity, while reducing the range of possibilities accessible or appropriate to each of a whole's parts. Each part's freedom of action is restricted, because its role is tightly constrained by its relations to others. The range of choices reduces to two: each part fulfills its nature as determined by its role, or it thwarts itself by renouncing its role. The first is necessary, if the second is self-extinguishing (hence, implicitly, a contradiction). Call this essential necessity. It compares to the existential necessity implied by the fact that no whole can exist without its parts. Here too, the negation is a contradiction, for the whole cannot be made of nothing. Essentialist necessity reverses the order of dependence: the character of the parts is determined by the task each is allotted by the form of the whole. Imagine a jigsaw puzzle. There is no puzzle without the pieces, but the shape of each piece is a function of the space left open when other pieces are assembled. Necessity of this essentialist kind is local—parochial—for its application is restricted to the possible world having this particular organization as its signature. Parts will have different shapes—different roles—in possible worlds that are differently organized. Parochial necessity is, all the while, the expression of a universal—logical—necessity. For it is true in every possible world that a whole's parts would be self-denying—they would lose identity— were they to reject their roles. Hence this cajoling, holist demand: do your part, fill your role. Be yourself when you can't do otherwise.

Communitarianism alleges that possibility and necessity are the complementary aspects of a thing's roles in systems. Pertinent necessities include the two-faced, existential and essentialist necessity shared with holism. A system's parts are existentially necessary for its creation: there is no system in their absence. But equally, a system's form determines the character and capacities of its parts: orchestras and teams lay down least qualifications for their members. For systems, like wholes, are not aggregates. The fit of their parts is a necessary condition for their formation. Fit may be static (the complementarity of parts in geometrical figures) or dynamic (causal reciprocity), but either way, fit is material, not definitional. Some things are anomalous: they don't fit. Here, too, existential necessity is universal and logical—no system in the absence of its parts—while essential necessity is both parochial and logical: roles are different in other systems, but it is true in every system that parts lose identity when a role is lost or denied.

Communitarianism nevertheless differs from holism in the relative weight it accords to possibility and necessity. Holism acknowledges the possibility of different wholes, each with its distinctive parts and organizational form, though each is exclusive of every other. Imagine, for example, the God who has no competitors; he is infinite because unrestricted. Possibility is more conspicuous in the mix of autonomy and reciprocity that communitarianism ascribes to every module, every system. Systems form, move in and out of reciprocal or nested relations to others, then dissolve. We, their human members, know the possibility that we shall participate in myriad systems, some stable (families or states), others ephemeral (conversations).

The modalities are just one of the critical topics for a comprehensive theory of categorial form. It would also acknowledge spacetime, properties of several kinds (mass and shape, for example), relations (including relative position and efficacy, hence energy and motion), systems, their hierarchical relations and emergent properties, dispositions, and laws. This is more than a laundry list of traditional, categorial features. Some are apparent within practical experience. Others have refined scientific descriptions. A few are considerations to which metaphysics extrapolates. All are topics for a comprehensive metaphysics of nature.

Is this project sabotaged by the simple objection that it implies ontological essentialism, the claim that reality has a distinct categorial form? I suggest that disparate categorial forms are contraries: nature embodies one while excluding every other. There is nothing odd about this: one chooses the design of a new house from an array of alternatives. The categorial profile of space, time, matter, causality, and motion may be equally singular and exclusive.

5. Antecedent Formulations

There are affinities between the idea of categorial form and Stephen Pepper's world hypotheses.[10] His candidates were atomism, mechanism, organicism, and contextualism, each defended by its proponents as comprehensive and self-sufficient. Pepper believed that the history of philosophy is the dialectic of these opposed conceptions, each belittling the others while justifying itself. Richard McKeon made similar claims about the sixty-four possible theories generated by joining the four expressions of his three rubrics: ideas, methods, and principles.[11] Or McKeon argued that there are four rubrics—the other three and interpretation, each with four expressions—entailing 256 possible philosophic views. Pepper and McKeon may have been inspired by Kant's antinomies.[12] Like him, they agree that we can use any consistent conceptual system—any consistent regulative idea—to think about reality. Yet, thought's plasticity doesn't entail that reality is formless or endlessly determinable. It may have a decided form, one theory (and translational equivalents) being true, while its contraries are false. The essentialism of categorial form is no more objectionable than that of chess or this building. Each of them has an essential form. Why shouldn't reality have one too?

6. Practical Applications

Metaphysical theories, like practical beliefs and natural science, should be empirically testable. Testability looks two ways: to the empirical evidence for truth and to cogency. We want empirical data for our claims, because we cannot know without it that hypotheses are true. We want hypotheses that are cogent, because metaphysics serves human aims: it is one of the inquiries that tells what we are, what the world is, and what place we have within it. Kantian world-making doesn't do as much. It directs that we think of the world "as if" it has a particular form, though fantasies don't appease us: we need and want to know what and where we are. Only truths can tell us.

A true theory of categorial form would be cogent in this way: it would enable us to locate ourselves in the world. We are well located already, in the respect that our bodies have position. But this is not the sense of location relevant here. Location of this other sort is a demand we make of self-understanding. Motivated by a combination of wonder and insecurity, we want to know our place in the world. A comprehensive, empirically and dialectically validated theory of categorial form would temper our hopes, appease some fears, and justify others. Wanting such knowledge is a first cousin to religious concerns, with the difference that resolution comes with inquiry, not dogma.

Categorial form is also cogent because of its implications for moral life, though the demand for acuity is reduced. Wonder about our place in the world deepens with precise information about its age, structure, and scale: think of the pictures of dust clouds trillions of miles high, newly formed stars blazing at the crests. Moral issues also want categorial direction, but they are insensitive to many such details. Einstein and the astronomers amplified Newton's claim without altering its moral implication: the universe is vast; we are small and ephemeral. Knowing the fine structure of spacetime adds little or nothing to this sober appraisal of our place and significance.

Each of the hypotheses summarized here—individualism, holism, and communitarianism—is morally germane though mute about such details. Individualism affirms our self-sufficiency and freedoms, both positive (freedom to) and negative (freedom from). It says that responsibilities are assumed rather than primary: they don't constrain us until we acquire duties to other people (as when contracts are made). Holism inverts the priorities. It emphasizes duty, saying that freedom is the opportunity to satisfy one's place in the whole. Communitarians object that freedom and duty are not contraries. They agree with holists that we are inevitably located within networks of obligation but add that some are freely chosen and that character emerges as we learn to fill and choose our roles. The moral quality of selfhood varies accordingly. Individualism avers that each of us is self-concerned. Holism supposes that the moral vector points beyond us to a corporate reality. Communitarianism acknowledges the moral conflicts that occur when persons located in several systems—work and family, for example—choose the order and degree of their commitments.

The moral determinism of categorial form is somewhat relieved, because each form may be expressed in several or many ways. Individualism affirms that bodies are separable and self-sufficient; it doesn't specify the number of bodies or the dimensions of the spaces they occupy. Holism doesn't detail the complexity of the system it postulates: there may be many parts or few; each may be connected directly to several others or to all. Communitarianism alleges that reality is an array of systems; it doesn't prescribe how many systems there shall be, the depth of nesting and overlap among them, or the number of mutually independent hierarchies.

Each categorial form is determinable. Contingencies—scarcity and crowding, for example—determine its lower-order expressions, hence their distinctive moral imperatives. Locke described a time when "all the world was America," a fruitful wilderness where individuals did as they pleased without affecting others.[13] Hobbes assumed that freedom is everywhere impeded by those with whom one competes for scarce resources.[14] One implied tolerance for people rarely or never met; the other described the perpetual war of each with all. Accordingly, we qualify the principle affirmed above: the generic imperatives implied by a categorial form are not rendered determinate and specific, until contingencies realizing the form are also given.

7. Which is the Better Hypothesis?

Each of the three hypotheses has supporting evidence. All agree that what we can and ought to do is determined by what and where we are. Each implies moral directives that are appropriate to its version of our nature and circumstances. So, young people behave atomistically in the void between systems they have outgrown and those they will make or join. They confirm a theory that encourages us to behave as if we were freer than we are, until these same people subordinate individual identity to the demands of a group by marrying or taking jobs that enforce duties and roles. We bend either way, accommodating ourselves successively to one theory, then the other. But how is this possible? Shouldn't we be incapable of satisfying directives from two or more of the hypotheses, if only one of the three contraries is true? I suggest this solution. Each of the hypotheses can be used effectively as a regulative idea, because humans are adaptable: our behavior is determinable within limits.

Does this variability disqualify human behavior as evidence for or against competing hypotheses about categorial form? Could we adapt to each form, like people who twist their feet into shoes more stylish than comfortable? Human malleability confuses the issue without altogether obscuring it. For behavior is distorted when hypotheses about categorial form are used as recipes to remake the underlying structures of social life. Organizations and associations of every intermediate sort (including families, teams, businesses, and states) may be misconstrued as aggregates bound by nothing but mutual advantage or fear. Or we may care only about the integrity of the whole, annihilating every lesser system, stifling the interests and initiatives of the people who join to create them. Both effects cripple personal development and vital social interests, because they disrupt or ignore basic systems.

Communitarianism is a better hypothesis about reality, human life and society included, because it predicts and explains the empirically justified aspects of atomist and holist theories, though they cannot provide for its claims. Systems are modular, and they behave sometimes as individuals. Systems are holistic, because they are comprehensive and totalizing, as businesses, states, or religious sects may be. Yet, atomism has no way of describing either the systems established by the reciprocal causal relations of their members or the hierarchies of nested, overlapping systems. Holism ignores both modularity, hence the individualism it promotes, and mutually independent hierarchies (Albania and Peru, for example).

Atomism and holism are, historically, the two principal ontological alternatives, because their theorists have hidden the evidence for communitarianism. Let Mill and Rousseau be our examples. One emphasizes autonomy, but ignores the families, schools, workplaces, and states where it emerges.[15] The other would force us to be free, requiring that we defer to the general will.[16] Communitarianism is more accurate: it describes the emergence of moral selves in contexts where autonomy and responsibility are acquired by infants, children, and adults engaged reciprocally to parents, friends, teachers, workmates, and fellow citizens. Atomism and holism are offsetting distortions of this more ample account. We may satisfy atomist or holist demands, but we are mutilated if they exceed the tolerances of our communitarian reality.

Moral implications such as these may trump every other motive for wanting to know reality's categorial form. What and where are we? What should we do and be? What is optional or required where *is* constrains *ought*? Hume's dictum—*is* doesn't entail *ought*—is true of particular circumstances (unhappiness or abuse, for example) but not of categorial form. Imagine that we reproach a breed of talking fish: "Why not live on land and breathe good air, as we do. You ought to try." "But we oughtn't, because we can't," say the fish. "Things we ought to do fall within the circle of things we can do because of what we are. *Is* limits *ought.*" Categorial form comprises the most general features of all that is. Anything that deforms these limits, anything contrary to them, violates us. Kant, the master deontologist, agreed. Morality, he said, is the imperative of our rational nature. We want maxims that are consistent if universalized, because universality and consistency are to reason as water is to fish.

The regulative implications for law and morality are clear, though complex. Categorial form constrains what we are and do. Yet, specific constraints are often determinable: there is variability within limits. No society survives without children, though rules and customs for marriage and child rearing vary. Any of several considerations may justify a variation, but each assembly of family members satisfies the relevant feature of communitarian categorial form: each is a system; each system is a module, nested within or overlapping others.

Hence, this finding. Variability is restricted. Categorial form is both its limit and the framework of norms—the *musts, shoulds,* and *oughts*—that regulate motion and practice in every domain.

CHAPTER TWO

Nature

Nature is often conceived in Humean terms as an aggregate. Think of marbles mixed and remixed in a drum that turns forever. There is sequence and conjunction, but no constraint except the contrariety enforced when every thing holds its ground, defending its identity by excluding every other. Nietzsche argued that freedom is maximized, constraint is minimal, because reality is formless but for the shape imposed when human will directs the choice of ideas used to differentiate and organize experience. Many objections to determinism justify themselves by making one or both of these assumptions. There is, for example, a view shared by neo-pragmatists and deconstructionists: science, they say, imposes the intelligible order of its theories on random phenomena, before mistaking its theories as representations of natural normativity. For science is only a version of literature or ideology; its claims have no more authority than the last interpretation of Othello.[1] A complementary view encourages us to deconstruct the natural laws responsible for normativity by reducing them to instrumentalities that are useful in local situations, though they are not generalizable.[2] But Earth turns perpetually around the Sun: this isn't an occasional thing, or one so peculiar that Newton's laws apply to the solar system but not to much else. Science, itself, sometimes invites interpretations that emphasize its indeterminist implications. Quantum theory is the conspicuous example, but there are also mathematical formulations that entail normativity's breakdown under specified conditions.[3] These are typically limiting cases incidental to a theory's principal aims and strengths (singularities that exceed the mathematics of general relativity theory, for example). They occur when the formalisms exploited by successful theories are pressed beyond the domains for which they were intended. They don't prove or imply that nature is essentially formless. Quantum indeterminacies are acknowledged below.

The following arguments for natural normativity are conceptual only, though their point of reference is always factual and empirical. They invoke considerations that are general and categorial, though this doesn't make them less credible than the equally metaphysical arguments of Hume, Nietzsche, or those who construe scientific findings for indeterminist aims.

1. Logic

There is a prejudice that logic comprises rules for ordering thoughts or sentences, never states of affairs. But why are there no contradictions in nature if the laws of logic—identity, non-contradiction, and excluded middle—do not apply there? Could it be that natural contradictions are rife, though invisible, because we can't think or perceive them? This is an odd debility for thinkers who easily recognize contradictions in thought and words: why are they harder to discern in nature? We don't find them, because there are none: the laws of logic apply there universally and necessarily, hence without exception. This is Morris Cohen's thought, one he shared with Santayana, Peirce, Leibniz, Descartes, Aristotle, Plato, and Heraclitus: "Logic may . . . be viewed as the simplest chapter in ontology, as a study of the exhaustive possibilities of all being."[4] The standard empirical test is inverted. We normally ask what empirical difference would obtain if a hypothesis were true. Now, we remark that an empirical difference is precluded: contradictions that might occur if logical laws did not obtain are not observed because they do obtain. The laws work perfectly: nature is sanitized by its logical norms.

But is this sleight of hand, is the very question—why no empirical evidence of contradictions—a category mistake, one similar to counting angels on the heads of pins? This would be a reasonable objection, if there were no plausible way of making logical laws pertinent to material states of affairs. But there is a way. Some general questions direct us: How do laws or rules apply to the objects of a domain? Are they conventions that apply, like the rules of grammar and games, when an intermediary—

a speaker or player—uses them to organize his words or moves? This way of construing logic's laws is inappropriate, because intermediaries aren't required to apply them: logical constraints are intrinsic to everything that exists in any way.

The laws of logic are grounded by a consideration implied by Bishop Butler's dictum: "Everything is what it is, and not another thing."[5] This remark expresses the law of identity—$(x)(Fx$ if $Fx)$—in material (as opposed to syntactic or abstractly logical) terms. Butler's formula implies this elemental, ontological truth: nothing exists without properties; every thing—simple or complex—is what it is by virtue of its properties. Each of the three laws of logic—identity, non-contradiction, $(x)-(Fx$ and $-Fx)$, and excluded middle, $(x)(Fx$ or $-Fx)$—instantiates this principle, though non-contradiction and excluded middle do not express it explicitly until the law of identity is elaborated to make these two claims: a thing's identity is a function of its properties ("Every thing is what it is"); and such properties as it has bar other properties ("and not another thing").

Pertinent others may be construed narrowly or widely. The narrower reading construes $-Fx$ as the set of Fx's contraries: something may be red or green, but it cannot be red all over while being green all over. The wider reading interprets $-Fx$ as the class complement that includes all properties other than Fx (where Fx may be simple or complex). Both readings assume that the number of properties constituting Fx is finite: each thing has some properties, but not all. Birds, but not numbers, nest and lay eggs; numbers, but not birds, are odd or even. Finitude is critical, for what would distinguish things from one another if each had a denumerable infinity of properties? One answer is that no thing can have all properties, because some properties are contraries. Contrariety would make things distinguishable, because things comprising denumerably infinite properties while red would be distinguishable from others comprising the same denumerable infinity while green. But this is not our world. The finite sets of properties constitutive of things differ from thing to thing; uniformity broken only by contrariety does not obtain here.

Notice that logic's ontological implications quickly swell, because Butler's formula converts difference into contrariety. For if each thing is what it is by virtue of its properties (including spatial and temporal location), then each bars every other from itself. In their simpler expression, contraries are the more determinate, mutually exclusive expressions of a higher-order determinable: red, yellow, and blue are the more determinate and contrary expressions of color. Now (after the second phrase of

Butler's formula), contrariety is otherness—difference—of any kind: every thing is qualified by a property or properties, Fx. It bars properties from Fx's class complement, $-Fx$.

This formulation is unproblematic when interpreted narrowly as a claim about the composition of things at any instant. It doesn't lead to paradoxes of the sort favored by Parmenides and Zeno,[6] unless we infer that the logic of exclusion bars change. Nothing changes—the inference goes—because identity-fixing properties bar all others. But this misconstrues the implications of identity. It obtains at every moment because of a thing's identity-fixing properties. Nothing in it precludes a property, Fx's, replacement by a property from its class complement, $-Fx$. But this is irrelevant to identity. It is satisfied by a thing's properties at a moment, whatever the properties and however they differ from those of the previous or next moment. Today's clear sky may be cloudy tomorrow, but that will be the effect of material, causal factors that are incidental to identity's character and condition. Identity rides the waves, oblivious to material conditions that promote stability or change.

The difference between identity-fixing properties and the properties thereby excluded is the complexity that carries the law of identity into the laws of non-contradiction and excluded middle. Having identity because having a finite number of certain properties entails not having others (all others or the contraries of a thing's identity-fixing properties). The law of non-contradiction, $(x)-(Fx \text{ and } -Fx)$, holds that something cannot be both itself and not itself: it cannot be constituted of a property or properties, Fx, and properties that nullify Fx's identity because they are members of Fx's class complement, namely $-Fx$. Constituting properties may be construed individually or corporately: a scarf can be red and green, but it cannot be red where it's green; if a donkey, then not a horse. The law of excluded middle, $(x)(Fx \text{ or } -Fx)$, divides the terrain: there are properties constitutive of a thing, hence of its identity, and the rest. Its affirmation—either/or—is unqualified, because identity is nullified if having a property is consistent with not having it. Identity is the ontologically prior law, because there is no traction for material applications of the laws of non-contradiction and excluded middle— $-Fx$ is undetermined (whether it constitutes all properties other than Fx, or Fx's contraries)—until Fx is fixed.

The force of identity's restriction is easily confused: it does not foreclose mixing the properties of different things to produce a third: mules. The point is narrower: material identity precludes, in that moment, that a thing be other than what it is. Why? Because every thing is what it is by virtue of its properties. Add, subtract, or alter them and one has a different thing. This makes difficulties for identity over time—one is different after a haircut—but not for these logical laws.

Property fields are another way to exhibit both the priority of identity and the complexity of the three laws.[7] Each field has a specific property—call it the *name property*—at its center. Every property, whether the name property or others, has three marks: quality, quantity, and relation. A property's quality is its manifest expression: this shade of red or blue, for example. Its quantity is the property's magnitude: size or intensity. (The number of its instances is incidental to property fields.) Relation has two principal expressions: a property's relation to itself and its relations—possible or actual—to others. A property's identity is a function of two factors: its distinguishing quality and the relations to other properties for which it qualifies because of its quality.

Other properties are arrayed about the name property in ways distinguished by the ways they relate to it. Red is the name property of its field, and every other property is arrayed about it in sectors appropriate to their different ways of relating to red. These are the categorial styles of the name property's possible relations to other properties, hence the limits on its possibilities for association with them. One style has an especially large constituency, namely, all those properties that cannot relate to the name property in any way. Rain comes in quantity, but "It's raining numbers" is a category mistake expressed as a grammatical error,[8] a mistake usually avoided because of our familiarity with property fields. Knowing their topography—by observation or by way of rules for using words that signify properties—we know that certain styles of association are barred. Solecisms are the red flag indicating that the limits on association intrinsic to a property field would be violated if the relation signified were to occur. But the contradictions thereby generated are only grammatical: it is talk about things—words alone—that sometimes violates limits never breached by things themselves.

This extends by one the number of factors critical to identity: a property's quality, the otherness of properties different from it, and its accessibility or inaccessibility to them. Butler's slogan—"Every thing is what it is, and not another thing"—signifies the first two considerations, but not the third.

Practical or theoretical interests sometimes challenge these elemental barriers to anomaly and contradiction. Does an electron violate the law of identity by having—short of the moment when the wave packet collapses—all the contrary states ascribed to it in probability? The fuzzy logics formulated to represent cases like this may be interpreted as tacit sabotage of the principle of identity (they tolerate contrarieties whose co-realizations are barred, for example, in property fields). But there is a difference in the practical uses made of these logics and the uncompromised principle of identity. Fuzzy logics are a way of compensating for our inability to describe the state of electrons prior to measuring their impacts. But this is a fact about us. It doesn't supersede the discriminations and exclusions on which the three logical laws are founded. The probability of alternate states at every next moment is consistent with having one state at a time.

Hilary Putnam objects to the idea that there may be something called "the logical structure of the world." Inferring that there is such structure is objectionable, he says, because

> (i) It posits something we have found no other need to posit (which is not, of course, observable by the senses—otherwise it wouldn't be a posit);
> (ii) It does no work for us, because we derive nothing from it but the very phenomenon we posited it to explain (it lacks "surplus meaning")—this also makes it unfalsifiable, of course; and
> (iii) Those who defend it do not suggest any way of extending it so that it will have surplus meaning—in short, it lacks fruitfulness ab initio.[9]

But the world's logical structure is not posited; this is not a convenient way of speaking, one stipulated to facilitate our thinking about reality. We hypothesize that this structure obtains while offering reasons for believing that the world would be otherwise if it did not. Accordingly, the hypothesis does significant work: it specifies a necessary and sufficient condition for the logical tidiness of things, the absence of contradictions in nature. Could we extend this style of argument, saying, for example, that the want of sightings is evidence for the invisibility of ghosts? We don't say it, because we have no additional leverage for the inference that ghosts exist. We have that leverage in the case of logical structure: namely, Butler's dictum and its foundation in the law of identity. Does nature's logical structure have surplus meaning? Think of

Conan Doyle's *Hound of the Baskervilles*: there is surplus meaning in a dog that doesn't bark and equally in violations that don't occur because of identity's implications for nature and discourse.

2. Possible and Actual Worlds

Imagine various games: rugby, polo, and baseball. Strip each game of contingencies that occur during play (including points scored, foul balls, and penalties). Then consider each game's essentials as specified by its rules. Each set of rules cites the conditions for playing its game (including the field of play, the numbers of players, and collateral equipment), and each regulates the flow of play.

Notice that all actual games were possible, in two respects, before their invention. It was possible, trivially, that inventors would formulate their rules: nothing in the games exceeds our ability to conceive or play them. This is material possibility: the capacities that enable human or other agents to act in specific ways. More important is this ontological point: imagining properties, inventing words, or formulating rules or laws does not create the possibilities thereby entertained, signified, or prefigured. The first person to draw a triangle expresses a possibility he has discovered, not one he creates. Rules, too, have existed as possibles before being formulated—cited—by people who make games.

The evidence for possibilities of this other kind is a simple logical principle: whatever is not a contradiction is a possibility or (equivalently) either a contradiction or a possibility. This is the principle of plenitude. It applies the law of excluded middle: either a contradiction or not a contradiction. Something may not exist because it embodies a contradiction or it may exist: it is possible. This opposition—either a contradiction or a possibility—is exhaustive: necessarily, something is either one or the other. Possibles that satisfy the principle are called *logical* or *eternal*. They are eternal, because anything that embodies no contradiction is forever possible, whether or not instantiated. This is possibility as a mode of being, the mode counterpart to actuality.[10] Reality has these two modes. Everything exists in the first instance as a possibility. Most possibles are uninstantiated, but some have one or more actual instances.

All the candidates for possibility are constituted of their properties, whether simple or complex. Actuality—these red spots, each having a specific size and hue—is qualitatively and quantitatively determinate. Possibility is qualitatively and quantitatively or only quantitatively determinable.[11] Possibles are qualitatively determinable when they are generic, as the possibility for color allows for further specificity: the possibility that color be red or blue. They are qualitatively determinate when specific to the last degree: for example, the possibility for a specific shade of red. Every possible, whether qualitatively determinable or determinate, is determinable quantitatively (numerically): it may have one, many, or no instances. Plato was flustered when asked if the Form for sail is a sail, but the question loses its sting if we answer that the possibility for sail is not a sail.

Every game, discovered and played or not, is constituted—defined— by its rules. Each game-fixing set of rules exists in the first instance, as a complex, eternal possibility. Such rules are norms: they regulate games played or those that would be played were the rules "formulated" and applied. Now consider the possible world instantiated as our actual world. It embodies ordering principles—natural laws—that have normative force within both the possible and actual worlds. The signature rules or laws of a possible world are its intrinsic constraints. They fix the limits of variation for the contingent detail of its qualitatively determinate expressions, whether possible or actual.

This point is qualified by the difference between two kinds of games—free-for-alls and those having rules. Some possible worlds—call them *Humean*—have no intrinsic regulative principles.[12] A coin tossed a thousand times comes up heads each time, but this is chance rather than evidence of an intrinsic constraint. Worlds of this sort are a montage of elements that are separable, because distinguishable: any arrangement is satisfactory, because none violates the principle of non-contradiction. Events in other worlds are constrained by intrinsic rules or forms that vary in three ways. First are rules or laws that cannot be breached, because their negations are contradictions: the three logical laws, for example. A rule that fixes the intervals between prime numbers would also be an example (if such a rule exists). Second are rules that allow no exceptions, though their necessity is parochial: they apply necessarily within a domain. The rules of Euclidean geometry satisfy this description, because its necessities do not apply within a curved space (except as approximations). The third alternative comprises worlds—games or practices—that are orderly because their necessities are enforced by the penalties threatened if their rules are broken. Accordingly, we have a threefold distinction: necessities that obtain in all possible worlds because their negations are contradictions, those applying within a world because of that world's distinctive structure (its geometry, for example), and the necessity that events should observe laws—as moves in a game are subject to penalties if they fail to satisfy its rules—though there is no basis in logic or nature for such necessities. A world is not Humean unless it lacks constraints of the first two sorts. Hume, himself, acknowledged stipulations we make and apply.[13]

Which is true: our world is a montage of accidental conjuncts, or it is intrinsically orderly in one or both of the first two ways? Hume argued for the absence of internal constraints: any event may have any antecedent or successor if their conjunction does not embody a contradiction.[14] Only existence and nonexistence are contradictory,[15] so any imaginable sequence is as possible as any other. It is incidental that the world looks orderly: it has no internal, constraining form.

A game that randomly mixes features of every possible game may be thinkable (not contradictory)—one can imagine home runs in chess matches—but this is not a game we play. Is nature more reckless? Does it, like Hume, conflate material possibility—meaning, possibilities founded in the structures and relations, hence the capacities, of material agents—with the absence of contradiction? Is it only an accident that gravitational attraction always falls off with the square, not the cube of the distance? The chance of a head on the next toss after a lengthy run of heads is one-half. But the chance of that run from its inception is very small. Is it just our odd luck that the Sun rises and sets in a sequence that repeats itself billions of times. We reasonably infer that regularities we observe—night and day, birth and death—have conditions Hume ignored.

Some sequences occurring in our world are accidental: whenever one of us breathes, everyone else also breathes. But every sequence—this one included—exhibits the constraining effects of natural laws: human metabolism converts oxygen to carbon dioxide, not the reverse. Every such law—its application restricted to a specific domain, hence to specific material conditions—is an instance of the laws of motion. They are exceptionless, but parochial, given that there is no contradiction to supposing that they are contravened in other possible worlds; things that are mutually repelled in our world are mutually attracted in others that are possible. This difference between universal and parochial necessity—hence, the contingency of parochial necessities—may have encouraged

Hume to believe that gravity signifies the regularity with which bodies fall, not an intrinsic constraint that explains the regularity. But Hume's interpretation is unattractive, because no one violates the laws of motion, try as he may, given that gravity is the normative effect of mass, energy, and acceleration in a curved spacetime. It is incidental to this parochial necessity that gravity is absent from or has different conditions in other possible worlds.

Suppose our world does embody its forms of order. Dress codes change irregularly, but often: are nature's laws more stable? There are possible worlds whose laws evolve, though evidence for the evolution of physical laws in our world is slight or equivocal. The material basis for their stability is, presumably, the stability of the dynamic spacetime in which they inhere. Does its form abide from the inception of the cosmos throughout its evolution? Maybe not.

3. The Actual World: Nature

Normativity's principal implications—limit, constraint, and regulation—are insufficiently exact. Standing in the middle of a crowd is constraining, but not normative. A pedestrian raises a hand to stop traffic after an accident: the effect is regulative without being normative. Normativity signifies regulation that is constant over time throughout a domain.

Stipulated norms—traffic and tax laws, for example—are critical to practical life, but they are incidental here where the topic is natural normativity. We describe it sometimes as natural or material necessity, but this is misleading (as argued above) if we suppose that necessity implies a norm or norms obtaining in all possible worlds. The laws of logic and their derivatives may be the only norms having this extended application. Other necessary constraints have a restricted domain: the inverse square law doesn't apply in worlds where gravity intensifies with distance. Hume's attack on natural norms—it is no contradiction to imagine that they do not obtain—is tendentious, because the necessity of nature's laws is local: they are the signature laws of our world, not principles that apply in every world. This is the contingency of natural laws: they apply necessarily in our world, but not others. Logical laws are founded in the properties constitutive of things. What is the material basis for natural laws?

A. Spacetime

Let motion be our point of reference. Space and time are its necessary conditions, so their relationship—no motion without space and time—is normative for every world where motion is present. The shape or structure of spacetime is also normative: trajectories have one shape or other for reasons intrinsic to its structure. Motion on a torus (doughnut-shaped) observes constraints that differ from those affecting motion on trajectories through Euclidean space: arcs or great circles in one are straight lines in the other. Normativity is the determination that trajectories shall have one shape or the other for reasons intrinsic to the structure of spacetime. There is empirical evidence for saying that its structure in our world has the variable topology and curvature described by general relativity theory. Its metric is implied by the difference of triangles inscribed in spaces that are flat or curved. The interior angles of the first equal 180 degrees; their sum is more or less as the curvature of space is convex (Riemannian) or concave (from Bolyai and Lobachevsky). Every motion—every process—satisfies each of these immanent constraints: topological, geometrical, and metrical.

B. Causality and Natural Laws

We reasonably believe that causality, too, is normative, though we suppress this belief out of regard for Hume's view that cause and effect are merely constant conjuncts in space and time. Finding no percept of power, process, or necessity between two sensory data, able to imagine either in the absence of the other, he argued that nothing binds cause and effect but the expectation that we shall perceive one when perceiving the other.[16] And he added, "There is no reason in metaphysics or nature that any event have an antecedent or successor."[17] Like the run of a thousand heads in tosses of an honest coin, every sequence is random. It is remarkable that sequences in our world continue to be orderly; but this is an accident to enjoy, not one having its explanation in the normative, productive relations of causes and effects.

This argument has been criticized many times from many perspectives. Five of its assumptions are relevant here:

i. Hume conflated extra-mental states of affairs (including causes and effects) with percepts on page 1 of his *Treatise of Human Nature*. This affirms Berkeley's (and Descartes') dictum—*esse est percipi*—without a single justifying argument.[18] Berkeley could declare it, because he happily turned the didactic skepticism of Descartes' first *Meditation* into a dogma, and because his skepticism didn't extend to his belief in God. Theory doesn't need an external world to stabilize human experience, if God can do it.[19] But Hume didn't invoke this prop. He reduced reality to sensory data unsupported by God, material objects, or minds that have a structure distinct from their sensory contents. He then made substantive claims—about causality, for example—after subjecting sensory data to four principles affirmed without argument: every thing distinguishable is separable; existence is nothing but the force and vivacity of our percepts; anything conceivable without contradiction can exist as conceived; we cannot infer what we could not perceive (mind cannot introduce ideas that are not copies of impressions). There is no contradiction if we imagine the idea of an effect without that of its cause or suppose that the force and vivacity of an idea is intensified to equal to that of the percept from which it derives. Hence, the claim that any event may exist as conceived, without a cause.

This argument is a withering application of Descartes' four rules for reconstructing confused ideas (of causality, for example): doubt them, reduce them to simples, construct complexes from the simples, then survey the ideas considered to assure that nothing is neglected.[20] This is well and good if ideas are constructs, each constituent distinguishable and separable from the others. It doesn't follow that this program for reconstructing ideas applies to the extra-mental states of affairs they signify. Hume wanted to preclude such speculations, because he supposed that the arguments of Descartes' first and second *Meditations* provide a self-sufficient ontology. There is mind and nothing more, or there is less: only sensory data and ideas. This posture dominates Western metaphysical thinking since Descartes, but it founders if mind is the activity of a physical system: namely, the brain and body.[21] We learn about their structures and dynamics—causality included—by using testable hypotheses, not by deconstructing complex ideas in order to reconstruct them in sober, a priori terms.

ii. Hume conflated causal and logical necessity (as argued above), though they differ as parochial necessity—determination within a domain—differs from the universality entailed by logical necessity. The sentence specifying water's boiling point is not a necessary truth, because its negation is not contradiction: there are possible worlds where water at sea level boils at more or less than 100 degrees centigrade. Though nothing is gained, and a difference is lost, if we amalgamate possible worlds. It is true that causal laws in each can be violated without contradiction—witness other possible worlds—but this misses a point: worlds are distinguished by their signature, parochial necessities—their laws—as games are distinguished by their rules. Cricket doesn't coalesce with baseball merely because it is no logical contradiction that some feature of one is intruded into the other.

iii. Someone defending Hume may respond that the variability implicit in the statistical character of many natural laws confirms that events in causal sequences are loosely connected and that the idea of deterministic—essentialist and exceptionless—Aristotelian templates misrepresents them. This supposes gratuitously that qualitatively identical things (gas molecules, for example) respond differently to qualitatively identical causes. Yet, this is not the implication of most statistical laws. They describe the behaviors of large arrays—of motorists, buyers, or molecules—when the variant details of particular interactions are incidental to a corporate effect. Such laws are consistent with the belief that things of a kind respond identically to causes of the same kind. The idealizations of quantum theorists are trickier, because indeterminist interpretations of quantum behavior are canonical. Physicists assume that particles described by a statistical law—the Schrödinger equation—are physically indistinguishable, though their behaviors differ: some jump randomly ("spontaneously") from one electron shell to another. But this is problematic as a final statement about the character and dynamics of the particles represented. For granting that these are particles of a kind (spectral lines identify them as an ensemble of particles of a kind), the random jumps suggest a currently undetectable difference in either the particles or their circumstances. The current inability to explain this difference (by complementing or superseding the Schrodinger equation) may explain the physicists' annoyance with objections that are merely philosophical.[22] But grant their assumption: suppose that quantum indeterminacy is not the artifact of a statistical law that ignores significant differences in the phenomena it represents. Causality is only slightly diminished. For boiling, not freezing, is the corporate effect of using heat to excite molecular motion. And similarly, there is a range of probabilities for specific quantum effects within an experimental apparatus, some more likely than others. Many logically conceivable effects have no probability in these circumstances, though they may be commonplace in other possible worlds. For this is the way—the inherent statistical norm—of causal processes in our world.

iv. Hume supposed that our naïve idea of cause and effect relations implies three things, each separable from the others: causes, their effect, and the necessary relation of cause and effect. He asked us to inspect the data looking for evidence of this third term and especially for evidence of its necessity. His assault on causality is partly the claim that we never perceive the alleged necessity, for it is not a contradiction that a cause have an effect different from the one to which it is typically joined. It is never necessary that one candidate win—given an electorate, voting, and other candidates—because it is conceivable that he or she loses. This is true, but too coarse a description of cause and effect.

Voting is accomplished when a person (qualified by age, residency, and citizenship) moves a voting-machine lever (in a place and time appropriate to an election). The voter and voting-machine are not causes unless and until they interact. Accordingly, the relation at issue, initially, is the interaction of the causes, not that of cause and effect. The decisive factor is energy exchange between or among the causes: there is no effect without it. This double relationship—of causes to one another, and of causes to their effect—complicates Hume's account. He emphasized the temporal relation of cause and effect implying their separability, as children are separable from their parents. (Hume's phenomenalist model assumes that time is the requisite ordering principle for all phenomena: first the cause, then its effect.[23]) But this exaggerates the independence of the effects. They are changes in the causes consequent on their interaction. The child to be is the synthesis of two gametes; voting is a change produced in a voting machine by an arm pulling its lever. Hume's emphasis—first the cause, then the effect—implies their separability, though the effect is an altered state of one or more of the causes: it is not a free standing successor or conjunct, a thing or event independent of them. It is relevant, too, that there is no impression of causal efficacy, for the reason that there is none of energy exchange. Where causation is explained by motion and energy transfer, Hume's phenomenalist scruples preclude him from locating the efficacy that makes causes of things that interact. Examples are close at hand. Igniting a bomb, we see the effect without perceiving the energy that brings down a building. Hume wrote at a time when many causal agents, including radio and sound waves were unknown. Does it follow that they do not exist, merely because we have no impressions of them?

v. Hume's assumptions were affirmed dogmatically, though he implied that his argument stands or falls with the empirical data. They include regularities that should be accidental and fragile if causes and effects are separable, because no power relation joins them. Any thing might come into being without antecedents; equally, it might lapse without affecting others. Uniformity should be ephemeral. There are 1024 possible combinations of heads and tails for a coin tossed ten times, hence one chance in 1024 that their be ten heads or ten tails in a row. Earth is several billion years old. Is the run of sunrises a sequence of separable, mutually independent events? This is, if so, a miracle that should amaze and terrify us. Could there be some better explanation for the sequence, one that invokes considerations additional to the empirical data: Earth's daily rotation and its proximity to the Sun, for example? This explanation exceeds the boundaries Hume prescribed; but it explains events that he reduced to mystery. Moreover, this hypothesis is empirically testable: we compare normal sunrises to those occurring when the Sun is eclipsed by the Moon. Humean empiricists don't require empirically testable answers for phenomena that would be miraculous were Hume's assumptions correct. Empiricists of a different stripe—Peirce is the best example[24]—suppose that empirical testability requires inferences from the data perceived to their extra-mental conditions. That effects of a kind are produced by causes of a kind is one such inference.[25]

Wittgenstein remarked that questions and answers terminate when nothing more is usefully said.[26] Hume is troubling, because the end of discussion in his case is also the beginning. We are to start and finish by observing the sequence of sunsets: don't ask for an explanation; there is none. Frustration is reduced, when we realize that the Humean idea of causation depends entirely on the stipulations just cited, all of them false. Needing a different hypothesis, I suggest again that interaction—implying motion and energy transfer—affects the agents engaged. Effects include the stabilization or alteration of a preceding state, property, or position. Possible worlds differ in the kinds of interaction they tolerate, the effects thereby produced, and the degree to which their causal relations are lawful. There are many possible worlds where regularity is neither lawful nor conditioned by energy transfer or motion. They differ from our world.

My conclusion seems oddly dated if one thinks of natural laws in terms of their modern expressions: $F = ma$, $e = mc^2$, or the Schrödinger equation. But comparing their covariant form with the conditional form of causal law statements—no effect without a cause—exaggerates the difference. These covariant equations are implicitly causal, in the respect that causality is responsible for the altered values of their variables. Flooring a car's accelerator augments the force with which the car surges, hence the altered value for acceleration. The difference between the two kinds of laws is diminished all the more when we use correspondence rules—bridge laws—to translate the terms of causal law statements into variables of the equations of motion or the Schrödinger equation.[27] Is a comprehensive reduction feasible? Two questions are implicit: is the diversity of causal laws reducible to a smaller number of causal laws; and is that smaller set of causal laws reducible to the laws of motion or those of quanta? Consider such causal laws as these: heating water to 100 degrees Celsius causes it to vaporize; increasing the pressure of a drumbeat increases the volume of sound; cars go faster as pressure on the accelerator increases. These are three expressions of a more generic causal law: increasing the magnitude of the cause increases the magnitude of the effect. Generic formulations reduce the array of causal law statements to a much smaller number. Are causal laws indefeasible; or do they reduce to the laws of motion? The qualitative diversity of causal laws makes this reduction seem implausible: heating, drumming, and pressing an accelerator are different in many ways. Yet, they are alike in this respect: each is a force applied over time with the effect that mass is accelerated. There seem to be no causal laws that are not expressions—however obscure—of the laws of motion or quanta, if matter is mass and causality is energy exchange.

How do natural laws relate to the phenomena they regulate? One may believe that laws float ethereally over their domains, somehow applying to things they cover. But laws need access to things to which they apply. Access might be satisfied by intermediaries, as chess pieces can't satisfy the rules of the game without chess players; but there is a better explanation: natural laws have no force or reality apart from things that act and interact. Being constrained by laws is identical, with behaving in the restricted ways for which things qualify because of their dispositions. What we call *laws* are constraints on motion and change founded in the dispositions of spacetime and things that move and act.[28] I shall be saying that dispositions (hence the structures, charges, and velocities on which they depend) are nature's regulators and the basis for its laws. This is so, because a structure's dispositions restrict the things it can engage, the manner of their interaction, and the range of possible effects.

Imagine a light switch: agitating a particle beyond a certain degree causes it to release a photon; less agitation, and no photon is released. A causal law statement signifies the parameters of this result and predicts its occurrence given appropriate values for its variables. What aspects of the particles determine this effect? Relevant features include the structures and charges of the particles and the spacetime in which they move, hence the dispositions that make particles responsive to one condition, but recalcitrant to the other. Where there is uniformity among particles—particles of a kind have the same character and dispositions and interact in the same ways—we have a causal law. Law statements report the relationships for which things qualify because of their dispositions. But law statements are not laws. Conflating the two falsely implies that natural laws are distinct from the phenomena they regulate, though laws are intrinsic to the phenomena law statements report: they have no reality apart from the properties and interactions of the things to which they "apply." Such laws are Aristotle's *universalia in rebus*.[29]

C. Dispositions

Think of grinding a key by cutting notches in a blank. Each cut changes one of the key's structural properties, thereby qualifying it to open locks of complementary shape. Suppose that structural properties—mass, and topological or geometric properties especially—are described as first order. Things are capable of, or disposed for relations with others because of their structures; hence, the conclusion that dispositions are second-order properties of structures. A knife can cut because of its fine edge. Eyes can see color because of cone cells in the retina. *Can* is materially significant, though dispositions are not separate, material entities. Writers wanting to avoid the contrary impression conflate them with structures they qualify.[30] But this reduction obscures a significant difference. Structure is the configuration—the organization—of matter in spacetime; dispositions are the qualifications for relation and interaction consequent on having a particular structure. Different structures are likely to have different capacities for action or reaction, as knives differ from forks. Speak to Japanese in their language, and the information is communicated. Talk to me, and the message doesn't pass.

It is physical structures—particulars—that have dispositions, but the emphasis on the structure of individual things should not be construed as a reversion to the atomist claim that material particulars are nature's only constituents. For there is this uncertainty: are particulars typically separable and separate, however qualified for relations, or do they usually or always bind to one another? Wittgenstein acknowledged this issue in his *Tractatus*, though his response was ambiguous. Are his *Gegenstande*—objects—ever separate, because unrelated to others? Or do they invariably participate in configurations where they display one or another of their internal (dispositional) properties? Wittgenstein's preferred answer was that we infer the circumstances of objects from those of their proper names. But there are, he said, no names apart from sentences, hence no objects apart from states of affairs: meaning, that objects are always configured.[31]

This is a dictum for which no empirical evidence is supplied. But we may regard it as a balanced hypothesis, one that resists the implications of logical atomism. Things exhibit some of their dispositions by virtue of the relationships that engage them. For none is freestanding: each participates in some of the many relationships for which it has qualifying dispositions. Hence, our uncertainty: are material things simply located or multiply located because of their effects on others? Is the character of each thing fixed by its mass and constitutive structural properties (they can be perceived and measured, like Aristotle's self-sufficient, primary substances[32]), or is its identity indeterminate or determinable, because many of its dispositions—its qualifications for relation—are currently unrealized and unknown. Things that are finite in themselves and specifically located may be potent centers of unrealized forces or properties. These two perspectives shift in and out, promoting confusion that quickly dissipates. For this is the difference of structure and function. Things are constituted of structural properties that secure them a specific character and place, though these same properties qualify them for myriad relations to other things. See them as structures, and we locate them simply. Inferring their dispositions—by seeing them function—we struggle to capture the amplitude of their powers. This is plainest when we think of other people: each is a finite body or a variable source of initiatives, provocations, and responses, some predictable, others not.

This hypothesis obliges us to look both ways: to analyses that identify the fundamental particulars of a domain (the proper parts of its systems) and to syntheses that create systems by joining particulars. Reduction fails if it identifies those individuals while ignoring both the reciprocal causal relations that create systems (molecules from atoms, families from their members) and the dispositions that qualify particulars for these relations. Ideally, we would decipher layers of synthesis in order to show that nature is the successive overlay of many orders, quarks to quarks, molecules to molecules, then cells, bodies, tribes, and stars to their others.

We are a long way from reducing the simplest of everyday complexities to this nest of orders and their reciprocal determinations, but this or something similar is plausibly our world's construction principle. Its design is more complicated than is suggested here, because this account of dispositions is partial: it emphasizes structure—the organization of mass (shape, for example)—rather than velocity, charge or spin, equally fundamental material properties, as the basis for dispositions. The same consideration—the difference between character and the relations for which something qualifies because of its character—justifies extending this account to them. But structural properties—geometrical properties, especially—facilitate discussion, because they are more graphic (and for a reason emphasized below). Remarks about them are generalizable to those other, elementary properties of material things.

Does or could it happen that objects of identical structure acting in identical circumstances sometimes exhibit contrary dispositions: matches are used to start fires or extinguish them, though we never know in advance that they will do one or the other? This scenario makes several assumptions. It hypothesizes, first, that dispositions are second-order properties restricting the causal relationships in which structures may participate. But, second, it postulates that recurring interactions of the same causes do not have the same effects, so, third, we infer that the dispositions of the causes were different, implying, fourth, that the structures of the causes were insufficient to fix their dispositions, given, fifth, that no additional factor intervened to cause the difference.

This outcome would violate the principle of sufficient reason, a principle of inquiry that has vast empirical support. But sufficient reason is not a necessary truth (its negation is not a contradiction). One cannot prove its necessity without assuming it, though a *reductio* is suggestive.

Suppose the principle is false: no effect has conditions sufficient to produce it. This loosens the dependence of effects on their causes, for none is sufficient to produce the change that occurs when they interact: fires don't start because of striking matches, locks don't open because keys are turned. We have a Humean world where no event depends for its existence or character on any other. But then we also have no explanation for regularities observed in our world. This much order, stable but accidental, embodies no contradiction, but it would be miraculous (as above) if it had no sustaining conditions. Wanting an explanation, we consider possible conditions for the regularities observed. They include a god who guarantees the order we observe, or causes qualified by their dispositions so events of a kind have causes of a kind. These are alternative versions of sufficient reason. The first—a god—is an ad hoc stipulation for which there is no independent evidence. Discounting it leaves the second: we affirm that things act as they do because of the causal relationships for which they qualify (for which they are disposed) because of their structures. This *reductio* doesn't prove the necessity of sufficient reason. But choosing instruments appropriate to one's aims is prudent good sense: no hammers to swat flies. Theory, too, applies this principle systematically: sugar is bad for diabetics; printing money recklessly is bad for stable prices. Hypotheses that violate the principle by assuming any cause may have any effect are quickly falsified.

Quantum theory challenges this Aristotelian assumption in two ways. It alleges that particles sometimes have different effects, though they and their circumstances are identical: the particles have identical values for their measured variables, mass, velocity, spin, and charge. And quantum theory avers that particles described exhaustively by the wave function of the Schrödinger equation do not have determinate properties short of the time when they are measurable because of interacting with other things. This entails that there are no determinate grounding structures for dispositions when the particles are not causally engaged. Talk of dispositions that qualify structures for interaction is altogether dispensable if this is so, because what particles can do is a function of what they do: structures and their qualifications for causal relations emerge—with the "collapse of the wave packet"—as particles interact with other things. Both claims are problematic.

The first—that identical particles in identical circumstances behave differently—is dubitable in five ways: i. The Schrödinger equation can't differentiate among particles of a kind in order to specify, at an instant, determinate values for all the pertinent variables of each particle. ii. Measured values said to be identical can only be identical up to the accuracy of the means used to measure: variations that exceed the means are not measured. iii. Heisenberg indeterminacy entails that one cannot measure momentum and position simultaneously. This entails that measurements are sequential, and allows for changes of a previously measured variable when measuring the other. iv. Physicists sometimes allege that hidden variables are precluded by quantum theory or its experiments. But how is it possible to "prove" that all of an effect's causes have been cited, or that nothing is unspecified when identical causes have different effects? Theory is rarely complete. The Schrödinger equation provides accurate specifications of many phenomena. It isn't necessarily the whole truth about them. Hidden variables could have either of two forms. They might be properties independent of and additional to those known. Or a hidden variable could be the corporate effect—the relationship—of variables already known: the configuration of a particle's variables, each with its particular value, may create a corporate property, one whose character alters with differences in the values or relations of its constituent variables. Balance is a corporate property consequent on the relationship of several others (gravity and bodily posture, for example). And, critically, balance has efficacy, as corporate properties need have if they are to have the effects predicted but not explained by the Schrödinger equation. Either version might explain the different behaviors of particles said to have identical values for their variables. Both versions are testable, in principle, though only with the greatest difficulty in practice. v. Can one discount the effect of spacetime on particles embedded in it? Could spacetime be warped in ways sufficient to explain the different behaviors of otherwise identical properties? This possibility implies or couples to the second version of hidden variables: particles may be variously deformed by the variable topology of spacetime, thereby creating different corporate properties. Such properties—comprising particular values for mass, charge, and spin embodied in a minuscule spacetime region— may be the elementary referents for things called *structures*. Or variability may be benign in this respect: topology regards a knot as the "same" as often as it is twisted or untied, so long as it isn't cut. Could it be that the different behaviors of structurally identical particles are variations within comparable topological boundaries? These would be differences that do not violate topological sameness, though they do appear and measure differently. This would reduce the disparity of things that behave differently while being otherwise identical. We would want to know the material condition for this difference, but inquiry would be redirected: to the topology and geometry of the spacetime in which particles are embedded.

The alleged indeterminacy of unmeasured particles seems to have no deeper basis that the reduction of ontology to information about measured values. We are to believe that the Schrödinger equation provides a comprehensive specification of particles, though it is mute about specific values for the properties—topological, geometrical, or otherwise—of particles that are not interacting with other things. There is only a probability density to mark their passage in the interim. Instrumentalist readings of quantum theory emphasize that there is nothing more to know: particles do not have determinate properties between interactions that are measured, hence observed. (It is incidental that the observers be measuring devices or humans.) This formulation nicely satisfies Percy Bridgman's operationalism,[33] and Berkeley's *esse est percipi*. But there is no explanation in quantum theory for the odd fact that aggregates or relationships of indeterminate particles are themselves fully determinate. Or should we assume that middle and large sized things also lose determinacy when unobserved. Do sleeping humans become indeterminate when they are unobserved by others or themselves? Or is it contact with mattress and bedclothes that makes them determinate? The indeterminacy of things unobserved is challenged in every domain but quantum theory: imagine parents terrified by the indeterminacy of their absent, perhaps unobserved children. It is tolerated as an interpretation of quantum mechanics, because this is a vastly successful theory of particles, and because criticism is paralyzed by the status of physicists. An ethos that demands a comprehensive metaphysics of nature would probe quantum theory dialectically, questioning its alleged completeness, requiring that it explain the emergence of determination from indeterminacy.

There is no demand for such a theory, because skepticism and instrumentalism dominate our thinking and because the debacle of the ether—a much amended mechanical explanation that failed—convinced physicists and philosophers that every such speculation is arid.[34] But there are questions to answer. General relativity—also a well confirmed physical theory—affirms that masses and their relations—both having fully determinate local properties—satisfy geometrical constraints. There is, presumably, no slippage in these constraints, hence reason to doubt that the indeterminacies of a statistical theory are the last word about nature and its norms. The internal, economy of every system (the system-sustaining dynamic relations of its parts) together with its geometrically or dynamically determined dispositions and the geometrical and dynamical character of its circumstances may determine its every subsequent state. Different outcomes for apparently identical particles may be evidence that they or their circumstances are not identical.

We sometimes misconstrue the structure of a representational mode as the structure of the things represented: Aristotle inferred the relations of things and their properties from the subject-predicate forms of Greek grammar. Is the Schrödinger equation the final truth about reality? Could it be true that the indeterminacy it ascribes to particles is an artifact of its statistical form, not an indeterminacy within nature, itself? Physicists ignore this issue, because they have no better theory and because they cannot design experiments that would test for differences among "identical" particles. Others can speculate: why don't we observe variability in the effects of identical causes at other orders of scale (meaning, greater size)? The familiar answer is: averaging. Small differences wash out in phenomena of larger scale. But the problem doesn't disappear. Imagine that physically indistinguishable things of any scale behave differently in physically indistinguishable circumstances. What would explain, what would preclude these variations?[35]

One answer suggests that dispositions are fixed by the geometrical and topological properties of structures, so that a structure's causal relations are constrained both by these properties and by the geometry and variable topology of their embedding spacetime.[36] This would preclude the contrary effects of identical causes: structurally identical keys would always open locks of a complementary shape given constancy in the topology and geometry of both structures and their embedding spacetimes. (Qualitatively different spacetimes—one Euclidean, the other curved—would have different structures, and sometimes or always require different keys.) Slight and variant topological deformations in particles or their embedding spacetimes would result in particles having different structures, hence different dispositions and different behaviors.

This account of dispositions requires additional details. We need, for example, a more detailed description of the relationships for which things qualify because of their structures, hence their dispositions. Some are static: one wears cloths that fit. Others are dynamic: energy is transferred. The difference between relationships of these two kinds isn't always plain. The relationship of iron filings arrayed about an electrified wire looks static, but isn't: stop the current, and the wire loses magnetic properties. We reformulate this distinction, saying that static relationships are limiting cases of dynamic ones, those where motion is reduced to zero. The skirt too tight for walking is fine if one stands. It is also relevant that dispositions are ascribable to space, time, or spacetime when we infer from trajectories they tolerate to the qualifications for relation conditioned by their structures. For there is a difference between a structure and the configurations or trajectories it may embody because of its structure. So, motion on a torus is channeled by its structure: straight lines there are arcs or circles. Motion on a twisted torus describes a figure eight, with effects on gravitation and acceleration, hence on structures moving along these trajectories. Dispositions vary with a spacetime's structure: each has qualifications for relatedness—dispositions—consequent on its form, so each accepts some motions and precludes others. One spacetime can't acquire the constraints of another because (it seems) neither is plastic.

These considerations complicate the story without compromising it. Now, as above, we locate dispositions in structures, and natural norms in dispositions. We infer that structures of a kind fix dispositions of a kind and that dispositions are qualifications for relation, so that identical sets of causal conditions are disposed to produce and do have the same effects: natural normativity is in the structures and dispositions of material causes. Every motion, like a child going down a slide, may exhibit the limiting effects of its spatiotemporal structure.

These suggestions are problematic: it isn't evident that topological and geometrical properties are paradigmatic, everywhere or often, of disposition-determining, structural properties. A structure's relation to its dispositions is most apparent in norms that are close to the surface of practical life: the relations of locks and keys, furrows cut by ploughs, or, more remotely, the formation of crystals. But the leap from such graded examples to the alleged geometric complementarity of sub-atomic particles or to the structure of spacetime is vast: a knack for pinochle or argument is not obviously a function of either. Yet, some dispositions are founded in the geometrical-structural properties of their hosts. Opium induces sleep because of its dormative power. But this is not a semantic play on *dormative*. It happens, because the geometry of opium's molecules is complementary to the geometry of the molecules of the neural dendrites to which they couple. Moliere would have been surprised. Physics and chemistry will likely surprise us more. Every such example exhibits nature's uniformities: same geometry and topology, same dispositions.

Add repeated interactions of structurally identical causes to get the same effects. This surmise is complicated by the difference made by velocity: the lightly blown stone that bounces off a window breaks glass when thrown harder. But velocity, too, has a geometrical component if inertial motion is accelerated on trajectories in a curved spacetime. The paths and velocities would be different in spacetimes having different geometries. Other factors—charge, for example—also complicate this surmise. Confirming it would vindicate the geometrical hypotheses of Plato, Proclus, Descartes, and Einstein.[37]

The hypothesis is "classical" in the sense implying *retrograde* when used by physicists, but their annoyance wouldn't last if theory could resolve every complexity—the sound of an oboe or loon—by embedding causality within the features of a dynamic spacetime, hence to motion, geometry and topology. Providing for natural normativity in this way won't please everyone. It is a red flag to those who fear that explaining complex uniformities by reference to a few foundational properties eliminates emergent phenomena such as life or mind. But their elimination is not implied. Life emerges with the creation of cells from molecules. Complexity's emergent effects are not diminished by locating the dispositions of molecules or cell assemblies in their geometrical-structural properties.

What do we lose if this account of dispositions is mistaken? The argument informing us has the same logic as the *reductio* used to defend the principle of sufficient reason: deny that dispositions are founded in the topological or geometrical structures of things, and derive the result: namely, the chaos where such factors as a structure's topological or geometrical properties and velocity are not necessary and sufficient to fix its dispositions and effects. Anything may happen when structures interact. This is perplexing, because it implies that identical structures and velocities do not entail identical qualifications for relation, or identical effects when interactions occur. One explanation for this imagined difference would cite the context of interaction: random intrusive events explain the disparate effects of otherwise identical causes. But there is no need to explain such effects by postulating interference, if structures are not uniformly qualified: same structure, but randomly varying dispositions and effects. A different response explains randomly disparate effects by observing that every structure qualifies for a diversity of interactions: move a person from the sauna where he perspires to the icebox where he shivers, and we have one structure responding differently to altered circumstances. Most things qualify for many relationships, some that never come to pass.

Those many relationships index the range of a thing's capacities, but they
don't explain the matter at issue: how things identical in structure might
have and evince contrasting dispositions in identical contexts.

This difference would be mysterious were it to occur. There is no
reason why it shouldn't occur if no material condition fixes the dispositions of things. What could that factor be if it is not the velocity or structural properties of things that affect one another by interacting? The
limited alternatives include mass, spacetime, and motion. But masses and
spacetime are structured by their dynamic, geometrical, and topological
properties. Motion—velocity—is constrained by the geometry of spacetime. There seems to be no alternative to dispositions that are founded in
the dynamic, geometrical, or topological properties of masses and spacetime. The explanation for nature's uniformity is here: same cause, same
effect. Dispositions are the critical mediating term: structures of a kind
qualify for relations of a kind.

We aren't close to confirming that myriad, complex, everyday examples are resolvable in this way. But the advantage of the surmise is apparent: grounding dispositions in these properties supplies the required
material basis for the parochial necessity of natural laws. The laws would
be different if motion, mass, and spacetime were different.

D. Systems

Dynamic systems—families and cells, for example—are created and sustained by the causal reciprocities of their parts. The parts of static
systems—geometrical figures, jigsaw puzzles, or melodies—are complementary: they fit. The parts of dynamical systems are themselves systems: molecules from atoms, for example. Every individual participates
in some system: the free hydrogen atoms in otherwise empty space are
bound gravitationally. Separate hierarchies of systems rise from this
common base.

Each system is a module, and each holds its place more or less
securely. Modularity has three implications: i. A system imposes least
constraints on its parts. These are forces embodied in the geometry and
motion of the parts in the case of atoms or molecules; they are organization, mores, and laws in the case of states. ii. The relations binding a
system's parts give it a degree of independence and an internal economy.
iii. The relations creating a module mediate the effects of things outside

the system by filtering, interpreting, or dissipating their inputs. Modularity is consequential for freedom: each module is free from the direct effects of many others and free within its space (however circumscribed) to fill its roles or pursue initiatives of its own.

One imagines possible worlds where nothing interacts or things are unaffected by their interactions. Compare the reciprocities and stabilities commonplace here. A system's parts are usually bound by gravity or electromagnetic force, less often by the stabilizing effects of negative feedback. Thermostats are the familiar examples of feedback, but others are closer to human experience: friends disappoint one another before perceiving the effects and altering their behavior to save the friendship; conversation flourishes when a stranger asks a question of one who stays to answer. Positive feedback also creates systems, though their reciprocities are unsustainable: heat that oxidizes something combustible creates more heat, burning through the available material until nothing remains to burn. Compare the solar system: the mutual gravitational relations of sun and planets stabilize this system for billions of years.

We usually suppose that constraint—normativity—is lateral: things interacting restrict one another, hence their mutual effects. But constraint is vertical in hierarchically ordered systems: atoms from quarks, animal bodies from their organs. The higher-order system would not exist if the parts were not reciprocally related, but it, once established, constrains them. Two sorts of cause—formal and efficient—are implicated in every such system. A system's parts are its efficient causes: the system is created by their interaction. Their organization is the system's formal cause. It regulates the mutual relations of the parts, hence the parts themselves. Imagine couples arrayed about a stage in the changing patterns of a dance. The moving pairs—the efficient causes—create an evolving pattern, but then the logic of the pattern determines relations among the pairs.

A rabbit is prior to its parts in the respect that each part's function and structure are conditioned by its reciprocal causal relations to the others. The heart pumps as its structure determines, though its rhythm and size are partly determined by the organs—brain, glands, and lungs—to which it relates dynamically. Why call this constraint vertical when the mutually constraining effects of organs are plainly lateral? Because vertical constraints have no efficacy but for the interactions of parts they constrain. A live heart beats as it does because of its structure and because of its accommodation to the internal economy established by the body's divers organs and systems, itself included. Vertical constraint is the complex effect of a system's mutually inflecting parts as they impinge on any single one. That part responds to an economy it has helped to create. Let civility be our example. Each person responds to another or others in ways calculated to provoke a similar response. The result is a higher-order system, hence the regulative force that every such system has on its parts. Children and strangers learn the expected responses; a few are stubbornly hostile and alien.

Constraint is layered. An orchestra's musicians regularly signal one another. There are cues appropriate to the music played, cues learned as one practices with others and cues that go back and forth during a performance. This system—the orchestra—is established and stabilized by the negative feedback of musicians who respond to one another. But the orchestra is not simply the system of its coordinated members. There are critical subsystems: first and second violins, brass, woodwinds, and percussion. Players learn to work together before their sections can achieve the integration—the discipline—required of the orchestra. The regulative effect of these normative relations is plainer if we imagine the difficulties of new members. Reading the score and playing the instrument are easy enough: these are accomplished musicians. Adjusting to the practices of a section, then the orchestra requires that a player's habits be modified by the expectations and responses of others. It takes a while before new members are integrated. But then the system's norms are learned, and these members are reliable guides to newer ones.

An agent falls under the control of a higher-order system when its behavior is altered by its reciprocal relations to the system's other part or parts. Jack and Jill are self-absorbed, until they meet and bond. Now, each attends to the other in ways that secure their friendship. For it is no mystery that successive higher-order systems differentially regulate their members, or that we can distinguish and explain a member's responses to the norms imposed by successive orders. Imagine a friend who participates in a system that requires discretion: a business, a church, or the FBI. "There are things you aren't telling me," you complain. "I can't," is the reply. "It's my job." Every behavioral nuance might satisfy a different level of the hierarchy in which a lower-order system is nested, hence a different norm. Yet, the ontological basis for this cascade of norms is never more complicated than the causal reciprocity of its constituent lower-order systems: atoms make a molecule; individual persons make families, tribes, and secret societies. Vertical relations often stabilize their proper parts: an obstreperous athlete is pacified by joining a new team, a child is secured by family, neighborhood, friends, and school. But conflict is as common as reinforcement: someone docile in his private life is moved to fury by a new job.

These are higher-order systems showing their normative effects. Regulation is achieved and maintained directly by the reciprocal causal relations of a system's parts, or mediately by the regulative effects of the hierarchy in which a system is nested. Join quarks or atoms in ways appropriate to their structures, and the effects are stable atoms or molecules—nothing adventitious. The efficacy of the causes is founded, in turn, in the dispositions—the qualifications or limits on relation—consequent on their structural and dynamic properties. An orchestral musician has the subtle mechanical and intellectual skills appropriate to his or her instrument. Given the occasion—a conductor and score—he or she responds. Skeptics deny the physical basis of norms, arguing that the regulative force claimed for them is nothing but an observer's expectation or prediction. But is this plausible: could anyone play as well? Let skeptics staff orchestras by recruiting random passersby: give each an instrument and the downbeat, then wait for the result. How many musicians would we discover? Why do we find any? Because of the self-regulation taught in music schools and the habits their students acquire. Regulation—normativity—is external in the respect that a conductor imposes his interpretation on the musicians. But it is also internal: musicians play as they do because of the patterns of excitation and inhibition acquired by habituated nerves and muscles.

Normativity's locus is more obscure when the dispositions at issue are those of systems. A knife cuts because of its fine blade. What is the comparable, disposition-bearing structure in a system of reciprocally related parts? Are there corporate dispositions: meaning, dispositions that emerge with the creation of a system, dispositions distinct from those of its parts? Where, if so, are they located: in the system as a whole, its parts, or their relations? Answers are implicit in the knife, for it, too, is a corporate entity. Its blade is a system of molecules bound by electromagnetic forces. Its capacity for cutting is the consequence of its rigidity and the form achieved by grinding away some of the molecules. Rigidity is, structurally, the tight packing and bonding of the molecules; this is, dispositionally, the structure's ability to resist an external force.

An orchestra that plays with a particular style is also a corporate entity having corporate dispositions. Compare its performances to recordings made by splicing the bits and pieces of musicians recorded separately. Taping solo musicians excuses them from needing the habits required were each to coordinate his or her playing with others. Many entities created by political or legal fiat disguise a similar incapacity. A nation's laws may seem to unify its provinces, though the uniformity of their responses may be evidence of the state's intimidating power, not the consent or cooperation of its people or provinces. We need a different, more subtle account when higher-order control of lower-order systems is natural, not contrived or coercive. For then, the higher-order system has no basis but the structures and interactions of its parts. Yet corporate dispositions should not be confused with the dispositions of an aggregate's parts. Grass looks green when all or most of its blades look green; but this effect differs from the impression made by a system of integrated parts: someone walking gracefully, for example. Clumsiness in any part makes the effect disappear. Compare frogs or crickets chattering at night. Let them stop, one at a time, and the sound is diminished, not stopped.

Nature is a network of systems, some that are mutually independent or aggregated, others that create higher-order systems (including, cells, bodies, tribes, and ecosystems) by engaging one another. Imagine that people meet and bond, thereby creating a higher-order system. A third person creates overlap by bonding separately to each of them: A-and-C overlaps B-and-C. Or systems nest in successively higher-order systems: Brooklyn and Manhattan are proper parts of New York City, in the state of New York, in the United States. Is there a single system that comprehends every other, either because of overlap, nesting, or both? Gravity binds the array of things in spacetime, but its unifying effect is limited. A thing affected gravitationally by those in its backward light cone affects everything in its forward light cone, but it cannot affect things that ceased to exist before it.[38] Nor is gravity sensitive to the emergent properties of higher-order systems: no intellectual attraction connected Moses to Australians of his time. These considerations preclude an overarching system, like the self-conscious Absolute, that gathers and acknowledges each system embedded within it.[39] We do observe hierarchies of nested or overlapping systems, but they—like towering clouds—rise separately from their common gravitational base.

E. The Whole

Is there an alternative perspective, one that exhibits the unity of the whole rather than its diversity? Is nature a unitary system in the respect that there are norms having regulative force on all its regions or parts? One clue directs us: Why don't laws vary from structure to structure, region to region, time to time? The likely answer is that the universe is one dynamic structure that differentiates and organizes itself until it is too distended to cohere, or until its many systems dissolve because the energy needed to sustain them has turned to heat. What is this one structure? The plasma-filled, electrified spacetime from which our universe evolved. Why is it one, rather than many? It is one, presumably, because of the unifying geometry and topology of its spacetime and because of the pervasive unifying effects of its electrical and gravitational fields. spacetime is the medium and form of the whole; gravity and electromagnetism are tensions that pervade and integrate the parts. The tensions are everywhere local, but they propagate throughout spacetime, either directly or by the mediation of intervening masses. The result is global cohesion with local dynamics and pervasive normativity. Regulation's principal sites are the layered fields established by the electrical and gravitational relations of particles, then by the successively ordered, material systems constructed from them. spacetime is the medium in which particles and higher-order systems are arrayed. Material reality has these three factors and motion as its only constituents.[40] Constraint is intrinsic to its form and dynamics.

This surmise is challenged by the indeterminacies of quantum theory, and by cleverly engineered violations of Bell's inequalities,[41] but supported by the implications of relativity theory. Physics tortures itself with this opposition, or ignores it. But no one, including quantum theorists, has a theory that explicates and confirms the indeterminacy of untested particles, their alleged spontaneity, or action at a distance.

4. Testability

Can one test these hypotheses about dispositions, causes, systems, and laws? Gravity's effects are familiar to everyone who drops a glass. The relation of dispositional properties to structural properties is also testable, as honing a knife enhances its capacity for cutting. But there is more to confirm: how do we establish that the normativity of natural laws is founded globally in the form and dynamics of spacetime and locally in the structures and velocities of individual things? We do it in steps: surveying the effects created by nature's self-differentiation—meaning, the systems formed successively when particles and their complexes are joined by reciprocal causal relations—we infer the properties of the whole from their character. Some of these properties (the shape of space, the direction of time) are corporate—they are properties of the whole—others (causal reciprocities) are distributed throughout its regions or parts. Observing these fragments of the whole, we find evidence for their sufficient conditions in the gravitational and electrical properties of masses arrayed in spacetime. We infer that the regularities observed express our world's essential norms.

This hypothesis will be resisted as another version of Aristotelian essentialism. Laws—already obscure in a world of particulars—are to be founded in the dispositions of structures that include spacetime and material particulars, though dispositions—qualifications for relation—are the ghostly "powers" of Aristotle's metaphysics.[42] This is a reasonable objection to Aristotle's partial characterization of dispositions: he didn't specify their material basis. But there is no mystery if dispositions are qualifications for relation founded in the structural properties of things, geometrical and topological properties, for example.

Seeing regularities we speculate about their structural, dispositional, causal, and nomic conditions, then look for the observables that would falsify or confirm the hypothesis. The procedure is unproblematic, unless we suppose that verification requires that dispositions, causal energies, and laws be perceived directly, rather than inferred. But many things we acknowledge are not perceived directly. We don't see black holes or radio waves, though hypotheses about them (inferences from effects to conditions that may or may not be observable) are confirmed when effects they predict are observed. Similarly, we confirm that dispositions are qualifications for dynamic relations—interactions—by seeing the difference made by altering a structure or its velocity: what does it do that it didn't do before?

There is also this question about the epistemological status of my inferences: are they hypothetical and contingent, or something other and more? I suggest, after Leibniz, that inquiries concerning nature's inherent normativities eventuate in judgments that are fully or weakly analytic a posteriori.[43] Studying phenomena that seem contingently related, we discover that they exhibit dispositions founded in the dynamics of a spacetime that has topological and geometrical properties. Their relations are necessary in the parochial respect described above: they are local to this spacetime, but necessary here. This is the weaker version. The fully strengthened one affirms with Bishop Butler that the laws of logic are universally applicable and materially immanent. These are necessities we discover, not the claims of a priori prescription.

5. Humean Objections

Compare two hypotheses. Change is constrained by dispositions founded in the structures and velocities of things. Or an event ensues—whatever its antecedents and whether or not it has any—though no constraints direct the evolution of things. The rationale for the latter view is the principle of non-contradiction: an event may have no successor or any partner to which it is joined in thought without contradiction. This is a permissive standard. There is no contradiction to supposing that my cat proves Fermat's last theorem; but this doesn't bring her achievement into the circle of plausibility or fact. Conceivability—non-contradiction—is a feeble test of possibility. It satisfied Hume, because he required little more: things conceived, whether ideas or percepts, lack nothing for existence but force and vivacity. But dreams and delusions of all sorts are evidence that vivacity is never a sufficient condition for the existence of things thought or perceived.

The deeper charge is that Hume's test for possibility conflates nature with logical space, material with logical possibilities. Material possibilities—possibles that may obtain in our world because they are founded in the dispositions of its structures or consistent with its laws—are a subset of logical possibilities. So, plays appropriate to a game are a subset of all logically possible plays; but no one plays baseball using marbles or a tennis racket. Hume might say that no contradiction results from mixing the plays of various games; and that is true, though saying it would confirm that he ignores the difference between material and logical possibility. Hume is also guilty of reducing all processes to the stream of sensory data entertained by a stripped-down Cartesian consciousness.[44] He described nature as a succession of events—like color spots or sounds—

each distinguishable and separable from the others, but ignored the abiding regulative conditions such events satisfy: the inverse square law, for example. Acknowledging them would have obliged Hume to distinguish material from logical possibility. For every regulative condition or property precludes its contraries: most possibilities consistent with an inverse cube law are uninstantiable in our world.

One imagines three principal objections to these remarks about Hume. Two were considered previously, the third is new: i. Redescribing *is* as *must* adds no content to the description of events. ii. Normativity—with its implication that events of a kind must occur—confuses the contingency of our world with the necessities that apply within all possible worlds. iii. What stabilizes normativity? Grant that natural necessity is parochial (restricted to a particular world), not logical, then consider: why couldn't dispositions—hence norms—change abruptly or continuously? The result would be a world that looks Humean—anything might succeed any other—but is not.

Imagine that the first objection—no difference between *is* and *must*—is applied to moves in a game: a batter runs to first base after hitting a pitched ball. We have no problem distinguishing what he does from a rule. For we see that what he does satisfies it. Let him run too far out of the base path, and he is called out for violating the norm. Why is the distinction of *is* and *ought* undisputed in games, but disallowed when norms are natural? Why can't the same phenomenon satisfy two assertions, one that tells what is, another that invokes the norm thereby satisfied?

The second objection is the familiar Humean move from nature to logic, though conflating the two is odd. We don't advise a chess player of logically possible moves he has ignored: he can't outflank an opponent by moving pieces off the board. Why is it inappropriate to acknowledge constraints in nature, given that we know the difference between norms and the moves they legitimate in games? One may respond that games are evidence both of norms and their violations: we know the rules because we know their breaches. Nature is different, because there are no violations, hence no evidence of intrinsic constraints. But this is an odd discretion. Should we infer from the absence of exceptions that the laws of motion don't have regulative effects? Why isn't the contrary as plausible: the absence of exceptions is evidence that the laws apply pervasively within our world? Imagine actors rehearsing a play. Each has learned his or her lines; rehearsals and subsequent performances go perfectly. Descriptions recount these successes. Transcriptions record them. But nothing said or heard intimates the inherent constraint. Should we infer that there is no norm—no script—determining what is said?

Where everything is logically possible, every event may have any successor. Regularity is miraculous, though nature continues its regular ways. Which is the better explanation: that events are random or that intrinsic constraints limit and determine the effects of interacting causes? Random sequences entail that we are unlikely to see or hear what we continue to observe. Intrinsic limits entail that we should observe what is observed. Inference to the best explanation weighs heavily against Hume, because it favors intrinsic norms.

The third objection—what sustains the normativities operating at any moment—is harder to answer, but tendentious. How norms are perpetuated is an issue separate from their presence in nature. The issues seem to elide only if norms change with every next event. This effect would preclude inductive generalizations: the future wouldn't resemble the past. The interpretation of such changes would, nevertheless, be uncertain: we couldn't distinguish a random sequence from one whose every event exhibits an intrinsic but different norm, as if the rules of a game were to change with every play. Nature is Humean in the first case; it merely looks Humean in the second. We might try to determine that nature is one or the other by estimating the rate and direction of change. Finding a formula that predicts the changes, we would infer that nature is not Humean. Or careful investigation fails to discover either a material basis for the changing dispositions of things or a formula that discerns their evolution. We wouldn't be able to tell whether nature is intrinsically Humean (it changes chaotically from moment to moment) or merely seems to be (because inherent ordering principles change from moment to moment). This is not our predicament: we do find the structural and dynamic bases for regularity.

What material factor accounts for the perpetuation of norms? This is the problem of induction—why the future resembles the past—formulated in ontological terms. I have argued that dispositions—qualifications for relation—are the basis for norms. The task of sustaining norms is, therefore, the one of sustaining dispositions. How is that accomplished? One may think to answer by imagining someone fickle: she loves me, she loves me not. Nothing is changed but her inclination. The answer is different if the bases for dispositions are structural or dynamic. Spacetime is supple, but topological and generic geometrical properties (space is flat or curved) persist through its transformations: think of string knotted, then untied. This is natural necessity: meaning, outcomes that are assured because their contraries are excluded by the persistence of nature's constituent or organizing features. The future will be like the past if material structures continue to qualify for the same interactions and changes. But why do they persist? Perhaps the route of spacetime's evolution—if any there be—is tightly constrained by its geometry and topology: given what it is, it cannot vary in the all but unlimited way that Hume postulates. Why this is so, or why spacetime has this form rather than another is unknown. Leibniz would have said that this form maximizes God's aim.[45] Spinoza would have inferred that no alternative form is logically possible.[46] But this entails that every alternative form embodies a contradiction, though alternative spacetime geometries do seem possible. Why our world has its form rather than another is, perhaps, unanswerable.

6. Natural Norms

The evidence for nature's inherent normativity is overwhelming. It includes the regularities everywhere apparent and our success at finding their material bases. Is the piano out of tune? Tighten and calibrate the strings. Do seasons recur predictably? Find the reason in Earth's rotation about the Sun. My argument reaffirms Descartes' belief that natural necessity is geometrical. This is a surmise, not a hypothesis we know how to confirm across the hierarchies of nested and overlapping systems: it isn't apparent that every disposition has this basis. My proposal cannot eliminate the possibility that things of identical structure have different dispositions. Nor is it proven that dispositions founded in topological or geometrical properties are secure: there is insufficient evidence that spacetime does not change, sporadically, spasmodically, or continuously. But my question is less ambitious: are there natural norms, and if so, what is their material ground? The evidence is considerable: their basis is dispositional, structural, and dynamic, more specifically the topology, geometry, and dynamics of spacetime and the systems arrayed within it.

We could surrender this hypothesis, and admit that we don't understand why the natural laws founded in dispositions should be as universal and stable as they are. We don't, because of the simplicity and power of an idea that runs from Pythagorus through Plato's *Timaeus*, Proclus, and Descartes to Einstein: we search for the geometrically constrained dynamics that creates the behaviors and effects observed.

CHAPTER THREE

Practical Norms

The phrase *practical values* is often used to imply effective solutions to problematic situations: we are hungry, lonely, or embarrassed; what's to be done? We assume that problems come and go: we solve a current predicament, then turn aside before the next one. This account is misleading, because problem solving is not sporadic. Every system—including human bodies and the higher-order systems having them as parts—is perpetually at risk of exceeding its range of viable, stabilizing behaviors. Need is ongoing. Everything that satisfies it, everything that sustains a system or facilitates relations with others has practical value.

This chapter identifies the parameters of practical value and the distortions introduced when atomist or holist ontologies are used to describe them. They are better explained by the communitarian hypothesis that nature comprises hierarchies of nested and overlapping systems. Two questions direct us: What are systems, and how are they formed and stabilized? How do practical values accrue as systems maintain themselves? Both answers speak to my thematic question: what is the relation of *is* to *must*, *should*, and *ought*?

1. How Are Systems Formed and Stabilized?

Consider the two parts of a cell: an osmotic membrane and an interior where nutrients passing the membrane are digested. The cells survives (as its separated parts would not), because the membrane prevents the protoplasm from dissolving into the surrounding solution, and because the

61

protoplasm supplies proteins that make the membrane elastic. This is causal reciprocity. Each of the cell's parts affects the other in a way or ways that establish and maintain the system.

Every living body incorporates structural parts or functional subsystems whose reciprocal relations have a similar, corporate effect: they establish or sustain it. Inside, the system channels sustaining resources—energy, materials, or information—through causal relations that bind its parts. The system thereby created is a module: the heart or solar system, for example. Each module may be separable from other systems, even from other parts of the higher-order system in which it participates (as heart and lungs are separable). Still, the modularity of systems or their parts (themselves systems) implies relative autonomy, not isolation and self-sufficiency. Not having an infinite supply of energy within it or information appropriate to all its aims, a module requires more or less frequent interchanges with other things. Equally critical is the hospitable environment where things of its kind are tolerated or supported by ambient pressure, temperature, and the chemical bath—water or air—where it stabilizes. No system survives, if its environment is altered beyond some degree.

The integrity of bodies is obvious, because their boundaries are visible surfaces. The boundaries of social systems (whether their proper parts are ants, bees, or humans) are hardly less conspicuous, though different. Fill a room with people who speak either of two languages, and require that conversation be their only means of bonding. Here is a case where the reciprocal relations that establish a system—communication in a shared language—are a sufficient barrier to other things: no additional boundary, no impermeable skin, is required. Imagine now that a bilingual speaker participates in both communities. This is an instance of nesting and overlap: one thing—one lower-order system—is nested in higher-order systems that overlap because they share this part.

Every system comprises the parts whose reciprocal relations create it, but there is this difference among systems. Organizations are established by the reciprocities of parts that have disparate but complementary roles: teacher and student, pitcher and catcher, for example. The members of associations have few internal offices to distinguish them, because these systems are created and sustained by the affinity of their members, not by the complementarity of their roles. A team's fans are functionally undifferentiated: the enthusiasm of each intensifies equivalent feelings in his neighbors; none has a role different from the others. Organizations require the relative autonomy—the modularity—of their members. Associations reduce autonomy: they don't survive if each member's beliefs, attitudes, or feelings don't mirror those of the others. Modularity is also sabotaged when it dissolves under the pressure of nesting and overlap. The American colonies regarded themselves as independent sovereignties and economies. Their political and economic merger—the United States—transformed a higher-order system of cooperating parts into a larger, more complex version of a single sovereignty.

2. Practical Imperatives

Three practical imperatives are common to all systems: sustain reciprocities that establish the system (roles must be filled, coordination assured); secure resources that maintain it (books, food, or nails supply information, nourishment, or materials required by people who need one or another to fill their roles); service other systems with which it exchanges resources. Things that satisfy or frustrate these imperatives are positive or negative utilities: trucks that deliver our goods shatter the pavement and pollute the air; music that soothes us bothers the neighbors. Value ascriptions are half-truths if they single out the beneficiaries without mentioning the victims. Details are familiar: Heart and lungs have practical value, because their relationship sustains human life. The quarterback or shortstop has practical value for a team that can't win without him, and also for opponents that lose when he plays. A system is valuable and valued when it relates to others by supplying a service or resource: feeding the doctor enables him to cure the farmer who supplies his food. The circle is not usually so small. A complex society is sustained by reciprocities that propagate in many directions and by nested or overlapping subsystems of many sizes. Practicality is dedication to these three tasks. Businesses are exemplary. They survive by promoting the reciprocal relations of their employees or parts and their bonds to sources and clients: the shoe factory needs workers effectively organized, leather, and buyers.

Practicalities are situational. A thing having instrumental value in one situation, loses it when circumstances change. Does anything have abiding value? People typically regard themselves or their systems as stable, intrinsic goods, some other people or things as lesser centers, and the rest as utilities. Each of us expresses this bias as a more or less consciously formulated map of intrinsic and instrumental values. The intrinsic goods are represented as foci; utilities circle them as iron filings ring the poles of a magnet. Probably, no map is static: each changes with circumstances, interests, and attitudes: we willingly make ourselves instrumental to another's well-being, if a minor focus—work or friendship—comes to dominate us. An accurate map acknowledges that things having positive utility for one interest are inimical for others: we burn ourselves on stoves that cook our food.

Comparing maps confirms their agreement about the positive or negative utility of instrumental goods—money or water, for example—and also accord about lesser goods-in-themselves: family, friends, fellow workers, congregants, or citizens, for example. But there is no consensus about intrinsic values, given that each person perceives him or herself as the primary good. This adversarial perspective is common to all or most of us. The benefit or cost is mine; other people and things have value because of their positive or negative effects on me. We notice that our actions have effects that ripple through others, but we, the intrinsic goods, can ignore them. For egoism is stubborn: each person feels his or her needs and pleasures more directly than those of others, and each is justified by the individualist ideology that justifies us when we act accordingly. This must surprise other people: perceiving themselves as intrinsic goods, they find themselves used as instruments. Their responses sometimes shame us, for we know that other people are legitimately self-concerned, and that they, too, have families and friends. We retreat to a qualified egoism—the people and things important to me. Yet, each person's belief in his or her intrinsic value is oddly schizoid: we acknowledge that our worth is self-declared, not intrinsic.

This bad conscience roils thinking about practical values: granted that we use other people and their systems for our purposes—often without regard for their aims—is practical value more than the shadow cast by self-interest? Do other people and things merely seem useful because of our self-concern, or is there an objective basis for saying that they have intrinsic utility? A plausible answer is closer to hand when moral ambiguities are put aside. For there is no doubt that water is good—useful—for putting out fires but useless for making them. Its practical value derives from the natural relation of cause and effect. Discount our aims, and the issue is only factual: does water extinguish fires, do fish need it to live? Answers invoke myriad causal laws—this is a cause of that—each applying to a specific array of utilities and their effects.

Looking for normativity in laws of this form is confounding, if we suppose that law statements do no more than signify correlations in data or events observed or predicted. But there is another way to read them. Each law signifies efficacy and constraint—hence normativity—in the relations of its variables. This way of construing the laws is anathema to Humean sentiments, but less shocking when we consider that apprentices spend years learning how to achieve specific affects. Bakers, carpenters, musicians, and dentists learn that certain procedures work, others not. The normativity of such relations is plainer, if we imagine the contrary. Suppose that everything works: one can produce any effect desired by any and every action. Imagine the relief of students when told that practice is irrelevant: they can achieve an effect any way that suits them. Nothing in our world justifies this assurance: normativity is an everyday feature of the things we do, because every specific effect exemplifies a law of the kind signified above: x is an effect of $a, b, c \ldots$ or n (but not of $p, q \ldots$ or z). There are several ways to do many things, but they compare to myriad ways that fail. The successes emerging from the backdrop of failures are the norms of practical life: achieve the effect desired by doing something that will produce it.

The instrumentality of natural relations is explicit in the biblical view that nature was created to satisfy human interests. Descartes, too, acknowledged their utility, but then he implied that the value of utilities derives only from their effects on us:

> All the preceding passions may be produced in us without perceiving in any way whether the object causing them is good or evil. But when we think of something as good with regard to us, i.e., as beneficial to us, this makes us have love for it; and when we think of it as evil or harmful, this arouses hatred in us. . . . This same consideration of good and evil is the origin of all the other passions.[1]

Material things, in themselves, have geometrical properties only. The values we ascribe to them have some other source: namely, our interest in using or avoiding them. This is a claim about judgment and will: each person affirms his or her value (though Cartesian thinkers are not gendered): other things are good or bad given their effects on us.

Western culture often bets its future on the assumption that we are the cynosure of all creation; the worth of other things is measured only by their effects on us. This persuasion is often expressed in heroic terms: we shall have an objective by willing it, whatever the means available, however adverse our situation. This slogan confuses stubborn will with the causal efficacy of its instruments, though one cannot empower the other. The effect desired will not be achieved in the absence of appropriate causes, however persistent we are and whatever the desirability of the aim. Desire may be one of the causes, but it is almost never the only one, and sometimes, it is incidental to the effect desired (good weather, for example). Practical reasoning makes the distinction explicit: this is what you do if you want this effect, though of course you may not want it, and for many effects you should not. Think of two recipes for baking cakes— one that correctly describes the procedure, another that misdescribes it— then notice that someone wanting cake will not get it if he uses the flawed recipe, however much he wills the aim.

Compare the many instances where desire makes a difference. A local newspaper has two pictures of an old book: one taken before, the other after the book was restored. There was an *is* but no *ought*, until a curator decided that the book should be restored. This is also the pattern when environmentalists argue that we should save an endangered species: take the moths' point of view, then demand action appropriate to their interests, because moths neither discern them, nor speak for themselves. We do both things for them. Hence the charge that my appeal to natural norms wrongly imputes to nature the values of its advocates. We are to believe that mind stands apart from nature and that we thinkers manipulate it as will and desire prescribe.

These distinctions—mind and body, valueless until valued—lapse if mind is the activity of a physical system. For values are not generated by a mind that issues decrees from a position outside of nature. Material systems are valuable, because of their effects. Every material difference has practical value—thought and desire included—because each is the effect of causes and the cause of subsequent effects.[2] Binders and librarians are good for books, music and fresh air are good for me; I have instrumental value for whatever things I affect, whether the effects are destructive or enhancing, adventitious or intended.

Human interests change; things gain or lose value as we use or abandon them. Isn't this confirmation that practical values are a function of human interest or desire? No, it proves only that we conflate two things when we think about such values. First is the factual question: what difference does something make? Second is a question about human interests or intentions: do we want this effect? The first consideration establishes the domain of effects that are or could be made, hence the array of things having practical value. The second identifies the much smaller class of current but changeable human interests. Technology is the engine that extends this subset into the larger domain of practical values. We learn to exploit causal relations that once seemed incidental to our aims.

Normativity is not exhausted by the controlling—determining— relation of efficient causes and their effects. Aristotle cited four causes: material, formal, efficient, and final.[3] Each is a dimension of practical value, and all are present in nature, hence in human behavior: material agents achieve an objective by acting in ways shaped by rules or laws. Games are played with material of some kind (bats, balls, or cards) in accord with rules that limit the field of play and the permissible moves. They proceed when players act in a way calculated to achieve an end (bidding or batting to win). Every causal relationship embodies norms that limit their effects, though we may not perceive the constraints until they resist us. Think of yogis trying to levitate.

Appealing to Aristotle may seem retrograde. Matter, motion, and laws are pervasive; final cause is not. The next section argues that teleology is intrinsic to mechanical systems in ways that are ontologically innocuous.

3. Ends and Aims

Practical values include but are not exhausted by materials, efficacies, and rules. Ends also have practical value, and they, too, are normative, though the issue is complicated by this difference. Some ends are achievable, because there is a causal trajectory that does or would realize them; others are ideal because there is no causal trajectory having them as effects. Ideals considered but never pursued may have aesthetic but little or no normative effect: we enjoy entertaining them, but do nothing to achieve them. The normativity of those we pursue has two expressions. First are the causal sequences that achieve an objective. Incorporating material, formal, and efficient causes, they are a lever for practical decision and action: if you want this effect, proceed in one of these ways. Second are the states of affairs thereby created. Recall Aristotle's metaphysics of nature and his belief that natural processes are guided by intrinsic aims (the caterpillar soon to be a butterfly, or things thrown from a window). Can we provide for the normativity of such outcomes without supposing that unrealized attractor states behave magnetically, drawing and directing the mechanical processes that achieve them?

Anyone wanting to save Aristotle's notion must answer to Hume. His claim—there is no reason in metaphysics or nature why any event should have a successor—entails that nature is a random walk devoid of inherent aims or objectives. Events of a kind may aggregate about a mean (misconstrued as an essence); they may recur (misconstrued as inherent law); but essence and law are ontologized descriptions for accidental conjunctions. There are similarities among phenomena, spatial and temporal relations, but there are no natural causes, generative kinds (essences), or inherent laws. A fortiori, there are no natural aims or ends.

Plato's views about appetite and the normativities they imply are accurate counterpoint. He said that appetites are cyclical, not "infinite" because unappeasable: we pass from hunger to feeding, quiescence, and hunger again.[4] These are stages in the cycles of a dynamic, steady state system. The system is stabilized if the relations of its parts do not deviate from a range of variation. Hunger is evidence of a variation that threatens to exceed this range. Feeding restores the system to equilibrium. This condition is an attractor: the system issues alarms (hunger) when it deviates from this state, but stops giving them when deviations are corrected.

This formulation saves us from having to say that attractor states are ideal (currently unrealized) objectives that signal, somehow, to mechanical processes that strive to fulfill them. Systems move to a steady state— the least energy state—for reasons that are mechanical only. Water cools to room temperature; ardor turns to patience. Least energy states are more stable than others, because their use of energy is more efficient; disrupting or destroying them requires more energy than sustaining them. Attractor states—personal health and civic harmony, for example—are states of greater efficiency, hence natural ends. Many things impede the realization of least energy states, but this is the implicit norm—the inherent, regulative principle—of natural systems. There are no inefficient atoms. Societies that seem primitive and static from our perspective are organized to assure the efficiency of a principal organizing value, be it a line of authority or a mode of production.

Is there an anomaly in coupling systems—each having a steady state higher than entropy—with a least energy principle? Why don't systems dissipate to entropy and heat death? The answer is that entropy is one expression of the least energy principle, though not the only one. Least energy is equally applicable to systems that are far from equilibrium (far from entropy). It requires only that they be established and sustained in ways that are energy efficient. Protons are energy efficient and self-sufficient. Living bodies and human social systems survive by diverting energy from systems they deplete (stealing from Peter to pay Paul). Satisfying this principle is no guarantee of a system's longevity, because no system is isolated from factors that disrupt it. The solar system will disintegrate because the Sun collapses, or because of a powerful intrusion; jealousies and inequities of all sorts promote social conflict. Every system—every least energy, far from entropy, attractor state—is a contingency that emerges and dissolves. The universe, too, is a least energy system. Will it collapse because of internal factors or because of its relations to other things, other universes for example? We don't know.

The equilibrium of a steady state system—its attractor state—is one inherent material norm, but there is a second. Each steady state system is a node: meaning, a condition that is richly consequential for others. This is plainer if we focus on one of the stages in the cycle from hunger and appetite to satisfaction. One step in the sequence—quiescence—stands out from the others because of its effects. Hunger and feeding are narrowly consequential, because they dominate attention. Quiescence—temporary exemption from the need to recharge the machine—is richly consequential, because this is the condition and context for satisfying life's many other interests and needs. Systems having such effects earn description as nodes because of their fertility. Many people have children. Only a few produce the Plato, Newton, or Mozart who subordinates an era. The solar system is more remote from human concerns, but also more consequential since its emergence from the chaotic, early universe. Disorganized, unstabilized interactions were superseded by the stable, more consequential system we have. This is the condition and norm for lives and cultures that were impossible before.

Not every consequential state or event is nodal. Accidents often have consequences that outrun the events provoking them: a carelessly thrown match starts a forest fire, a careless word starts a war. Why not say that these too are nodes? Because nodes have an additional attribute: they or their heirs endure and prevail. A church endures; Plato prevails because thinkers who learned to think as he did perpetuate his ideas. The node is regulative, because it controls the character of its effects, and because it standardizes them over time. There is, nevertheless, no obvious least time for either a node or its consequences. A soloist spends months preparing for the hour of song that moves her audience. They are changed, though the resonance in them may not last the day. Some nodes—prosperous economies, for example—require human intervention; many others—cycles of days, seasons, or tides—do not.

There is no essential tie between nodes and the stability of attractor states. Rogue bankrupts (Enron and WorldCom, for example) are unstabilizable, but perniciously consequential. Least energy systems are normative in both respects: they are richly consequential, attractor states. So, the stability of many families and friendships is both a least energy state sustained by the causal relations of the members, and the generator of valuable effects. One thinks of Dewey's emphasis in *Experience and Nature*: every consummation is an attractor state, and a cause of subsequent effects.[5]

4. Consequential and Instrumental Values versus Intrinsic Values

The difference between things valued instrumentally and those valued for their consequences seems unstable. Systems or persons are valued consequentially as nodes, because they are ample sources of effects. Or they are valuable instrumentally because of satisfying the needs or interests of systems or their members. Let freedom be our example. As instrument, it has utility value for systems and their members; as node, it is the source from which these consequences derive. Like a change of state—liquid to gas, or gas to liquid—either becomes the other. The difference between these descriptions—node or instrument—is principally one of perspective and emphasis, but there is also the rhetorical effect of using one honorifically while reserving the other for things diminished by saying that they have utility—practical value—only. Ambulances and wrenches have instrumental value; universities are nodes. Some things are classified both ways depending on our orientation and purpose, will, for example.

Intrinsic value is not pertinent to this difference, because its alleged sites are persons who claim it for themselves and preferred systems. Their self-appraisal is better understood in nodal or instrumental terms: persons are causes; they have effects on themselves or others. This leaves us without an example of intrinsic value or content for the idea of it, though both are ready to hand. Music is good in itself when melody, harmony, rhythm, development, and instrumentation are effectively integrated. These are music's essential ingredients. Candidate scores or performances are more or less good as they meet these requirements. People are good, in themselves, when they satisfy criteria such as efficacy, honesty, and generosity. This formulation locates intrinsic value in the constitutive—essential—properties of things said to be good in themselves. It makes goodness derivative: a thing is good, because it satisfies the requirements of its kind. This criterion is demanding in a way Plato would have approved: a good painting is all the things something must be in order to fulfill the conditions for being a painting.

This formulation seems to entail that paintings less than good are not paintings, though many things incontrovertibly identified as bad art are paintings. More, this notion of goodness—good as a version of its kind—is needlessly Procrustean. Many things are good, because unclassifiable: they break established formats. But neither of these objections is decisive. The first misconstrues the claim: it doesn't disqualify inferior versions as instances of their kind. Given, say, five criteria to satisfy, something is an inferior version of its kind if it satisfies less than five, though it is something of the kind—it is good enough to be one of them—if it satisfies two or three. Or it satisfies all five, but does it poorly. Bad paintings are paintings; they are bad because of failing to satisfy the criteria to a high standard. (Poor students pass their courses with low grades.) The second objection fails, because it confuses goodness with novelty. A cello concerto requiring that musicians sit quietly, doing nothing for four minutes is not music, whatever the scandal it provokes. (Would one buy and listen to the recording?) Innovation is exciting because different, not because novelty is good in itself. We don't know its worth, until novelty proves to be more than flutter by achieving a viable style. But then, innovation proves its force by moving the standard. Criteria for things of a kind change: paintings don't have to be representational; dissonance isn't inimical to music. Ossified kinds—especially moral and aesthetic kinds—break up under the pressure of altered criteria. Repeated changes eventuate in family resemblances: there are different kinds of music and paintings and alternate sets of criteria. Things that satisfy all the criteria in one set satisfy none or a few in the others. But each is, nevertheless, better or worse as an instance of one or another of these fractionated kinds.

Something good in itself is, by this telling, a good of its kind. It is good as a streetlight, good as a parent or proof, good as sculpture. Intrinsic good implies something more: that such things are good unconditionally. But this is an illusion. Each kind determines the parameters—the

attributes of form—to be satisfied by its instances. The perfect crime is
not an unconditional good, but merely an optimal realization of its kind.
Every such thing may be appreciated for the achievement it is, but then
we ask or imply this other question: for what is it good? No matter now
that we understand the question in nodal or instrumental terms: no
matter that we value a thing as ground of its consequences or as cause of
its effects. Either way, we consider its relations to others. Goods of a kind
are turned back into the procession of causes and effects: every fulfillment is or can become the means to a subsequent effect.[6] This is consequential for aesthetics. For given that something is a good of its kind,
what is its effect on other things? Beauty is, more amply, the- experience-
of-beauty (chapter 5). It requires both a thing that is good in the way of
its kind and a cultivated perceiver, someone who resonates when perceiving it.

5. From *Is* to *Must, Should,* or *Ought*

Going from New York to London, one takes a boat or plane. If the distance is shorter—from here to the next room—we walk or crawl. Either
way, one is impelled by three imperatives: you should go (because of duty,
desire, or whatever); you must choose one of the available means of going
(because there are no others), and you ought to acknowledge and con-
form to the *musts* and *shoulds* of your situation (because you will be frustrated, embarrassed, or confounded if you ignore them). There may be no
obligation to choose any particular objective: nothing may entail what
one should do or be. It is true, nevertheless, that we have limited options.
The *is* of our circumstances restricts our choice of ends. The *is* of causal
relations restricts our choice of instruments. These two are practical
values: namely, what we can do or be, and what we can use to do or be it.

Constraints on *what* and *how* are familiar to everyone who takes the
measure of his or her situation before acting. Why should anyone accept
his lot if he couples American initiative to Nietzschean will and our ever
more potent technology? Isn't every barrier temporary, if we are inventive
and resolute? This is partly true, but mostly false. Some critical barriers
fall when challenged. Most never do. The practical problem is more
often one of judgment than will: which barriers yield, which do not?
Freedom tests the difference.

CHAPTER FOUR

Moral Norms

This chapter is a study in ethics, meaning theories or interpretations of morality. Ethics is contentious: there are several ways to construe it. Should it formulate principles that prescribe an ideal moral order, whatever changes of habit and conduct they decree? Or is ethics an empirical science, one—like sociology or psychology—that makes testable hypotheses about the formation of moral systems and persons? An a priori ethics is no more attractive than an a priori physics. It would be paradoxical if moral thinking and practice were determined by a theory that starts—as Kant does—by declaring the irrelevance of human needs and interests.[1] What and where are we? What can we do and be? Significant answers cite our nature and circumstances. But ethics is more than an empirical theory if—as proposed here—it has a moral aim: ethics commends morality by emphasizing the material conditions that make virtue exigent.

I shall be saying that morality's inception antedates both moral reflection and the rules or laws introduced to regulate behavior. We learn viable styles of moral behavior—and acquire moral sense—in core systems that include families, friendships, neighborhoods, businesses, and schools. The habits and inclinations learned in these circumstances are sometimes elaborated or reformed by rules and laws, but morality gets its leverage in contexts that are particular and local. Compare an ethics that issues a priori decrees: proud citizens of an abstract moral universe, we lose our way in local streets.

1. Semantic Preliminaries

Should and *ought* have four principal senses. "You should (ought to) go," says a friend commending a restaurant or city. He means that I would be pleased were I to go. His suggestion applies Aristotle's practical syllogism: if you want this, do that. Go, because you want pleasure and this will provide it.[2] Call this the pragmatic *should* or *ought*. It is distinct from both the deontological or universal *should* or *ought*, the categorical-situational *should* or *ought*, and the legal *should* or *ought*.

The deontological *ought* requires each person or rational being to will or enact only those rules or practices that all could will or enact without contradiction. One who accepts credit cannot refuse to repay it, for the reason that no credit would be extended if everyone refused to repay creditors: willing both an action (not repaying a debt) and the absence of its necessary condition (being given the loan) is a contradiction. We universalize most proposed rules or acts without entailing this logical impasse. So, conflict doesn't arise if we will that opposing lines of traffic be divided as they move on a two way road, because the effect willed (traffic flow) doesn't entail a condition (head-on collisions) that would preclude it. Legal *shoulds* and *oughts* are contingencies of this sort. Their negations are contraries rather than contradictions: the law could as well have required us to drive on the left.

The pragmatic *should* or *ought* is particular and conditional; do this to get that. The deontological *should* or *ought* is unconditional and universal. The legal *should* or *ought* is conditional—England or France—but universal within a domain. The categorical-situational *should* or *ought* is unconditional, but particular and existential: "You should (or ought to) do this, irrespective of what others do or ought to do." This dictum is addressed to someone having responsibility for a role—parent, teacher, or judge—or a responsibility consequent on an ephemeral situation, as one thinks "I ought to apologize" after an unintended insult. A particularly situated person is made responsible for an action he should or should not perform.

Pragmatic, legal, and categorical-situational *shoulds* and *oughts* are everyday features of practical and moral experience. It isn't plain that moral life justifies the priority Kant ascribed to deontological *shoulds* and *oughts*. For there is moral justification for practices he faults. Kant believed that lying has the same moral status as breaking promises or failing to repay one's debts: every such act sabotages a necessary condition for the act, namely, the mutual confidence—the trust—its performance requires. He denied that trust may be abused for a moral aim. So, one lies to thugs who come to the door asking if people they are looking to kill are hiding in the basement. These are honest thugs: never lying or expecting that others do, they believe it when you tell them no one is hiding downstairs. This result satisfies the pragmatic *ought* (Kant's hypothetical imperative[3]): lie, if you want to save innocents. It also satisfies the categorical-situational *ought*: you (not, more vaguely, anyone) ought to save the people hiding below if you can. Lying might even have legal sanction: lying to avert harm might be an extenuating consideration when the law otherwise requires truth-telling. Does this imply that everyone should lie whenever it suits him or her? No, truth-telling is a policy of inestimable practical value; trust in the word of others is a condition for cooperation and the ordinary business of life. We honor the rule without blinding ourselves to honorable exceptions. "You ought to lie" is, sometimes, one of them.

It is plainer now that legal and categorical-situational *oughts* are not distinct genres. Legal *oughts* (conditional because universal within a domain) are promoted for their consequences, as traffic laws promote safe passage. The unconditional categorical-situational *ought* is shorthand for this longer assertion: you ought to do this, given your circumstances, if you want that. These, too, are pragmatic *oughts*.

There is, however, this finer point. Categorical-situational *oughts* are distinguished from other pragmatic *oughts* by this double emphasis: "you ought to do this because you ought to want that." What justifies the second of these *oughts*: why should you want that, whatever *that* is? One answer might be that not wanting it is a contradiction, so wanting it is necessary. But this is false of categorical-situational *shoulds* and *oughts*. Their negations are contraries, not contradictions: not wanting vanilla, one might want chocolate or strawberry. A firmer answer supposes that an unimpeachable authority requires you to want it and will not heed the objection that wanting or having it is bad for you or others. Only God could make such demands, though the categorical-situational *ought*—you ought to do this, because you ought to want that—is not demonstrably God's will. *Demonstrably* needs emphasis, because numerous people, citing passages from privileged communications or the Bible, claim to know what God wants. Never mind that their claims have no supporting evidence, or that texts they cite are mutually inconsistent: killing is bad (abortion), but killing is good (capital punishment). Accordingly, the second *ought* of categorical-situational prescriptions—"because you ought to want that"—is still problematic. What could justify it? We glimpse the answer by looking more closely at things we ought to want. They are typically mundane, but fundamental to the well-being of people or interests for which one is responsible. This is what you ought to do, we say, because you ought to want the best for your children (spouse, friends, comrades, country). Categorical-situational *oughts* are emphatic versions of the pragmatic *ought*.

This reduces the fourfold division above to this simpler alternation: *oughts* are pragmatic or deontological. Kant distinguished them as hypothetical and categorical imperatives.[4] It was plain to him that the goodness of the will is founded in its commitment to reason. It requires that ideas, rules, or principles be universalized (in contrast to the particularity of things perceived), and it prizes consistency. A will constrained by reason resists impulse. It affirms only those plans, projects, or "maxims" that are universalizable without contradiction.[5] Neither reason nor will can guarantee that mind's intentions shall determine the shape or direction of material circumstances, but morality is served if mind controls actions within its power, principally those of thought and will.[6]

Kant's moral theory is oddly schizoid. It requires that practical life be governed by the a priori mechanics of reason, will, and deontological *oughts*, though Kant's pragmatic motives are explicit: he would avert the effects of cheating and lying—they disrupt or preclude the cooperation, harmony, and free choice vital to human flourishing—by using reason to discipline the will. Which is the dominant consideration, his characterization of reason and the good will or the importance of harmony, freedom, and cooperation? Suppose, as a test, that reason and will provoke social conflict. Which would Kant have sacrificed, his a priori mechanics or these humane values? Other evidence—his essay "Perpetual Peace"[7]—leaves no doubt that the practical conditions for autonomy and community are the touchstone of his concern. From which it follows that Kant's appeal to reason is pragmatic: morality can be grounded in reason and the categorical imperative because consistent, universalizable maxims would produce social harmony. Exploiting our rational nature is morally right, because this is the only propitious way to achieve individual well-being in the context of mutual reliance. We are successful to some degree, because there is public memory of practices that work, and because evolution has made us interdependent by nature and need. Our calculations are pragmatic. In public policy, as in personal life, we decide what to do after considering our needs, aims, and resources, then the likely effects of acting in particular ways. And usually, we infer that cooperation is the condition for freedom and harmony.

Should and *ought* have only this pragmatic sense when used in this chapter. *Should* is sometimes used with the full force of *ought*, other times as a softer commendation. This variability is sensitive to the circumstances where morality—duty especially—is learned and practiced. *Must* is used only incidentally in this chapter. It is never used to imply moral equivalents for the universal necessities of logic or the parochial necessity of natural laws.

2. The Context of Morality

If I look at forks and spoons asking what moral imperative follows from them, no answer is forthcoming. This is one of myriad states of affairs from which there is nothing to infer about the good or the right. But suppose the question is embedded in a larger story: we are having a family dinner, people are seated, food is served. Now, the details are sufficient to specify some duties. One shouldn't throw cutlery at the other guests, because it would wound them, break plates, and ruin the occasion. Why is that good or bad? Because of its effects on this family. Indifference and hostility are mostly alien here. Members like and rely on one another. Their dinners are frequent, and every member believes that these are important expressions of family devotion. What are the members' duties? Act in ways that respect and preserve this union and one another. Why? Because members achieve personal identity and well-being by way of their mutual relations. Their self-love derives in part from this system's binding force. Why call this *duty*? Because this is all that natural duty is: one is obligated by feeling, habit, and idealization to do such things as sustain prized systems and their members. Throwing spoons violates these duties, because it damages the family, other members, and oneself.

Participation in systems one values—especially such core systems as families and friendships—is the natural, unconsidered basis for both character and morality:

> Where after all, do universal human rights begin? In small
> places, close to home—so close and so small that they cannot be

seen on any map of the world. Yet they are the world of the individual person: the neighborhood he lives in; the school or col-
lege he attends; the factory, farm or office where he works. Such
are the places where every man, woman and child seek equal justice, equal opportunity, equal dignity without discrimination.[8]

Character forms close to home in families, friendships, neighborhoods,
and schools. Valuing ourselves, we value these systems, or we value them,
hence ourselves. The order of priority is hard to fix, because we emerge as
persons within systems we sustain. Knowing ourselves, we acknowledge
our duties to them. The duties are *oughts* that derive from the *is* of affiliation. They have instrumental—practical—value both for systems and
their members.[9]

This is a different context from the legalistic one usually assumed
when duty is invoked. We legislate to protect people in core systems
(marriage laws), to defend the parties to contracts, to create duties in
classes of people covered by a law (car owners or airplane pilots), or to
establish common rules across the divide of communitarian differences.
Fall within a law's domain, and you inherit a duty; fall outside its frame of
reference—refuse to sign a contract—and you are exempt. This alternation also holds if there are systems of two sorts: core systems to which we
have duties because we are formed by and value them and those in which
we have roles but no duties because our participation is forced. I have a
duty to family and friends, but not to an occupying army. This difference—voluntary loyalty or coercive law—confirms the impression that
duty is radically ambiguous.

Hegel's *Philosophy of Right* is the apotheosis of this difference. He
would have us believe that reason and law supersede mere tribal loyalties,
though life's dynamic comes from the network of systems that law displaces or reforms. Put all the emphasis on law, and we ignore or suppress
the systems and interests that give law its traction and point. For morality has its principal basis in the duties and dignity of people and systems
that make life viable. Law can rationalize old duties, or create new ones.
But it cannot supersede duties to core systems without becoming arid or
irrelevant to most of life's concerns.

Emphasizing law to the exclusion of the morality learned in systems
distorts duty in three ways. It ignores duties to core systems that antedate
the laws introduced to enforce them. It conflates duties to systems created
by the reciprocal relations of their members (including families, friend-

ships, schools, religious sects, work teams, and states) with duties created
by subjecting classes of people to laws (taxpayers, dog owners, or polluters,
for example). It obscures the grain of moral practice by opposing the high
morality of reason and law to the low morality of habit and inclination.
This opposition distracts us from graded duties created by affiliations that
are unrefined and undistorted by laws. For systems are more or less
dependent on the work of individual members, while members are more
or less dependent on their systems. *Degrees of dependence* implies the variability of the effects systems have, and consequently variability in the
degree to which members are duty bound to fill their roles. This implies a
version of gravity's inverse square law: obligation falls off sharply with the
diminished difference that systems and their members make to one
another. Duties to one's family exceed one's obligations to strangers.

Duties to core systems are natural in this way: we affiliate because we
must. Every such practice is a solution to a human interest or need. Solutions are variable. Who sits at the head of the table? Or there is no
favored seat, because tables are round. A culture's solutions are formalized
but not usually invented by the laws enforcing them. For the relationships establishing core systems are not originally contractual, whether or
not legal fictions and sanctions are later devised to protect participants.
Legality seems alien when a family, job, or friendship shapes one's hopes
and identity: members feel and believe that duties to the system are all
but indistinguishable from duties to oneself.

It may be said that I erroneously mistake the surface appearance for
the deeper truth about fact's relation to value. Focused and active,
keenly feeling our needs or interests, we see things as good or bad, useful
or not. Stepping back, separating our purposes from the means used to
achieve them, we easily distinguish things as they are (this glass) from
our valorizing aims (holds water or wine). These two perspectives—
reflective or engaged—shift back and forth, like a Necker cube. Many
believe that duty is similarly ambiguous. Seeing ourselves or others as
duty bound, we falsely interpret commitment or passion as obligation,
though, in itself, membership in a system is morally neutral. This persuasion rightly asserts that many things have no moral attributes, until we
legislate for or against them (sticks and stones, for example). It wrongly
denies that passion or habit, causal relations, and utility are sometimes
the sufficient basis for those attributes. So, morality is one domain of
utility: meaning, practical value. The relations of a core system's
members are a conspicuous example. Duty, at its inception, is nothing

more or other than the mutual expectation and intention created by interdependency. Fulfilling duties makes us useful to those who depend on us.

Individualists (the atomists of chapter 1) don't share this understanding of morality. Endorsing Hume's deflating analysis of causation, they cannot acknowledge that systems are established by the reciprocal causal relations of their members. Ignorant of systems, committed to privacy and the self-sufficiency of the Cartesian ego, they will not acknowledge that people acquire personality and the rights and duties of moral agents by virtue of their roles in core systems. They reduce morality to individual sentiments (Hume) or to respect for law (Kant and Hegel), though we bootstrap ourselves to personal, social, and moral identity by participating in systems that create and sustain us. Duty to systems and their members is evidence to others and ourselves that we are altered by our roles. Hegel condemned these virtues as subjective or tribal. He emphasized their contingency and insecurity short of the time when reason, law, and the state have bestowed their imprimatur.[10] But Hegel was too quick to subordinate the contexts where character and duty form to the imperium where they are rationalized and defended.[11]

Duty, freedom, trust, and respect express morality's inception in core systems. Duty includes the obligations of members to their systems and systems to their members, and duties to one's self. (Legal duties are considered below.) Freedom is moral to the extent that one must have it if duties are to be chosen or accepted and affirmed, rather than coerced or satisfied mechanically. Trust is confidence in one's partners. Respect is recognition that someone—initially a core system's other members or oneself—has worth because he or she is a reliable partner and because of the emotional or intellectual depth that makes him or her reliable. I shall be saying that duty, freedom, trust, and respect imply *oughts* and *shoulds* that derive from the *is* of systems and the selfhood that emerges with participation in them.

3. Ontological Assumptions

It was true until recently that human biology was fixed, evolution aside. Altering the anatomy and physiology of human bodies was mostly beyond our powers. The stability of our nature was often distressing—there was little we could do to avert sickness or death—but rhythm and strength reliably mitigated disappointment and decline. Now, when molecular biology threatens this stability, we feel vulnerable: what will anchor us, if our animal nature and social arrangements become fluid? Could biological tinkering or cultural variation eliminate all the features from which reliable values derive? This is possible: growing humans in the style of oysters (on strings in vats of amniotic fluid) would alter personal development and character by eliminating families. It wouldn't alter our need for schools, businesses, or states. The theories of reality mooted in chapter 1—holism, individualism, and communitarianism—would be as relevant then as now. What do they imply for morality?

Holism proposes that reality is a network of integrated parts, and that each part's identity is fixed in two ways: by its constituent properties and by its relations to the other things of the network. The first is conditioned by the second, when the information, attitudes, and habits of one are an accommodation to the other. For I am what I do, where the particular character of the doing is a function of my place in the whole: I know myself by knowing my station and its duties. Compare the person who has no place in this or any network: the conditions for his identity lie altogether within him. He resembles the odd piece found in a drawer: we turn it about, unable to imagine its use.

Holism may have originated in organic metaphors (the reciprocity of heart and lungs, for example), but its justification in our time leans equally on mechanical systems. Atoms and universal gravitation fall at the two extremes of spatial scale, but both illustrate systems having constituents that are only apparently self-sufficient. Holism is nevertheless contentious. It ignores the modularity of systems whose internal economies make them somewhat exempt from one another. So, each human perspective—including its thoughts, feelings, and attitudes—is distinct from every other. Holists resist. Anything said in our common language is never more than embroidery on ideas generated in the cross talk of interested parties: think of Newton standing on the shoulders of giants. Feelings, too, implicate our relations to others: we are angry because bruised; affectionate because encouraged. Individuals are the material sites of thoughts and feelings, but these are effects of our relations to interlocutors, partners, or adversaries. The pertinent domain for some effects is the entire network of systems; the smallest domain is never less than a region that includes the reciprocal relationships of several or many agents.

Holism may seem to imply that individuals have no freedom of action, given that each is constrained by its relations and duties to the others of its domain. But this ignores the two kinds of freedom present within networks of efficiently organized roles. Negatively, agents are free from having to do the work of others. Positively, they are free to do their own work, with appropriate talent and resources, and without interference. Other needs are satisfied by other members of the system, or by complementary systems (the grocery that supplies food to musicians who entertain and pay the grocer.) For the self-sufficiency ascribed to a network's parts is illusory: everything is as it is because of its identity-sustaining relations to other things.

Every such relationship—students to teachers, citizens or friends to one another—fixes the character of the agents engaged. Each does something to or for its partners, and each expects that the other or others will respond appropriately: perceiving your effect on me, I affirm our bond by organizing myself to do as you expect. This is a first expression of moral will or sentiment: I acknowledge my responsibility to a system and its other member or members. What do I owe them? Just such actions as affect them in ways appropriate to my role. These responsibilities presuppose that agents are empowered for the effects expected or required of them. For there is no responsibility without the opportunity and means—the power—to satisfy it. Power is a function of character and context. Character forms when talents are educated; context may supply opportunities appropriate to character. Power's exercise is an expression of freedom, though freedom is usefully ambiguous: it signifies circumstances where agents are empowered by talent and education (hence character) and by opportunity (contexts where resources are appropriate to character); but equally, freedom signifies the moral demand that one be empowered to satisfy a role. I need be free to do what my role requires of me. We suppose—if we are holists—that reality is a network of reciprocally related roles, each filled by an agent qualified to support the others. We also make this more or less explicit demand: let reality achieve its essential form. For duty brings a complex imperative to action: let me want to do what duty requires, then allow me—enable me—to do it. This demand implies four principal moral values that holists emphasize: duty, trust that one's partners are also duty bound, and a will that freely chooses to satisfy companions one respects.

Holism is a first account of normativity as it emerges—without a hint of magic—in the midst of practical considerations. *Is* entails *ought* when truth conditions for a descriptive theory include conditions that satisfy moral imperatives: I behave morally when I act in ways appropriate to my role. This may seem to be sleight of hand: linked but different factors—I have a role, I ought to fill it—are conflated. Ignoring their categorial difference encourages the false impression that the state of affairs satisfying the description also satisfies the prescription. But this objection merely affirms the point in doubt: it declares that *ought* cannot reduce to *is*, though we have evidence to the contrary. For the obligation to do one's duty is just the effect of two material considerations: the system in which one has a role will not work or survive if the role is not satisfied; the person having the role identifies with the system, its members, and their common aim. He or she has acquired the information, attitudes, and skills required to do the system's work, and he or she approves its aims and values his or her relations to its other members. Add the contingency that resources required to do the work are available. For then conditions are sufficient: the system's moral economy is satisfied, because the work is done.

A critic may hope to trump these considerations by asking if members should be duty bound to a gang of bank robbers or to a conspiracy working to poison the local water supply. This fair question is answered by acknowledging that one may have conflicting duties, duties to a gang voluntarily joined (duties not derogated by their pernicious effects) and duties to the community that support one's other interests. Such conflicts—duties to a system versus duties to the wider community—expose a flaw in the holist assumption that the interests of each subsystem are consilient with the interests of every other. But that consideration (relevant below) distracts us from the question at issue here: are the material facts of a matter sufficient to generate the *oughts* of duty? Holism says they are. It invites us to settle the issue with a direct question to the members of the whole: why do you do the system's work? The likely answer will go as follows: there is work to be done by a system I admire, this is my job, I gladly do it. Why does *ought* require something more than this description of relevant states of affairs? Why should such a person need a deontological thunderbolt to impel him? Does it add something to his sense of obligation? Or is it rhetorical only: we appeal to reason or God to legitimize a duty that is established and fulfilled for reasons that are social and material?

Social atomism—individualism—opposes holist claims about reality and values but shares its format: specify the categorial features of things, then derive the consequences for value. Atomism affirms that reality is the aggregate of self-sufficient entities, be they minds, souls, or material substances. Relations—principally, spatial and temporal relations—are incidental to the character of things. They may be altered when things interact but every thing is self-stabilizing, so each resists forces that would destroy it. Protons and living bodies have this force for a while, because internal organization stabilizes and sets them apart. People who survive wars and other disasters testify to this natural bias for sustained, self-regulating autonomy. Sustaining principles are obscure when the alleged individuals are minds or souls.

Individualist morality avers that positive and negative freedoms—freedom to choose and pursue one's aims, and freedom from interference—are the natural condition of every thinking, willing person. But many things deter free choice. Nature is overlaid with abusive compromises and contingencies, so we require a political and moral agenda for recovering the freedom to do or be as we choose. Why require this change? Because of the teleology that animates each of the three theories of social reality. Expose and eliminate distortions: let the nature of things be uncovered and seen. Here too, there is no *ought* but that of an idealized *is*: see what the self-directed man or woman is and does.

Is there empirical evidence for either of these theories? Holism postulates a single network of mutually dependent roles. God is, classically, the one in whom all other things are connected; or the one is consciousness, the many being ideas or thoughts so inflected that each contributes to the coherence of the whole. There is no evidence that wholes of either sort exist. God is a surmise; discordant thoughts and feelings are everywhere familiar. There is one whole—namely, spacetime—and there is one relation—gravitation—that connects everything within it. Yet, they, too, are imperfect evidence for the holist thesis. It requires universal mutual dependence, either directly or by way of intermediaries, though every entry in a telephone directory could be spelled differently while the others remain as before. Even gravitation fails this test, because the reality of time entails that things created late—plants and animals, for example—have no effect on things that have already disappeared.[12] Nor is holism confirmed by the fact that spacetime is a whole of universally connected places, for there are relations additional to spatiotemporal ones. The members of a band share the crowded benches of a subway car, but their mutual relations are different from and additional to the spatial relations shared with other riders. Holism requires pervasive internal relations. When those relations fail, the "one" dissolves into an array of clustered systems (galaxies and cities, for example), each a module that is unaffected by changes in many, most, or all others (gravity apart).

Is atomism more successful? It proposes that reality is an aggregate of self-sufficient entities, whether bodies, minds, or souls. Diversity implies their separation and autonomy, hence the space or time where they stand apart. Mill is emblematic: he emphasized thought, deliberation, and choice, then added that each of us should be free to join others in projects of mutual concern,[13] though children aren't free to do any of these things until nurtured and educated. Mill anticipated this objection by saying that he is speaking of "human beings in the maturity of their faculties."[14] But this is less a defense, more an admission: individualism has a narrow range of applications. It works for solitary thinkers or ambitious innovators, but not for the give and take—the interdependence and reciprocity—of the families, friendships, businesses, schools, and states where most interests and needs are satisfied.

Causality subverts individualism, because changes induced by interaction imply dependence: each cause depends on others for some aspect of itself. Yet, this implication is challenged by some classical notions of cause and effect. Aristotle acknowledged efficient causes, but emphasized the stabilizing effect of formal causes—essences—implying that change is accidental to the character of interacting substances.[15] Descartes argued (after Galileo's house arrest) that finite substances do not affect one another, God being the only cause.[16] Hume eliminated efficacy altogether: contiguity in space and time are (with similarity) said to be the only relations binding phenomena.[17] Generations of philosophers genuflect to his argument that no contradiction accrues if we imagine effects having a succession of different causes, or changes that occur in the absence of any cause. But fantasy isn't reality. We may imagine Athene born from the forehead of Zeus, but no one—not even Hume—proposes that biology be reconstructed from such figments. His positivist heirs prefer a circumlocution: start from a well-confirmed scientific theory—it reports constant conjunctions—then derive specific truths about embryos and their carriers.[18] Does this imply that spatiotemporal contiguity is a woman's only relation to her unborn child? Or imagine a conversation or comics trading insults. Is either an overlay of monologues, each oblivious to the other?

We have copious evidence that causes make a difference, and that some differences are constant and sustaining, not sporadic and incidental. We see and participate in relationships generated when these efficacies are reciprocal. We know, for empirical and practical reasons, that many things distinguishable are not separable, and that causality is not reducible to spatial or temporal contiguity. Efficient causation is energy transfer. We can have no idea of energy, on Hume's terms, because we have no impressions of it.[19] But this is a flaw in Hume's account of ideas, meaning, and knowledge, not a failure of causation. Atomism—individualism—lacks credibility, because (the universe apart) there are no freestanding, self-sufficient substances of greater complexity than protons, and because Hume's theory of cause is the artifact of his phenomenalist theory of ideas and its cardinal principle: separable if distinguishable. Individualism is a moral, political ideology, not a well-founded ontological hypothesis.

Holism, too, is embarrassed, though for this other reason. It supposes that some principle or activity instantaneously knits every bit or aspect of the whole to every other. Causality cannot serve this function, because contemporaries cannot be causally related in less than the time it takes for one to affect the other. Worse, causation has restricted effects, because causes are filters for the motion and energy they transfer: my telephone doesn't ring to calls you receive. Add that the effective trajectory of most causes is short: their energy often dissipates within the modular systems where they act. Causality is a pervasive feature of natural relations, but holism and atomism are materially false because they misconstrue it for moral or political aims.

How do theorists respond when their hypotheses are falsified? They adapt by exploiting an ambiguity in *theory*. It implies hypotheses tested against states of affairs, but also interpretations that construe "evidence" in ways congenial to themselves. Hypothesis is subordinate to ideology when theory has this second implication. For then interpretations are used as recipes for remaking the social world: rather than test a theory against the reality that stands apart from it, we engineer a society that satisfies a formula. Is it raining? Step outside: you'll soon know. Theories used ideologically are undeterred by states of affairs that deviate from the theories' prescriptions. For every such theory is a demand that reality be remade to satisfy it. Holism requires that social life be remade to establish a system of comprehensive relations and duties: atomism prescribes that we be free from constraint. Passionate exhortations to achieve one condition or the other are evidence that our actual character and circumstances do not confirm either theory: we are insufficiently related and duty bound, or insufficiently free. This is further evidence for the conclusion of the last paragraph: anything that frustrates a theory used ideologically is evidence that falsifies the theory construed as a hypothesis.

Do we want holist responsibility or individualist freedom? Having neither, we need a different ontology to account for the responsibilities and freedoms we have. The communitarian alternative avers that every thing is a system, or an aggregate of systems (a living body is one, a crowd the other), and that every system is generated and stabilized by the reciprocal causal relations of its proper parts (the next, lower-order systems that are its parts and members). Eyes and ears, nine planets, and four infielders are the proper parts, respectively of human bodies, the solar system, and baseball teams. Some systems have many members, others one or a few. Some (conversations) are ephemeral; others (molecules and some families) endure. All are distributed, like myriad islands, in spacetime, some steeply hierarchical, others flat. Spacetime is the only totalizing system, and gravity the one dynamic binder.

We expect that higher-order systems will be less stable than their parts (as when alliances of states are less stable than their members); but the reverse is true if the higher-order system secures an energy source more efficiently than its parts. Animal bodies are more stable than their separate tissues or organs; protons are more stable than their constituent quarks. Or higher-order systems endure, because dissolving them requires more energy than the supply available. Every system is stabilized in two ways: by the reciprocal causal relations of its parts and by the environment that supports or tolerates the system. So, every animal body is sustained by its sources of energy and by supporting physical variables that include temperature and atmospheric pressure. These stabilizing conditions are often ignored, until disrupted. Think of houses built on hillsides or seismic faults.

Nature is an array of systems; human societies are systems having humans or systems of humans as their proper parts. These examples—however banal—are unusual in the respect that we have words to express them. For the absence of such words is one reason for theory's neglect of systems. There are proper names—New York, Paris, Rome—and some descriptive terms—family, school, business, and state, but there are no words that designate many other familiar systems, including those having two or more nested parts (a business, its suppliers, and customers, for example), or those that signify overlap (the daughter- or son-in-law claimed by two families, the city astride a border that falls within competing jurisdictions, the Russian and English speaker who participates in two cultures).

The constraints systems impose on their members may seem perplexing. Why do people cleave to one another, when each could walk away? Because of animal needs that include food and defense, and because of habits that emerge in relationships where personality and culture flourish. Plato's remark is cogent: "The origin of the city . . . is to be found in the fact that we do not severally suffice for our own needs."[20] Adults could try to do everything for themselves, but they would do much of it badly, and some not at all. More, none of us starts as an adult; we pass a long apprenticeship in dependence or interdependence. The result exceeds the need that provoked it. Wanting relationships that replace the ones of childhood, we become stabilizing members of systems we join, or those that form about us.

Communitarianism is resisted, because its ontology is misconstrued or because atomists and holists reject its moral implications. There is little patience for the idea that things are joined in communities of spirit or feeling or collected in the mind of God. And there is the persuasive (individualist) idea that we satisfy the requirements of sociality if we are neighborly or civil. But communitarianism doesn't need mythic foundations, given its empirically testable claim that systems are established and sustained by the reciprocal causal relations of their proper parts. It doesn't need a sentimental rationale, if causal reciprocities created innumerable systems—human bodies and societies included—well before civility was imagined and approved.

Critics may respond that communitarianism is essentially obscure. What, for example, is a system's corporate identity? Is it established and known by a group mind? Are members conscious, because the system is conscious? Fantasies like this have sabotaged the communitarian views of Leibniz and Hegel[21]; but no one is obliged to think of human systems in their terms. Corporate properties and interests are perplexing if we imagine that they imply a corporate thinker or group consciousness. But the truth is simpler. Friends alter their relationship by actions that affect it and themselves. This doesn't imply that a system's every member is aware of its corporate identity, or that each member finds some hint of him or herself in it. A business pays advertisers to project an identity. Yet, the image presented may have little relation to the character established by the reciprocities of its members, suppliers, and clients. Indeed, members who formulate the image or advertisers who do it for them may have little idea of the system's corporate identity. For it may be very hard to discern. Formally dressed or checking a new haircut, one looks in a mirror; but there are no mirrors that accurately reveal the corporate identity of systems as small as a family or friendship, let alone a corporation or nation state. No corporate mind creates or perceives them. They are too complex, both internally and in relation to their partners, to be fully comprehended by individual minds.

4. Signature Values

Each of the three ontologies—holism, atomism, and communitarianism—has a small set of signature values.

Atomism emphasizes the self-sufficiency of the individuals it postulates. Each is said to be freestanding; some are also self-starting. We humans are both: our bodies are separate from one another and the things we use; we initiate thought and action for private aims. We are, by nature, free to do such things as we choose, and, conversely, it is unnatural that we be confounded by the interference of others. (This is a moral application of Newton's first law: unrestrained bodies move in uniform rectilinear paths.) Mill is simple and direct: "The only purpose for which power can be rightfully exercised over any member of a civilized community, against his will, is to prevent harm to others."[22]

Individualists (or the ethical theorists who speak for them) are emphatically self-conscious. Why be moral? What does morality require of me? These questions are obsessively pondered. For it is only an inquisitorial conscience that vindicates the claim that I am more than a creature of impulse, or one who finds good reasons for doing bad things. This reflective posture seems liberating: bad motives are scrutinized and purged, or one wills the categorical imperative, hence such laws as all could will without contradiction. This exalted perspective is, nevertheless, a mark of estrangement. One climbs a tower with a view, achieving unchallengeable moral virtue by overseeing and overriding impulses, motives, or self-serving reasons. Other people and the intensity of one's affiliations are considered from a distance: they disappear into a generalized, disembodied other.[23] But self-scrutiny is isolating, however satisfying the virtue it confirms.

Compare holism. It emphasizes affiliation and duty. The efficient operation of the whole requires that agents filling its roles are free from interference and able—because of skill and resources—to perform them. Neither sort of freedom—freedom to or from—implies the atomist exemption from unsolicited duties. For if no one is self-sufficient, need obliges us to acknowledge and engage those who support us. Atomism and holism are also differentiated by their perceptions of conflict. Individualism expects conflict and explains it as chronic bloody-mindedness, or as competition for scarce resources. Holism regards conflict as a curable distortion. It wouldn't occur if roles were efficiently organized, or if sufficient resources, effectively distributed, enabled each person to fill his or her role. There is also this corollary. Agents filling roles in well-organized systems needn't subject themselves to the atomist's self-flagellating inquiry: they are already doing the right thing. Their morality is assured by the plan enacted by the whole. Think of Plato's *Republic* as it realizes the Good: artisans and guardians, even philosopher-kings don't need a private interrogation to reassure them that their purpose is good and their motives pure. Atomism is a secular version of Protestant conscience. Holism is not. More than a context and support for its members: the whole is their rationale. Outsiders (if any there be) may want to confirm its worth. Participants aren't usually asked to justify it, and don't assume they should.

Communitarianism—systems theory—gives equal prominence to the obligations that bind us to core systems (they satisfy basic needs such as nurture, education, and protection), and to the freedom acquired as we move among and appraise systems that engage us. How shall we do justice to diverse commitments and ourselves? How shall we rank their needs against our interests, deciding the time and energy to be devoted to each? Systems theory avoids atomist isolation, because reflection is never more than a step away from the core or other systems that incite it: being their member requires that one answer to them, if only to announce one's resignation. This is a saving defense: reflection can't easily lapse into an obsessive, hermetic search for virtue's justifying, intrapsychic grounds (purity of will, for example). Communitarianism also avoids holist insouciance, because prioritizing diverse commitments—to family, work, and friends, for example—requires deliberation and hard choices: how much time, how much energy to each of one's commitments?

Communitarianism agrees that conflict is endemic, when systems having disparate aims compete for resources. Or conflict results because individuals engaged in two or more competing systems are divided against themselves. How should conflict be alleviated or averted? There are only these possibilities: festering conflict turns violent, power to stop it is vested in a person or role (a tyrant), or people set aside their private, sometimes opposed interests to legislate procedures for defusing it. A deliberating, self-regulating public emerges when individuals and systems acknowledge their conflicts while respecting the integrity of adversaries and the interests of systems that are adversely affected by the actions of others. Its aim is civic, social health: that state of affairs where individuals and critical social systems are secured by deliberations that eventuate in self-regulation.[24]

All three ontologies acknowledge this task. But individualism and holism are impaired. Cooperation is essentially alien to individualist ideals, because it frustrates initiative by obliging us to curtail our aims. Holism requires cooperation, but it postulates that persons are identified with their roles, hence all but precluded from choosing new roles or from legislating for the welfare of all. Communitarianism is not restricted in either way: individuals cooperate to create systems, but each person moves among various systems—from home to work, from family to friends—so there is less difficulty distinguishing oneself from any particular role. Communitarianism also has this unique advantage: it acknowledges, as atomism and holism do not, that each of a system's members (infants apart) is accustomed to negotiating with others to achieve the system's corporate aim. For there are publics of many scales short of the public constituted of a state's citizens or the public comprising all mankind. Most every member of small systems—a family, business, or school—has learned to join with others to legislate or revise its practices or rules. This experience prepares us for civic affairs and incubates the moral skills and virtues required there. One is not always happy with his or her partners in systems, or with the many others with whom one creates a public. But the aim is clear, and experience in core systems teaches us to negotiate for a common good in the face of discord.

Difficult adults are prefigured by irascible babies. They don't grin with pleasure; their caretakers are angry; neither trusts the other. Compare the positive feedback of successful feeding: one smiles and presents the spoon, the other gurgles and accepts it. Each enjoys his or her part, enjoys pleasing the other, and does it again. There is eye contact, warmth, and comfortable reciprocity. There is duty because each wants to satisfy the other. This desire is partly a self-directive: let me help to make it work. The self-directive in a baby is surely rudimentary. But it evolves, so that feeding has an established format after several months: you get my attention; I get yours. Engaging one another, we cooperate. There is freedom, because each is more or less aware that he or she may or may not cooperate. Yet, freedom is disciplined by duty. Each does cooperate: one because he or she is hungry and doesn't want to distress the caretaker; the other because he or she is responsible for this child, and because these moments of togetherness are intensely pleasurable. Trust and respect are also apparent: confidence, patience, and tranquility are measures of trust; affection expresses gratitude and respect. One who likes his dog or canary may exaggerate its subtleties of thought and feeling. But the evidence of depth in the give and take of one's relations to other people is compelling. Dogs register emotional changes in their caretakers; but babies do it better and faster, with emotional nuances of their own. Parents see the amplifying emotional and intellectual power of their infants, and match it with their responses. Joined by the reciprocities of feeding and playing or holding and being held, each recognizes depth in the other, and each experiences the other's response to his or her expressions of respect.

These two—learning to create and sustain reciprocities and learning to recognize the affective and cognitive states of one's partners—are the complementary aspects of relations that join us, practically and morally, to others. This is the trajectory of a child's socialization and self-discovery. Responsive to others, in control of ourselves, we learn to cooperate. But equally, we anticipate conflict, and know how to resolve it. For conflicts within core systems are mitigated somewhat by our respect, however grudging, for their other members. Conflicts provoked when systems share a member or members are reduced if the members can affirm their loyalty to each of the systems and respect for their members. Solutions to other conflicts extrapolate from this store of information and attitudes: other people also value their core systems, and we imagine that they too—perhaps strangers to us—are worthy of respect.

This is the perspective that evolves as we move beyond personal and private concerns to the moral attitude of a public's citizens. The uncertainties and vulnerabilities are mostly the same when strangers meet to negotiate the rules or procedures intended to avert or mitigate their quarrels. Infants are only reactive at the beginning. But very young children begin to distinguish their own needs from the affective states of their caretakers, even to the degree that one sees them caring for their caretakers, if only by responding in ways that gratify both. This regard for the other's needs is the step beyond self-concern to the perception and self-control required to sustain a relationship. Later on, this will be the knack of wearing two hats: one private, the other public. Satisfying a role, we think and act in ways appropriate to its objectives. Participating in the deliberations of a public—whatever its scale—we put these interests aside while considering procedures and laws that would enhance the system and all its members, or—if this is the public formed by the citizens of a state—the many systems and their members. Imagine that all the legislators responsible for traffic laws are drivers and that each enjoys driving fast. Speed kills, so these lawmakers reduce the speed limit, then suppress an inclination to exceed it.

This trajectory extends from personal to civic affairs, despite detours, potholes, and blind alleys. We don't like all our systems or all our partners; some or many of them don't like us. Coercion often displaces duty and freedom; we respond by sabotaging our abusers. Yet, we do respect some of our partners, and when committed to them and free to chose, we act as our roles require. Most of us are frequently moral, because we are socialized to this degree at least: we freely satisfy duties to people we respect. Law, habit, and the moralizing stories of patriotism and popular religion fill in the gaps by universalizing the lesson of this developmental experience. They extrapolate from experiences where each person learns to trust and respect a few to the essential trustworthiness of all. This is less naïve than practical: we extrapolate from local conflicts and local solutions to the community at large, the state. Its formation presupposes both a deliberating citizenry and the politics that crystallize its organization, discussions, elections, and legislation.

This trajectory, stripped of embellishments, is critical to moral development and civil order. Neither atomism nor holism can plausibly account for it. Atomism reduces systems to contractual relationships. It eviscerates duty and trust by replacing them with the threat that legal damages will be awarded for broken contracts. Holism can provide for duty and trust, but not for freedom: I am free only to fill my roles; anything less invites coercion. Communitarianism proposes that reality is an array of systems and that individuals acquire character—selfhood—by virtue of the reciprocities that bind them to other members of core systems. The trajectory from impulse and self-concern to effective socialization is also the trajectory of moral character: it emerges in self-regulating core systems.[25]

Ontologies purport to tell us what we are essentially. Yet, their competition sometimes resembles the jostling of decorous advertisers: each ignores the other while holding up a picture of the way one would look if dressed in his formula. Is autonomy imperfect? Are social connections loose or troubled? Alter them in ways the favored theory prescribes. For every such proposal may be construed as an idea, an ideal, or an ideology. An idea characterizes some actual or possible state of affairs; an ideal favors it. Ideology converts the ideal into a recipe for altering our circumstances in ways signified by the idea.[26]

Norms are intrinsic to each of the three hypotheses. Atomists needn't emphasize that self-reliance is good and dependence retrograde once they say that we are essentially self-sufficient. Holists don't have to extol cooperation. It is critical, therefore, that both theories misrepresent our circumstances. We are neither self-sufficient, nor soldered to all of humanity. The truth about us lies somewhere in the middle: modular but nested systems fill the space between the abstractions mooted by atomists and holists. We cripple ourselves if we live as their ideologies commend.

Characterizations as general as mine invite a skeptical question: does any thinker espouse one or another of these cookie-cutter, conceptual styles? I concede that almost no one is doctrinaire in the narrow ways they prescribe. Yet, the thinking of almost every moralist is dominated by one or another of them. For these are the established options—the templates—for thinking about reality of any sort, morality included.[27] Differences among some notable representatives of the three types are considered below.

5. Moral Psychology

Contemporary ethical theorists emphasize reflection,[28] because they suppose—with Kant as their example—that a moral justification for behavior (actual or intended) requires an intrapsychic foundation. This would have surprised Plato. His philosopher-kings were to see the Good and act as it prescribes; others would be moral because their characters (hence their dispositions) would be acquired in social circumstances formed in its light. Conscious intention or approval would be incidental. Aristotle agreed that character is the basis for morality and that habit is its stabilizer. Aristotle's modern readers commend his ideas about character and virtue but forget that his *Ethics* is the propaedeutic to his *Politics*: the two were divided by an early editor. This is germane, because Aristotle, too, understood character and its morality in practical terms: the good man, be he a landed citizen, mechanic, or slave has attributes that fit him for his social role. Reflection is incidental: people, like carburetors, are made for the work they do. Aristotle suspected that immoral people are badly made and not easily fixed. Certainly, reflection isn't likely to fix them, because their attitudes—their social orientation—are pathological. There may be no lever but punishment to change or deter them.

These views contrast with those fostered by the evolution of religious thought since the Old Testament. Successive prophets deplored the morality of their people. For they knew God's commandments directly, presumably by finding them engraved in themselves. This is an abiding influence, one apparent in Augustine, renewed by Luther, then secularized and generalized to ideas of every sort by Descartes. Thinkers of this lineage would have us scrutinize ideas to confirm that they are clear and distinct. This is a standard better suited to ideas than passions, but they too should be disciplined, first by seeing them as they are, then by using will to inhibit or release, deny, or affirm—them. Inhibition is the prior and primary moral task, because impulses are often sinful and because sinners will not be redeemed. Self-scrutiny is urgent.

Descartes characterizes mind in a way that supplies its model. There is lower-order awareness (of reasons and desires, for example) and the higher-order awareness—self-consciousness—where standards of meaning, truth, or virtue are affirmed, then used to test or discipline phenomena of the lower order. And critically, nothing can happen in either order unless awareness of the other is concurrent: one is never conscious of any content without also being self-conscious, and equally, there is no self-awareness without awareness of some lower-order content. This structure and the reciprocity of its parts is the guarantee of moral scrutiny. For there is no way to obscure one's actions or impulses—"I wasn't paying attention"—because there is no way of hiding from oneself. The atomist bent of these reflections is not incidental to religious interests. For it is individuals, not whole societies or systems, that are judged and saved.

There is little explicit reference to these historical considerations when Descartes' successors searched within us for moral motives or a test that would validate our moral judgments; they may have been familiar to the point of being commonplace. Hume was content to describe mind's structure and virtues, distinguishing things favored from those abhorred. Kant described them, too, but the faculties he specified were to be used, in the traditional way, to suppress or approve desires. Nothing is good, he said, but the will that subjects itself to the logical rigor of the categorical imperative. One thinks of Luther, the demands of conscience, and the rectitude of a soul turned to God. This introspectionist style—"individual rational reflection"—disqualifies some motives for will or action, while promoting others: yes to some reasons, desires, or attitudes, no to impulse. Notice that theorists who favor such deliberations suppose or imply that they may be pursued at a distance from the other people with whom one lives and acts: concern for or engagement with them promotes reflection, but virtue's ground and justification are exclusively personal and private.

This internalist version of atomism emphasizes autonomy and responsibility. Hobbes, an externalist, emphasized fear. Power is the only justification law can have or require: we don't need reflection if intimidation creates an orderly, moral society. The moral psychology of holists is equally uncomplicated. "My station and its duties"[29] is an exact précis of the reflections encouraged or permitted within the whole. I don't need to reflect, because I don't need information additional to three considerations, all cut and dried: What things are legitimately presented so I may act on them (who can put work in my in-box)? What work am I to do with or on them? To whom is my finished work passed (who can rightly take it from my out-box)? There is no reason for me to trouble myself with pointless and obsessive self-scrutiny if I do my work, others do theirs, and the whole is well organized. This was the message to the artisans and guardians of Plato's *Republic*; it works as well in armies and corporations. For holists are consequentialists. The travail of people introspecting—Is my will pure, are my reasons good?—is incidental, if the self-stabilizing whole supports and defends its members.

Communitarian moral psychology joins aspects from these three theories: holism and the internalist and externalist versions of atomism. It says that virtue is the reliable performance of one's duty: doing what you have learned and agreed to do. The result is efficacious because useful to a system or systems and their members. This effect is perceived and acknowledged by others, not only by a mind turned on itself. Socializing the perception enhances mutual trust and respect among people joined in work of mutual concern; privatizing it—confirming in reflection that I am moral—has no consequence but the one of vindicating my worth in the disembodied abstract. This was important to Calvinists who feared eternal perdition. It needs a different justification for secular thinkers. But communitarians, too, emphasize reflection, moral justification, and moral choice. That is so, because everyone engaged by several systems has to decide the degree of his or her commitment to each of them, and because each of a system's members has responsibility for the system's effects, whatever his or her role in producing them. The regular morning chat with a neighbor makes little difference. Work done in a weapons factory or political prison has implications that need consideration.

This is content for private deliberation, but it differs from the reflections of introspecting atomists. They struggle to appraise the moral value of an act or aim, or they take a morally virtuous posture in regard to it. Communitarians usually have simpler questions to answer: What are the consequences of doing the work? What effects would there be if one stopped doing it? These are demands for information, first about this undertaking, later about one's attitudes and desires: what is proposed, what effects would there be, which of these actions and effects do I approve or disapprove and why, what should I do given the answers? One continues as before, if the predicted effects are consistent with one's values. One is slow to participate, if they are not. Or there is conflict, because one has several interests, one served, another offended by a system or role. Firm ground may be hard to find: there may be no easy resolution when attitudes conflict with needs (work, for example), or because the effects are uncertain or unknown. Still, the vector is plain. Action, not reflection, is morality's primary site. Reflection is critical but secondary. It considers the effects of actions proposed, then appraises both in light of attitudes that are socialized by one's roles in systems, then confirmed or not by one's reflections: what does this system favor, what do I want? Approving or disapproving, I return to the task at hand or refuse to participate.

There is a further possibility, and it carries the reflecting communitarian to the extremity familiar to atomism. Suppose I step back from an attitude that impels me to abandon my place in a once treasured system. Why defer to this attitude, given its disruptive consequences for me and others? First attitudes are learned in core systems. They are contingent— other families or societies, different attitudes—but compelling. How can they be superseded by attitudes of reflection? Before I counted on my training in particular core systems to form attitudes appropriate to tasks and their contexts. They prompt me to consider the good for all, the good for some, or principally the good for me. This comfortable assumption is deflated, because it is just such attitudes that are now interrogated. But this critical posture is itself in doubt: what leverage enables me to validate attitudes sanctioned by reflection?

There is, or seems to be, no way to stand apart from every attitude to justify one or more others. The unresolved dialectic of the atomists implies the perpetual retreat of solid ground. For they don't agree about an ultimate justifier for moral norms: no test is universally acknowledged as the validator. Every thinker with a preferred test evades the issue by making a substantive, attitude-resolving assumption. Hume supported good reasons for moral attitudes by postulating an inclination to sympathy for others. Kant said that material expressions of the formal contradictions loathed by reason are intolerable social conflicts—universal lying or cheating. Both introduce a substantive, consequentialist claim to decide the issue: our nature and circumstances give us information we don't suppress. Yet, this intrusion is subversive, because the question at issue—which attitudes to approve or reject—is begged. The answer introduces information that expresses a favored attitude: show sympathy, avoid conflict.

Stepping back to appraise all one's attitudes from the standpoint of none is ill-conceived, because retreating from all to justify one or a few leaves no attitude with which to appraise the others. We respond by smuggling in the necessary starting point. It may favor self-interest or the good for all, but either way, the choice is surreptitious and arbitrary if the aim is a disinterested appraisal of all one's attitudes. It is better to acknowledge our predicament: there is no a priori test for all attitudes. We are trapped in the attitudes we have. Juggle them, play one against another; but don't scuttle them all. And don't be surprised that others, especially people of other societies or cultures, have attitudes different from one's own.[30] They, too, make action and its effects the test of reflection: things go better, because the gods approve, or merely because foresight improves both efficiency and the decent treatment of all concerned.

Communitarians can also deliberate in a way that is available to holists, though barred (in principle, but not practice) to atomists: difficulties may be discussed with others. This isn't effective, if the one who provokes reflection is alienated from all the others of a system. But it is a viable way of resolving moral issues, one that takes advantage of reciprocities that already bind a system's members. This can be an enabling strength, as it is in marriage or family counseling and the discussions that precede an election. Other systems—businesses and schools, for example—might try it more often than they do.

This use of reciprocities already in place is relevant for a methodological reason. Cartesians would have us believe that reflection reveals a domain of easily differentiated mental faculties, states, and content; but this is moot. Will is inhibition or excitation triggered by muscular, neural, or hormonal stimuli. It isn't an inspectable power suppressed or released by an intrapsychic pedal, like the break and accelerator under the foot of a nervous driver. Attitudes, too, are dubious candidates for inspection. They are known, behaviorally, by way of the feelings, thoughts, or behaviors provoked when they are aroused by circumstances. One proceeds accordingly, trying to identify his or her attitudes by imagining scenarios where they are variously aroused. This isn't useless, but it is less efficient than exposing oneself to trying circumstances or challenging conversation. For then the evidence is plain: how do I respond? Reflection is empowered by the answer. For attitudes are a synthesis of information, judgment, and affect. Information that falsifies a judgment may change an attitude. Feelings persist, but they are harder to sustain when the truth-claim is discredited.

Attitudes are habitual. Some are easy to change, because they are relatively superficial and lately acquired. Others, learned early in core systems, resist change. Atomist reflection is often superficial, because it occurs within boundaries established by attitudes that are deeply fixed and poorly discerned. Socialization may alter them; monadic reflection is less successful. Why couldn't one change a deep-seated prejudice (supposing that reflection alone could identify it) by applying the categorical imperative? Because that principle embodies one of Kant's attitudes: he favored harmony and cooperation. A contrary prejudice may not capitulate to a test that expressed his bias.

6. Thick Moral Concepts: The Cognitive and Emotive Aspects of Moral Norms

Heidegger believed that we see things as ready-to-hand before abstracting from our interests and their uses to see them in themselves.[31] He rightly supposed that most perceptual discriminations are suffused with the aims, interests, or anxieties of people working to make circumstances congenial to others or themselves. Rare phenomena—flashes of lightning or unexpected sounds—evade immediate classification, but they are incidental to the point: most differences and relations perceived, thought, or named are saturated with human perspectives and interests. Every term signifying such discriminations is "thick": it signifies a property, thing, or relation while expressing an appraisal.[32] This elision—fact's "entanglement" with value[33]—is the effect of our full time dedication to the work of sustaining ourselves and our systems. But the word *entangled* signifies a relation without clarifying it. Nothing in the word implies that reality is intrinsically infused with human aims.

Idealists think otherwise, because they suppose that reality is a function of the ways we think or talk, and because they believe, after Kant, that values determine the conceptualizations used to schematize a thinkable world.[34] But reality is not the contrivance of human thinkers or the languages used to differentiate and organize experience; it doesn't elide with our needs and interests. Bending a wire hangar, I reshape it to open my locked car door. Someone oblivious to my aim and annoyance sees the wire as it is, thinking, perhaps, that a hangar is ruined. He doesn't conflate this fact with my values, and neither should I. There may be entanglements that defy separation because valuation leaves the presumed facts unspecified: "You are wonderful (odious)," for example. But disentanglement is usually unproblematic. This is good or bad, I say. You look to see for yourself. Disagreeing in our judgments, we nevertheless agree about the relevant facts. "Hot," I say. "Yes," you say, "too hot."[35]

Suppose, however, that we accept thick concepts as they are. Allow that they express attitudes by virtue of combining affect with cognitive content. Which of the two is dominant when something is described as civilized or barbaric, crude or refined? Are the words used descriptively, so that one might be charged with error: it isn't as you say? Or is it usually or always true that such words are used and heard as appraisals? No evidence justifies dogmatism in either direction. Context is decisive as the words are used descriptively, evaluatively, or in ways that mix the two: "Dogged," we say, with or without admiration.

Words critical to morality are also thick concepts, with this significant difference. Usually, one can distinguish a word's cognitive content or referent from its evaluative use. And often—especially with responsibilities one resents or rejects—one makes this distinction when using such words as *duty*, *right*, and *moral*: circumstances oblige me to do this, but I don't approve. This distinction is often suppressed in moral contexts where responsibilities are affirmed. For then, the content of cognition includes the perception of a duty. Saying that I ought to satisfy my role as worker, parent, citizen, or friend, I acknowledge duty as a feature of my circumstances: I don't distinguish having the role from affirming my obligation to fill it. Moral intuitionists are succinct: the facts, themselves, prescribe one's conduct.

This conviction is familiar to everyone loyal to a family or friend: seeing them and their situation, I know my duty. One may have several or many such foci of conviction, each justified by pointing to a confirming state of affairs. For I am who I am by virtue of participating in systems where these duties are second nature. Knowing these roles, favoring these systems, knowing that other members rely on me, I perceive facts and duties as indivisible. Not seeing obligations in the facts would be a derogation of myself. A cynic might regard me as brainwashed. Someone more sympathetic would say that I am well taught or socialized. He would mean that I cannot stand apart from the systems to and for which I am responsible, distinguishing what they would have me do from what I want to do. But duty is learned. The righteous feelings aroused when others are threatened, affronted, or disappointed may be quashed or reconsidered with time and disappointment. Fact and value will seem less entangled then.

Think again of the priority Heidegger ascribed to things seen as ready-to-hand:

> The kind of Being which equipment possesses—in which it manifests itself in its own right—we call "readiness-to-hand". Only because equipment has *this* 'Being-in-itself' and does not merely occur, is it manipulable in the broadest sense and at our disposal. No matter how sharply we just look at the 'outward appearance' of Things in whatever form this takes, we cannot discover anything ready-to-hand. If we look at Things just 'theoretically', we can get along without understanding readiness-to-hand. But when we deal with them by using them and manipulating them, this activity is not a blind one; it has its own kind of sight, by which our manipulation is guided and from which it acquires its specific Thingly character. Dealings with equipment subordinate themselves to the manifold assignments of the 'in-order-to'.[36]

Heidegger reduced the practical value of things—the uses of hammers—to the aims for which we use them. Though nothing that is ready-to-hand would have utility if its causal role were not a consequence of its structure, hence its possible relations to other things. The hammer's possible relations—founded in its dispositions—prefigure its causal properties and practical value. These properties are content for cognition, hence for truths, irrespective of our aims. For it is incidental to them that we have a use for hammers. Accordingly, ideas of such things are thick, primordially, in the respect that their practical value is implicit in their causal properties and prospective practical uses. This point generalizes to moral norms, including cooperation, trust, respect, freedom, prudence, and efficacy. No human system works optimally without all of them. But there are such systems, so, a fortiori, it is a fact that these norms operate within them: their value—introduced by their causal powers—is not a gratuitous, emotional projection.

This point—value's basis in fact—ramifies. For the values constituent in thick concepts have disparate origins. Simplicity and consistency are values in practical and scientific inquiry for the good reason that bloated or inconsistent plans or theories are an obstacle to engaging or understanding matters at issue. We have learned that nature is both consistent and simpler than it looks, and we modify our hypotheses accordingly. Equally, hunger, safety, and cooperation are valued, the first (negatively) because it is life-threatening, the second because it reduces our vulnerability, the third because it is a condition for reciprocities that secure and satisfy us. These are disparate values, each having a different ground in matters of fact. Simplicity is a procedural value for scientific theory, because the nature it maps is itself simple: few variables and styles of relation generate the diversity of natural phenomena. Hunger is an alarm. It has value as a sign in negative feedback systems where it promotes behavior that returns living systems to a steady state. Various expedients make us safe; all are objective, but they differ as houses differ from laws. Cooperation is a procedural value: there is no reciprocity without it.

Every such value is firmly rooted in a state of affairs: nature and the practice that discerns its form, living bodies, laws, and reciprocities. Compare them to thick concepts that are expressions of taste, where "This is beautiful (stylish, desirable)" means only that I like it. For there are two kinds of thick concepts. Simplicity, hunger, safety, and cooperation are values firmly rooted in fact. Taste—in fashion, for example—has its origins in preference or whim. Where thin concepts have objective content only (content cognized), thick concepts of the first sort are relatively thin because their constituent values are objectively founded: in materiality or law, for example. Thickness of the other sort is bloated, because the affective—value—side is poorly rooted in the cognitive—factual—part. Last year's dress will be unwearable next year.

James obscured the difference between thick and thin concepts:

> Our passional nature not only lawfully may, but must decide an option between propositions, whenever it is a genuine option that cannot by its nature be decided on intellectual grounds.[37]

Putnam rejects it:

> I'm going to rehabilitate a somewhat discredited move in the debate about fact and value, namely the move that consists in arguing that the distinction is at the very least hopelessly fuzzy because factual statements themselves, and the practices of scientific inquiry upon which we rely to decide what is and what is not a fact, presuppose values.[38]

Putnam acknowledges a difference between epistemic and ethical values—two procedural, cognitively based, thick concepts—but then he obliterates the objective, material ground from which they derive:

> The claim that on the whole we come closer to truth about the world by choosing theories that exhibit simplicity, coherence, past predictive success, and so on, and even the claim that we have made more successful predictions than we would have been able to obtain by relying on Jerry Falwell, or on imams, or on ultra-orthodox rabbis, or simply relying on the authority of tradition, or the authority of some Marxist-Leninist Party, are themselves complex empirical hypotheses that we choose (or which those of us who do choose them choose) because we have been guided by the very values in question in our reflections upon records and testimonies concerning past inquiries—not, of course, all the stories and myths that there are in the world about the past, but the records and testimonies that we have good reason to trust by these very criteria of "good reason."[39]

This formulation is half-right: we can only bootstrap ourselves to knowledge of the ambient world by applying one or another set of procedural values: simplicity and cooperation, for example. But this choice implies a criterion for appraising the result: does the information acquired enable us to adapt ourselves to our circumstances while making accurate predictions about them? For if so, these procedural values have enabled us to engage other people and things effectively: principles expressing the values—simplicity, coherence, past predictive success—have passed a cognitive, objective test.

Putnam has a different aim: namely, dissolution of the fact/value dichotomy. The vulnerable points of entry are objectivity and value. In mathematics and logic (his paradigms) there is "'objectivity without objects.'"[40] There is value—as in ethics—without ontology. Kant and Carnap direct us: everything objective is the creation of data-organizing conventions (including semantic and syntactic rules) driven by values, some epistemic, others that are personal or ethical.[41] Kant was explicit:

> I have been reproached for . . . defining the power of desire as the power of being the cause, through one's presentations, of the actuality of the objects of these presentations. The criticism was that, after all, mere wishes are desires too, and yet we all know that they alone do not enable us to produce their objects. That, however, proves nothing more than that some of man's desires involve him in self-contradiction, inasmuch as he uses the presentation by itself to strive to produce the objects, while yet he cannot expect success from it.[42]

Data alone are not sufficient to create the experience of objectivity. Putnam, like Kant, requires that there be a rule—a schema—to differentiate and organize the data:

> What I am saying is that it is time we stopped equating objectivity with description. There are many sorts of statements— bona fide statements, ones amenable to such terms as "correct," "incorrect," "true," "false," "warranted," and "unwarranted"— that are not descriptions, but that are under rational control, governed by standards appropriate to their particular functions and contexts.[43]

One can agree with every word of this passage without conceding either that the extra-mental, extra-linguistic world is thought's contrivance, or that one cannot distinguish the navigating values of inquiry—simplicity and fruitfulness, for example—from both regulatory, moral, or social values (observe traffic laws) and from personal desires. There are the two kinds of thick concepts just described, some that root values in facts, other that merely elide fact with value. Thick concepts of both sorts can be appraised: do they enable us to engage other things in predictable, effective ways? Both may have that effect, but the former do it over long periods of time because nature and many ways of engaging it are stable. Simplicity, hunger, safety, and cooperation are enduring values, because their objective conditions endure. Taste and style are unstable; their "entanglement" with fact is unreliable because shallow and ephemeral. No one who is embarrassed by last year's passion has any trouble distinguishing it from her altered feelings.

7. Duties to Systems, Their Members, and Others

Duty is a thick concept of the first kind: it signifies values embedded in facts, values that are moral, but practical, too. They are practical because there are no systems without members who honor their duties to one another, and because life is unsustainable without critical systems. They are moral because participation in systems enables us to benefit others as they benefit us; and because we humans are socialized and civilized by our participation in systems that secure or please us. Practicality and morality are complementary perspectives from which to answer these elementary questions: what do we need or want, and what do we owe to those with whom needs or wants are satisfied? Answers emerge in the core systems where principal needs or wants are satisfied and principal duties learned.

We may say with Plato that the Good is the highest Form[44] or with Kant that only the good will is absolutely good,[45] but these refinements disguise morality's vulgar origins. For duty, described behaviorally, is the reliable performance of tasks on which others rely. Reliability is a principal moral virtue, because most human needs cannot be satisfied without the cooperation and assistance of other people. Systems are the organized expedient that solves this problem. Reliability is the virtue—the habit—acquired when individuals are acknowledged and rewarded for actions that fulfill their roles in systems. But machines, too, are reliable. Duty expresses the focused demand that humans should reliably satisfy the expectations of their partners. Mere habits at first (in childhood, for example), duties emerge when reflection, freedom, or respect for one's partners converts habit to choice.

Duties are differentiated by origin or objective. There are seven variants to consider: i. members' duties to their system; ii. systems' duties to their members; iii. the duties of a system's members to one another; iv. systems' duties to other systems or to people who are not their members; v. the duties of people to one another irrespective of their membership in systems; vi. duties to oneself; and vii. duties prescribed by laws.

i. Members' duties to systems. Systems are nodes, hence richly consequential. Imagine medical researchers who make discoveries working together that neither would have made alone. Their partnership is an accident, the result of sitting together at a meeting to which neither was invited. Both affirm responsibility for their friendship, and each says gratefully that thinking flourishes as he responds to the other. Each construes his partner's intention as a norm: respect and sustain the friendship. Habits or intentions of this sort are familiar in core systems where each member affirms the system's aims and values and believes that other members share this commitment. Either may precede the other in time—there may be expectation but no habit or intention, or the reverse—but these two are coordinate: each provokes and enforces the other. For duty is not alien: we are not typically uncertain or confused about duties to core or other systems, and, mostly, we perform appropriately.

Is one exempt from duties to systems, even to core systems, if he or she doesn't acknowledge the duty? We know people trapped in systems, with onerous duties and no desire to satisfy them. Or we emphasize a member's alienation from his situation by imagining him parachuted into a system he doesn't know or choose; what should he do? This situation, however uncomfortable, is an odd point of reference for someone having duties to core systems, because it is vanishingly likely that their members are unfamiliar with either their partners or the needs or interests that bring them together. Members who perceive a system's advantages make this mutual demand: do what is required to sustain a system whose consequences we approve. Infants don't start by knowing their mothers or nurses, but they do experience the needs that require partnership, and they soon know their caretakers. Expectation is experienced as the demand—however gently expressed—that each should coordinate his or her role-filling actions with those of a system's other members. It happens rarely, if ever, that one is dropped into a situation and instantly required to act from duty. People take jobs they don't like with little notice, but their responses to fellow workers are impelled by needing money, not by duty to the system.

Duty first emerges when mutual need or interest provokes the cooperation of people who do the work of vital systems. Each member qualifies his or her commitment by testing the others: do they respond in kind? Duty is the forming habit or intention that secures the reciprocity of the partners by justifying their responses. The habits are complex: they qualify one for a task and for cooperating with others who do the same or complementary things. So, children fill roles in families, friendships, or schools while seeing the individual and corporate effects and benefits, seeing too that doing less reduces the welfare of all because it disrupts these systems. Parents or priests may announce the moral principles that prescribe our duties, but moral habits and attitudes are validated by conduct, not commentary. Children know the difference.

Let truth telling be our example. This is a responsibility—a duty—because misinformation sabotages communication, hence the work that systems do. But is the injunction—tell the truth—generalizable? Need one speak truly to a system's fellow members about matters incidental to it? Is there a duty to tell the truth to everyone, including people with whom one shares no affiliation? Or is truth telling required principally or only of actions that would otherwise be detrimental to systems that satisfy critical human needs? These questions invite us to draw a line around systems vital to human welfare, thereby limiting the duty. But the line is hard to draw, because systems have effects that ramify. We don't usually know how far the effects extend within a system and across societies. There are other complexities, too. Systems are often at odds, because they compete for scarce resources or because of having contrary aims. Telling truths to all may subvert one or several for the benefit of others. Is the Gestapo at the door? I don't tell them of friends or family in the basement, because here, as before, duty is the imperative that emerges in relationships one makes and sustains. All its force derives from the relations of systems and their members. Kant may respond that duty to a lower-order system cannot override one's duty to practices that serve the interests of all. But this is problematic. What is the sequence in which duties are generated and learned: are they universal, then instantiated, or local, then generalized?

Children learn the virtue of truth telling in particular relationships, especially those that arouse the expectations of parents, friends, and teachers. They hear the universalizing slogans of moral life—don't lie or steal—but they practice these virtues in local contexts. We want them to apply the slogans in situations they cannot foresee: "Do it everywhere, always," we tell them. But this is rhetoric, because we know there are circumstances where such rules would be pernicious. Indeed, we want children to learn something more difficult than an exceptionless rule: namely, the judgment of knowing how to apply rules and when to break them. Judgment is critical, because the proliferation of systems exceeds anyone's imagination, and because conflicts among critical systems preclude a moral principle that paralyzes action, one implying that doing nothing is always preferable to choosing one side at cost to the other. Behave honorably, we say when there is no other rule to vindicate us: consider the benefits and costs to vital systems, their members, other people, and yourself.

ii. Systems' duties to their members. Perspective shifts with this question: Do systems have duties to their members? We say they do: families have duties to their children, schools to teachers and students, companies to their employees. But this is ambiguous. Do corporate duties reduce to members' duties to one another, hence to the reciprocities that maintain core systems? Or is there a duty that a system owes its members by virtue of its corporate identity?

Suppose that schools don't charge tuition (to avert questions about the contractual terms for fair exchange). Does it follow that students have no complaint when teachers don't teach? Hasn't the system presented itself as a school, thereby implying an essential, identity-affirming task? People who respond—members or clients—expect to engage the presenter on its terms. This is the factual basis for a system's duties to participants: it presents itself in a certain guise (a matter of fact); others perceive it accurately, agree to participate on those terms, and expect it to respond appropriately (also matters of fact). Obligation, too, is a matter of fact. Its sufficient conditions are a system's self-presentation and the expectations it provokes in others. For systems, too, are responsible for truth telling. Evoking the expectations of others makes the system responsible to them for actions consistent with its self-presentation. Some people take advantage of the social tide by misrepresenting themselves: they rightly suppose that others are credulous, and they profit from the deception. But credulity is more than naïve. We normally expect people to do as they say they will: cooperative activity would be sabotaged if we were mistaken. Trust in a system's intentions has equal force. We accept its self-presentation, agreeing to participate as members or to engage it, say, as customers, because systems typically satisfy the expectations they encourage to some acceptable degree.

Breaches of expectation are graded in proportion to their effects. Seeing an appropriate sign and shoes displayed in a store window, we enter and wait for a salesman's attention. "No," says the man who approaches, "we do this for display only. Sorry to have misled you." We leave bemused, careful not to say that the store ought to be and do as it presents itself. But we are annoyed and betrayed if a more consequential system—a family, friendship, or employer—fails to act as its self-presentation implies it will. For we commit ourselves to their work, as members or clients, believing that they will be as they present themselves. Disregard for members and their legitimate expectations is costly to those deceived, because wasteful and distracting. It is also immoral, because faithless and disrespectful.

One may argue that our disappointment is foolish: there is no corporate reality, hence no one or thing responsible for the things systems do. But this would be true only if systems were aggregates, as they are not. One knows the duties that come with membership in a system and the betrayal experienced when a system organizes itself to the detriment of members. Governments that abuse their citizens, schools that fail to teach: these failures of duty are pernicious in two ways. They sabotage a system's members, and, thereby, the system, itself. Satisfying a system's duties to its members—including respect, resources, and opportunity (freedom) to fill a role—is a condition for the cooperative activities that make social life possible and private life viable. We are reminded that corporate failures are more serious than personal failures, because more people and systems are damaged by them.

Reifying corporate entities nevertheless offends our individualist scruples. How shall we justify it when a system is nothing other than the network of its reciprocally related members? How can a system be morally responsible if moral qualities—duty, freedom, trust, and respect—are acquired as members relate to one another by filling their roles? It is members, not their systems, that have roles, and members, not systems, whose intellect and sensibility qualify them for moral responses to others and themselves. Moral agency would imply that systems are persons. But they are not. How can they be moral, hence morally responsible for their effects on members, other systems, or people who are not their members?

We usually answer by saying that systems can be obliged to act in ways prescribed by law. But legal duties (satisfied under the threat of punishment) differ from moral duties (obligations acquired when reciprocal engagements join us to others as we satisfy shared interests or needs). Legal obligations are incidental, if members make their system morally responsible. More, they deflect us from the point at issue: are systems moral agents, or is moral agency restricted to their members? If the former, we have still to tell how systems can possess the qualities of moral agents: namely, duty, freedom, trust, and respect. If the latter, we concede that systems, per se, have no moral integrity, thereby implying that duties to their members are legal, not moral.

A better answer amalgamates these contraries. A system is only its members, but with this difference. An aggregate is the sum of its parts. Systems are complexes created by the reciprocal relations of their members; they embody their members while having a distinct identity. Members who collaborate to create a system may also deliberate in its name, as family members or citizens deliberate about the conduct of their systems. How, for example, shall its duties, wealth, or opportunities be divided: how shall it treat them, its members? This is not the task of deciding how members should respond to one another, absent the system. Nor is it the issue of satisfying worthy but aggrieved fellow members: if I deserve more, so does he or she. Instead, members (or their representatives) deliberate and act in the name of their system. Are its burdens and benefits distributed equitably, given some reasoned policy for dividing them? Should they be distributed equally or proportionately, lawyers more than messengers, home run hitters more than fielders? Bureaucracy may paralyze these deliberations. Mindless pursuit of corporate aims—victory or profit—may preclude them. But systems can be organized to treat their members morally. Families, friendships, and schools do it often; some states and employers do it, too.

The corporate deliberations of the members look both ways: to the welfare of the system and the welfare of its members. The morality of the members expresses itself in the duties they freely satisfy and in the respect they show for others and themselves. Their system inherits these moral attributes when it (the membership acting in its name) freely acknowledges and fulfills obligations to its members, including respect, trust, resources, and the freedom to use them appropriately. Who deserves reward? Who is unhappy, and why? Claimants may be unable to distinguish ambition from achievement. They may confuse distress they bring to the system with frictions it provokes. But members are helped to make pertinent distinctions if they scrutinize the system's aims, efficacy, and organization while meeting in its name. This is the self-conscious self-control of individuals extended to the corporate deliberations of members who create norms of behavior for their system.

This process may seem awkwardly self-conscious: just get on with the work. We ignore the advice, because the conversations of a system's deliberating members makes them the agents of corporate self-regulation. Consulting with partners, discerning their emotional and intellectual depth, makes members responsive to and responsible for one another. Before, a system's responsibilities to its members may have seemed formal and abstract: members stabilize the system; let it behave responsibly to them. Now, the responsibility is particular, personal, and shared by members who meet as a system's corporate public. Families, friendships, and schools accept this responsibility for self-regulation: differential responses to their members are principal reasons for their being. Armies, states, and many businesses are more cumbersome, less responsive, and less moral.

iii. Duties of a system's members to one another. Duties to a system's fellow members are mediated by their system. But this is odd: making a friend, having a child, I seem to be responsible to him or her without mediation. That impression elides a significant factor. For it is responsibility to their system that creates members' duties to one another. This is apparent when we consider that responsibility to a system's members for acts appropriate to the system does not extend to people who are not its members.

Still, the issue is uncertain: is membership in a system a sufficient basis for duties to its other members? Are the members of a conspiracy duty bound by their partners? Are there mutual duties among the members of a drug lord's murder squad? Duties are obscured when the systems generating them are repugnant. Yet, the origin of mutual duties is straightforward, though complicated by three steps. The first is mechanical and amoral: there is a system in which members participate, one whose existence depends on their reciprocal causal relations. Members are responsible to the system for filling their roles, in the respect that the system degrades or dissolves without them. These are duties ascribed (so to speak) to the members by the system: do such things as sustain me. Second is a question from the members: Do we value the system? They may not, so the system's tacit demand has no affirming response. Or they do its work, because they admire its aims or because of advantages to themselves. Only the latter two conditions move us to the third factor: members who value their relationship also value one another instrumentally. Each sees the other's actions as a condition for achieving a shared or complementary aim.

This formulation may seem to confuse two kinds of friendship, hence two bases for duty. One is the utility a member may have by virtue of his or her role in a system; the other is his or her value as a person of distinct qualities and capacities. Shouldn't utility value be incidental to the properties that bind a system's members; wouldn't it be finer if people were valued for their virtues? This might be true if personal relations were dominated by the aesthetics of virtue, but this isn't the glue the binds us. Many people have virtues that others would admire and value, but one is not devoted or duty bound to all of them. For duty to others has this complex condition: it is mediated by mutual interests or needs, though it is not incidental that we know and value the persons—workmates, spouses, or teachers—to whom we are coupled. Fidelity to utilitarian duties comes to be enlarged by the duties of respect. This transforms relationships without diminishing their utility: one expresses commitment to a friendship by addressing the friend.

iv. Systems' duties to other systems or to people who are not their members. Satisfying a system's duties to others is problematic whether it relates to other systems, or to individual persons. Such relations may bestow no duties, because neither side couples to the other: like ships passing in the night. Or reciprocity establishes a new system. A foreign traveler comes ashore. He isn't and won't be a citizen, but he and his host have acquired duties to one another. Immigration officers greet him in appropriate ways; he responds in kind. He will pay his bills; this state will give him some of the rights guaranteed its citizens. He may freely walk its streets; it won't capriciously injure or jail him. Or it does abuse him, thereby exhibiting the contempt for duty that is familiar when some systems address other systems or persons who aren't their members. For having duties isn't a guarantee they will be satisfied. Fulfilling obligations requires, additionally, that there be freedom to satisfy them (implying the power to act and necessary resources), respect for the other system or person, and a system's acknowledgment that it has such duties.

The duties may seem contrived, because here, as above, it isn't plain that systems (not only their members) have duties. What is the referent, the responsible party, when we say that General Motors has obligations to its customers and suppliers or that an all-night bar has duties to its neighbors? Duty seems to be the moral demand made of conscious beings able to feel its weight. Human social systems are relationships of subordinate systems down to and including the people who are their proper parts. How can a system acquire or be made responsible for duties to others if there is no superordinate mind to acknowledge and requite them?

A system is an appropriate subject of duties because of its reciprocal causal relations to other systems or individual persons—it affects them as they affect it—and because its network of constitutive relations gives it a corporate identity. A system satisfies its obligations by exploiting its sustaining resource: the relationship of its members. So, a conversation is a system. Each person makes himself responsible to the other for a pertinent response, and each is responsible to their system, hence to one another, for the civility that maintains it. This example of duties acquired and satisfied by individuals is paradigmatic and not more obscure when generalized to more complex systems. But systems are not conscious in the way that persons are, so where do their duties lodge? In the organization of their parts. General Motors doesn't quiver with awareness. But it does have duties, and it is organized to satisfy them. Individual persons represent the system by virtue of their roles (engineer, salesman, or treasurer, for example). They have authority to act for the company; and they do act, using the system's network of members to satisfy its obligations.

The allocation of duties to members having specific roles is a commonplace of organized social life and evidence that a system need not be conscious to have duties. Even the fulfilling of duties may not require it. A light railway posts a schedule and keeps it, out of duty to its commuters. They respond by buying tickets to support the company and by appearing on platforms at the times announced. The railway is entirely automated. Passengers enter their schedules into an automated system; a computer program sorts the requests, establishes its schedule, and programs the trains. There are no train drivers, but trains come and go as the schedule says they will. The railway satisfies mechanically the duty that comes with promoting commuter expectations.

Fulfilling duties is a complex achievement. But this isn't surprising, if duty and its recognition emerge in the reciprocities that create systems. For the reciprocities binding systems—whether their members are persons or other systems—are complex and morally demanding. There may be no respect for the other, and no acknowledgement that reciprocity creates expectations and the habit or intention to satisfy them. Laws and penalties are introduced just because systems and persons fail to acknowledge their acquired duties, though deference to law has an off-setting liability: we come to believe that there are no duties in the absence of enforceable laws.

   v. Duties to other people, irrespective of shared systems. Duties to others may be founded in either of three considerations (reciprocities apart): their particularizing existence; their specific history, context, or character; or the generic personhood abstracted from the specific *that* and *what* of individual lives.

   Is there a duty to sustain life for the sake of life, without regard to its character? Life is awesome, perhaps all the more because of being the effect of coupling atoms, molecules, and cells in hierarchies of reciprocally related functions and parts. But is the magic of life—its existence—sufficient to generate a cascade of duties to individual persons? Are we duty bound, for the same reason, to respect and preserve every life—every virus and bacterium, included—whatever its condition or prospects? Nothing good can be done if one is not alive to do it. Yet, there are existences that promote no duty. I have just thrown a large, dying roach over the garden wall. Was I duty bound to avert its death? Asking the questions expresses my troubled conscience, but this may be sentiment only, the lingering persuasion that life is sacred. Suppose the roach had been a human stranger, one whose character and deeds were unknown to me. My behavior would have been different; but would I have been duty bound to save him?

   We want an answer that applies universally, an answer as sweeping and confidently grounded as Kant's categorical imperative. But there may be no unqualified answer. A desire to live is plausible, and everywhere apparent. A duty to preserve life—one indifferent to the character of the existent—seems ungrounded, if we discount traditional stories about a god's valorization of every life or human life only. For bare existence is the place marker for a possibility: namely, the character that uses its talents and opportunities to engage its holder in personally significant and effective reciprocities. Sartre remarked that existence is the necessary ground for human projects.[46] But this concedes that existence is an enabling, instrumental value, not a good in itself. Physicians demur. They save lives, irrespective of the personalities, relations, or purposes of the lives saved. But doctors would be shaken if told that all or most of the people they save go on to do horrible things. It might make a considerable difference to clinical practice if there were a test that identifies hopeless recidivists. There is no test, so medicine gambles that most people will use their lives constructively. This is also social policy. Laws everywhere proscribe murder (though not war). Life is precious; we defend it so the living may profit themselves and one another by the manner of their living. But this is a consequentialist gamble: given that nothing of value can be done without life, we bet on its good uses.

This concession—life is critical for what we make of it, not in itself—has implications that are carefully circumscribed: it isn't license to dispose of people who use their lives in ways we don't approve. Democratic societies find ways to tolerate divers characters and projects. Others may judge the utility or quality of the work we do, not usually our right to live. Behaviors that are odious or destructive can usually be deterred or redirected without annihilating the people responsible. War and heinous criminals alter this bias by threatening the lives of others.

This leaves two principal, alternative bases for duties to others: their particularizing context or history, or their generic personhood. The idea of generic personhood implies that duties are owed to any and everyone, irrespective of history, context, or character. But why is that so? What is there about each of us that compels attention, if bare existence is insufficient to generate duties? Is it recognition of each person's capacity to valorize life by his or her way of conducting it? Recognition is already a moral attitude, because it combines acknowledgment with respect: seeing the capacity, we defer to it. Almost no one is devoid of this valorizing power, implying that respect is appropriate to everyone. Yet, respect is not duty. The duties that concern us—first-order duties, we may call them—emerge within relationships that bind people or systems. Each person's character and duties are a history and map of his or her engagements, a kind of fingerprint distinguishing him or her from every other. It is these contexts—the natural history of our lives in core and other systems—that generate duties of three critical sorts: to systems, their members, and oneself. There are also second-order duties: respect the Constitution and pay taxes, for example. These legislated duties overlay the others because of our practical interest in the organization and coherence of society at large. But the stipulated character of the second doesn't obscure the local, affiliative origins of the first.

Where in this story are the duties that each person owes to every other? One way to identify them requires that we extrapolate to duties to persons in general from duties to systems and their members. Doing this requires that we be more specific about the latter. Having duties and acting on them is often unproblematic. One asks what a role requires, then, having been taught or told, one does it. Or one doesn't ask, because he or she knows and does what a system requires. This is true whether roles are affirmed or merely accepted. Either way, the reciprocities of the members are sustained. Yet, affirmation and acceptance are different: one is assertive, the other acquiescent. There is a continuum between these extremes, because members are sometimes ambivalent about their system or their roles within it. There are, however, pure cases of acceptance, and they are an intimation of the difficulty of supposing that each person has duties to every other, irrespective of the systems that bind them.

Imagine someone who fulfills duties to his or her spouse and children while feeling suffocated (not abused). Describing such a person as trapped, we imply that he or she hasn't the means—the money or strength—to go. But many people who have resources don't leave, some because of habit, inertia, or fear, others because duty precludes it. But duty to what? The example assumes that marriage has failed this partner. Why does duty survive the death of the system that nourished it? Because this man or woman sees past the system to its other members. Having learned to care for them, seeing the system's benefits to them, he or she chooses their welfare over the impulse to damage it more. I infer that concern for other people is mediated by the systems in which we relate to them, and that this concern endures when the contexts of affiliation have all but dissolved.

This implies a simple test for one's duties to other people: imagine anyone dear, identify the system in which they are partners, then ask if this person would provoke a similar response if he or she were the stranger with whom one shares the seat on a bus. Of course not, you say. Strong affinity is based on familiarity; this seatmate is unknown. Fair enough. Modify the example: we know the person well, if partially, because of frequently seeing him or her in films, on television, or in newspapers. Something is still missing: familiarity without affiliation does not generate the affinity acknowledged at the start. What explains it? Principally or only, it requires relations to the members of core or other systems. Those are systems in which we evolve psychologically and morally. Knowing their other members is a condition for being and knowing oneself and equally for acquiring the moral sense that includes duties to them.

This consideration impedes relations to people with whom we share no system, core systems especially. They are alien and seem to have little or no value for us, hence the division between these two classes of people: those to whom we relate within valued systems and those with whom we share no affiliations. Relations of the first sort are often affectionate; the others are civil but formal. Civility is a learned response to every stranger, whether fellow citizen or foreigner. Why treat foreigners as well as one treats the strangers with whom one shares a state? There isn't a uniform answer. Some cultures encourage hostility: no quarter given, because no interest is shared. Others treat visitors with the exaggerated respect that caricatures the respect that family members express to one another. Both responses enforce the point at issue by resolving it without ambiguity: you are not one of us, or you are, if only temporarily.

Some people reject both alternatives and by implication my claim that affinity depends on shared membership in core or other systems. They say that one system is ontogenetically prior to every other: namely, the family of man. Respect for others is a duty first acquired as we learn to respect our partners in core systems. But it is quickly and rightly extended to the generic personhood of every man and women. For affinity to parents, siblings, friends, and associates is an accident of birth and place. Each of us would have had other caretakers and friends in other places, and each can find or imagine in every person a germ of the qualities that he or she esteems or adores in the few people known well. Respect is and ought to be generalized, because everyone is worthy of it. The teleology of moral life may have no other vector, yet resistance grows geometrically as we try to perceive everyone in this light. Several things impede us. Core systems have failed: they didn't teach respect for fellow members, they qualified the condition for respect in narrow ways (men but not women, women but not men), or they implied that our style of communal life is the only context that generates people worthy of respect.

Morality derives from the demands that systems' members make of one another. This, its tribal origin, was suitable to the practicalities of lives whose commitments, affiliations, and loyalties were almost entirely local. Economy and technology have altered our circumstances without changing either the wants and needs that provoke affiliation, or the localized systems where they are satisfied. Embedding local systems in global ones—selling African bananas in Europe—doesn't change the look and feel of the supermarket or stall where they are sold. Moral development doesn't keep pace with trade. We try to regularize their different rhythms with laws, but legal sanctions or demands are a step beyond morality, the step we take and enforce when the morality of core systems loses its way in the wider, impersonal world. The natural—developmentally acquired—norms of one are superseded by the penalties of the other. We notice the difference without being able to integrate duties to law with duties to respected others. We may hope to mitigate this effect by creating a global village, though this is more rhetoric than reality: it confuses the homogenization of styles and information with the intimacy of core systems.

What saves us from tribalism, hence the mutual alienation and hostility it implies? Law (discussed below) is one consideration, though its effects are external. We learn its standards, but the duties it carries are formal rather than particular: they are duties to anyone, not obligations to these particular ones. We shouldn't expect such duties to be keenly felt, and usually they are not. Consider again that one's partners and companions are a contingency: most any person could have performed the roles of people known to us in core systems. Fantasy helps to make the point: imagine any stranger as one's parent, child, friend, or partner. Doesn't this make their unfamiliarity—their exoticism—less disconcerting? It doesn't, because we grasp the point intellectually but not affectively: the person imagined doesn't feel like a parent or friend.

Are there duties to strangers or remote others? We appreciate that their lives are valuable to them; we are horrified by their misfortunes. But this is respect or sympathy, not duty. We acknowledge their vulnerability without feeling responsible for allaying it. Should we nevertheless respond to them as understanding warrants? We may consider this a duty, and act appropriately. But we shouldn't be surprised when this rational policy founders in the absence of strong feelings. Duties we acknowledge are founded principally in our affectively nuanced roles in core systems. We also understand duties to law, or merely the penalties of violating them. A generalized duty to persons unknown is a weak extrapolation from our reciprocal relations to persons known better. But this is not indifference. Sympathy—fellow feeling—and respect are motives no less powerful than duty. They, too, engage us to other people, near or remote.

vi. Duties to oneself. Duties to oneself might have either or both of two origins: we create or discover them without regard to systems that engage us, or they emerge as we discover ourselves within systems. The first possibility is Cartesian: each of us discovers him or herself by direct self-inspection. Descartes, like Augustine, invests this discovery with self-love, hence with an inclination to preserve and gratify oneself.[47] The effect is asocial, a result all but entailed by the argument that I exist, though perhaps nothing else does.[48] Yet, this is a fragile basis for claims about the inception of selfhood. Descartes requires that we detach ourselves—if only reflectively—from others. He forgets or ignores that thinking of oneself perpetually implicates the people to whom we are joined in core or other systems.

Children are better evidence of selfhood's formation. They discover themselves in the midst of other people. What explains the perception that a child is separate from the systems in which he or she participates? The likely cause is deliberation provoked by choice or conflict, not Cartesian self-inspection. An argument disrupts his relations to a system's other members, or he is distracted by responsibilities to a new friend. Either way, the child withdraws to observe others and himself. What are we doing? Why do we do it? What do I want? These are questions about matters of fact. Their answers require information about the system at issue and its effects, but also information about the child and his or her circumstances. The questions are tentative when the child's psychic perimeter is vague. They persist as other relationships—friendships and school, for example—evolve. Identity crystallizes amidst the cross talk of these systems, each pulling to some degree against the others. For no system engages us without provoking these standing questions: What are my commitments to other people and systems, social norms, and myself?

Questions of duty are answered by citing pertinent facts. But where among the facts are duties to oneself? We find them by looking more carefully at the deliberations where questions are pondered. Adults, as much as children, often act without considering their circumstances. A situation requires that we behave in appropriate ways, and we do. Like the parts of a creaky machine—tired and distracted, but acceptably competent—we fill our roles. Our partners are satisfied, because we provide enough support for them to do their work. No one obliges us to consider what we do, our motives for doing it, or its effects on the system or ourselves. We don't think to ask. Perhaps, we dare not ask, because this is a job that supports a family or the role in a hierarchy that brooks no challenge. But sometimes, we withdraw from a role, while satisfying it, to consider our circumstances. In frustration, anger, or fatigue, possibly in a moment of joy, I perceive that a role is good or bad for me. *Good* and *bad* are words of appraisal, but nothing in this application implies considerations additional to matters of fact. The badness of a system that overworks, underpays, and abuses me is inherent in its effects. Nothing additional—no qualifying, appraising mental intention—is required to inject value into a situation that is otherwise value-free. This system, or my role in it, is a practical disvalue for me. I can make this judgment, because reflection has sensitized me to a distinction that was previously invisible or suppressed. Before, perhaps as a child, I was content in roles and systems that satisfied me, or I wasn't pleased but knew no other way to be. Pleasure or oblivion reduced the need to distinguish those systems and roles from myself. Self-referring duties may originate in satisfying affiliations: let me do what I can to sustain or repeat their effects. But now, less content or more aware, I perceive the discrepancy between my experience in a role and my hopes or desires for myself. Duty's objective alters accordingly: let me do what I may to establish or reestablish links to the people or things that will enable me to satisfy myself by achieving my aims.

Which has priority, duty to myself or duty to systems and their other members? This contrast emerges when a child falls out of harmony with parents or teachers. It is sharper still as he or she reflects on systems that are punitive or otherwise unrewarding. One's role may be significant, even essential to the work being done. Yet, the role gives no satisfaction. What shall a member do if he or she is responsible to a system for actions that are critical for the system's performance and aims, though the system is inimical to him or her? Soured friendships, marriages or partnerships gone awry: these are systems that strain the loyalties of members who want to do justice to the systems and themselves. Duty turns problematic, because the neat elision of role and well-being is ruptured.

The conflict is resolved as much by habit and feeling, hope or fear as by reasons and evidence. The tension is keenly moral, though it may lack—as surely it does with children—any awareness of moral theory or moral ideas: duty, for example. One knows the opposed factors: the system of reciprocally related members, and oneself. Shall I do justice to one or the other when I cannot do justice to both? Filling one's role in a system is onerous if the cost is the diminished self-esteem that goes with secret alienation from oneself. But saving oneself is equally costly if abandoning the system is experienced as disloyalty to others, or as self-betrayal. Either way, there are two losers: the system and its member.

This dialectic—whose welfare, the system or mine?—is everywhere chronic and familiar. It is resolved when people find congenial systems, systems that engage their affective and cognitive skills. Family, friendship, business, and school are universal templates, but their individual expressions are as idiosyncratic as their members. For there is no system without members who relate distinctively to one another. Each person lays down his or her terms for participation, and looks for compatible partners. The result is a singular alliance that satisfies the members while achieving their system's corporate aims. Its members rightly say that they fulfill their duties to the system, and to themselves.

Duties to oneself can seem ennobling or perverse; but either way, these expressions of self-regard are only matters of fact: the *ought* is only an *is*. No matter that there is a gap between what I am and what I propose to do or be. The *ought* is incipient: this is what I want for myself, given what I have learned to be. I have or am it already, just by virtue of having its seed within me. More than idea or ideal, this is my *telos*. Does everyone discover the same trajectory, the same duties? That might be so, if all were to retreat to the standpoint of an immortal soul or transcendental ego; but each person's discoveries are shaped by his or her history, context, and idiosyncrasy. Each discovers expectations that are encouraged as he or she participates in core systems—family, friendships, neighborhood, work, and school—where distinctive talents, attitudes, and intentions are developed and tuned.

There are, nevertheless, some similar conclusions about self-regarding duties, including satisfaction of one's needs, work appropriate to one's talents, liberty to choose affiliations appropriate to one's nature, circumstances, and wants, and charity for one's shortcomings. Being vulnerable, having distinct capacities and specific needs, each person searches for and establishes those practices and relations that will secure and satisfy him or her. These are generic truths about our material nature and circumstances. They all but guarantee that people everywhere will come to similar conclusions about the character of self-regarding duties.

Are there circumstances so chaotic that no duty to oneself is satisfiable, because every social system has disintegrated? This is possible, though horrible to imagine. Wouldn't one duty remain: namely, survive. No, because survival is more a principle of inertia than a duty: go on living, because one lives. Character would be more relevant. We would expect people to affirm themselves by reestablishing the systems that were once the context of duty and identity. Every refugee from the demise of core and other systems would look ardently, if carefully, for partners with whom to recreate centers of attachment and cooperative activity. For we don't like being singular, alone, and free from duties that bind us to esteemed people and systems.

vii. Duties to law. This is not the whole story about social life, because it isn't always cosseted in well-oiled systems. Think of crowded streets where people mingle and move in opposite directions. Foot traffic divides, but some people walk across the grain, and others stop to think or gawk or meet. Gas molecules often collide, but these pedestrians rarely run into one another. Each goes his or her way, taking care not to hinder others. The effect is considerate and moral—live and let live—but no one organizes the flow. Here, too, morality emerges in the midst of inter-action when people learn to behave in ways that serve their interests while interfering minimally with others. We do as we should, because of the animal radar that enables us to move safely among others and because of the simple rule: stay right.

Most duties to family, friends, or community are not legislated. We perceive and honor them anyway. One may object (perhaps thinking of Hegel) that these are proto-duties, not yet the real thing: authentic duties are those sanctioned by reason's transcendental laws, a holy source, or by an authority that legislates for the public good. We are to believe that duties are too august to have conditions—affiliative, advantageous, or altruistic—that are only practical. This is homage to a dogma, the refusal to acknowledge that many duties have just four aspects: the per-ception that a system depends on one's participation, affirmation that the system is worthy because it has worthy consequences, loyalty to its other members, and the habit or inclination to perform accordingly. This expectation and commitment may be strongly felt and firmly articulated: we may use the language of duty to express the quasi-legislative force of a personal intention: participating in this system may be a law for me.

This does not imply that every significant duty needs legislation to confirm it. Law is an afterthought when habit, inclination, and persistent practice have acquired a style that a system's members acknowledge and apply. Regulative principles—enforced by habit, inclination, and expec-tation—determine what is done, how, and by whom. So, the division of labor by gender or class is sometimes rigidly enforced, though no legisla-tor formalizes it. Think of preparations for dinner. Who cooks, sets the table, or cleans? Some variations are ritualized, others are fluid and infor-mal. The task is largely the same; styles of doing it vary.

Most of life's practices do not have or need any other principle to regularize them: we learn a style and apply it. Law becomes an alternative source of duties when unformalized regulative principles fail to secure us, or when loyalty to systems or their members is too parochial to guarantee peaceable or efficacious relations among people who share no core system. Child abuse is proscribed; we prescribe laws to regulate activities that vastly outrun the scale of local systems: trade or traffic, for example. We drive on the left or right, but we do it because of law and habit, not because our actions are regularized by the causal reciprocities that bind us to other drivers. Duty to laws may seem to be shorthand for fear of the penalties breaches invite; but these obligations are, more fundamentally, commitments to social coherence. So, Kant would have us test the universalizability of maxims:[49] consider the effect if people were to drive randomly on the left or right. We don't do it, because we shun the chaos it would provoke. Laws limit freedom, but they facilitate choice by regularizing social behavior. We gladly accept their constraints in return for the predictability introduced by cogent laws rigorously enforced.

Can we rightly ascribe normativity to laws that are regularly broken: traffic or tax laws, for example? This is not unreasonable, if we contrast actual behavior with its self-correcting trajectory. For we often make ourselves responsible for standards we don't meet. We respect the emotional and intellectual depths of other people, especially our partners in core systems, but the response is inconstant; we lose sight of a moral demand imperfectly learned. Laws oblige us to do some things we would otherwise forget. They establish a norm, then use practice or intimidation to stabilize it as habit.

Philosophers diverse as Hobbes, Kant, and Hegel have believed that laws equitably applied are the principal defense against abuse and the only source of legitimate duties.[50] Fidelity to law implicates reason and the individual's freedom and power to suppress inclination and self-interest in the name of principle. Social atomism postulates that character and law are the only bases for social order. Duties to persons and systems consequent on our roles in systems are mistakenly deemed irrelevant. Hegel, no atomist himself, served individualist aims by describing the trajectory from tribalism—with its emphasis on core systems—to the laws formulated by universalizing, enlightened reason. This nicely confirmed atomist prejudice by supposing that duties to systems and persons are replaced—not transformed—by duties to law, the local and tribal made rational.

This individualist/atomist emphasis is costly, because it ignores reciprocity and respect for others as alternative bases for moral behavior. The difference is a chasm in moral life. On one side are legal norms; on the other are norms founded in the duties and respect for partners acquired in core systems. We who live in systems made fragile by our mobile society incline to think of normativity in legal terms only. We deride or neglect norms learned and enacted when core systems are stabilized by their thoughtful, mutually responsive members. The combination of reciprocity, perception, and deliberation is the inception of morality's four conditions and virtues: duty, freedom, trust, and respect. Law is the preferred expedient when organization—by traffic laws, for example—is the only or best solution to the scale and complexity of social life. But law comes later: it cannot displace the core and other systems where morality is first learned.

We don't acknowledge the eclipse of duties acquired in core systems, because *duty* is usefully ambiguous: it signifies both responsibilities commanded by the state's laws and obligations to systems or oneself. Eliding the two is doubly unsatisfactory, first because it masks the evasion of duties to core systems, second because it obscures the common root shared by duties of these two kinds. For the state, too, is a core system, one that forms when the public of deliberating persons extends itself beyond neighborhoods, villages, cities, and regions to establish a constitution, legislation, and officers. The state is the premier expression of corporate self-regulation. Yet, citizens too easily lose touch with the levers—the reciprocities—of social control. The sclerotic public withers and dies, but the state is still a system, one that is bureaucratic or tyrannical, rather than democratic. Obligation in these circumstances is the product of coercion or fear, not the affirmation or acceptance of a system that is good for its members. This is a perversion of duty and a reason that a state's citizens cannot discern their core system—the state—in people and institutions that abuse them.

Conflating moral with legal duties—better, displacing one by the other—has a corollary in deontological interpretations of public policies that satisfy the requirements of distributive justice. There is, for example, talk of perfect justice with the rights and duties it entails. Rawls avers that every person has a right to resources sufficient to subsist, and that others—better off—are duty bound to make this possible by sharing their resources or opportunities.[51] But what is the factual basis for policies that ascribe such rights and duties? Are they descriptions of actual qualifications—innate rights—or is talk of this sort a rhetorical device used to encourage compliance when legislation transforms recommendations into enforceable obligations? People playing a game—cricket or baseball—also have permissions and obligations ("Your turn at bat," "Cover the base"), but these rights and duties are creatures of the game and its rules, games supervised by referees and umpires. Policies that oblige us to tithe one's salary for the benefit of fellow citizens or people in other states have no authority but the power of the enforcing authority. Sympathy and respect for others may commend such policies—it would be good if everyone were to enjoy health, civility, and the cultivation of his or her intellect and sensibility—but the rights and duties postulated by deontological projects are honorific only: we imagine a utopian scheme, then postulate the rhetorical leverage—those rights and duties—that can be used to oblige conscientious people to behave as the scheme requires. Deontologists, whether religious or secular, should cite evidence for the perfect justice, rights, and duties they invoke. That evidence should have a basis that is independent of the stories deontologists tell.

There is, of course, this other possibility: talk of justice, rights, and duties may be hectoring shorthand for the observation that all of us live better if we have the means to satisfy and secure ourselves while cultivating our talents. Wanting this effect for everyone, we invoke rights and duties to achieve it. But this practice—use rhetoric to promote a desirable aim—doesn't entail that each of us has an innate right to subsistence or flourishing, or that others, however remote, have a duty to help us achieve it. Rights and duties are negotiated and legislated, or they are effects of the reciprocities that bind us in systems. They are not innate qualification that ground and justify a priori claims on the goods or good will of others. Universalizing—"cosmopolitan"—deontologists think otherwise, but one sees the merely stipulative basis for their claims in their disputes with one another. What do the rich owe the poor: subsistence or the opportunity to flourish? Should public policy about such matters be determined from the standpoint of an ideal principle of distributive justice or one that is more sensitive to our disparate circumstances? Deontologists hope that obligations they invoke will seem intuitively compelling, but that effect is precluded by their disputes about strategy and tactics.[52]

These disputes, so reminiscent of people designing a game, remind us that such policies are rightly appraised by their consequences, not by citing postulated rights and duties. A priori talk about them is the shadow of our theological past: justify every claim by invoking its transcendental ground. We don't need that backing to justify our concern for human well-being: grant that everyone wants to thrive, then consider policies that may enhance it.

8. Moral Flashpoints

Needs are mostly unfulfilled apart from the core systems—families, schools, teams, businesses, and states—where specialization, self-control, and coordination enable us to do together what we cannot do alone. We underline the significance of these systems by saying that their actions or relations to others are *moral*. The word is a sign of alarm: don't trifle with vital social relations, persons, or viable laws, because these are the conditions on which human well-being depends.

Moral tension exposes *shoulds* and *oughts* that are strained or confounded by these five points of conflict: i. systems, including their relations to members, other systems, people who are not their members, and the natural environment; ii. the conflicted duties of individual persons; iii. relations between or among persons; iv. conflicts between legal and other duties; and v. conflicted laws. There would be no moral tension if every such factor were not laced with inherent moral constraints.

i. *Systems, including their relations to members, other systems, people who are not their members, and the natural environment.* A system may be regarded as an array of parts—its members—or as a corporate entity. Taking the perspective of the parts, we remark that a system's members are its existential conditions: it would not exist without them and their reciprocal relations. But systems are not aggregates. A triangle has properties (angles and the relation of sides to hypotenuse) that its line segments alone do not have. Systems, too, have corporate properties, needs, aims, and effects: it is cells and bodies, not their molecules, that live, and teams, not their members, that win or lose games. The reciprocal causal relations of the members create a family, friendship, business, school, or state. Every such system has an emergent character and economy of its own, hence interests distinguishable from those of its members.

Relations among systems are frostier than those of mutually responsive persons. People are interdependent across a swathe of interests, feelings, and activities; interdependent systems have but one or a few principal tasks. Focus isolates them, or they cite it to justify their neglect of considerations other than the workers, resources, or information vital to their aims: "We do steel, not milk or the environment." Affirmation and respect are personal responses to social engagements. Relations among systems require pragmatic surrogates, especially the practices and rules that maintain reciprocity while defending each system's integrity, task, and distance.

Autonomy is, nevertheless, qualified. Businesses, for example, are stabilized and sustained by the reciprocity of their parts, and by relations to their clients and suppliers. Mutual reliance becomes a moral demand—interests become duties—when each side acknowledges that mutuality is the condition for the existence or well-being of both itself and the other. Duty's inception may seem vulgarly self-concerned, but then we need to tell why its origin couldn't or shouldn't be pragmatic. Or we relieve the uneasy feeling that utility is an insufficient basis for duty by remarking that altruism emerges when self-concern is transformed by mutual interest: systems satisfy their mutual duties even when doing so is costly, because defaulting would damage partner systems or because systems are sabotaged by failing their partners.

This result is half commonplace, half ideal. Human social systems are organized hierarchically, each overlapped or nested by others. These networks are sustained by the negative feedback relations that make selfish behavior costly: each system responds to its partners by encouraging responses that maintain their stabilizing relations. Yet, complicated networks are hard to sustain. Resources are unevenly distributed, communication breaks down, interests diverge, internal disruption prevents systems from sustaining their relations to others. Or systems behave cynically, taking advantage of the generalized naïveté—the vague presumption of mutual reliability—that is a condition for doing one's own work in a hierarchy of interdependent systems.

Networks of systems, like particular systems, often verge on breakdown, usually in small precincts, sometimes more globally (civil war is a limiting case). But there are measures to take. Build tripwires or fuses into the network: extrapolate from the modularity of individual systems to the modularity of higher order systems in order to reduce the risk that failure in one will bring down others. Design practices that reward reciprocity but punish unreliable behavior. Deter cynicism by making clear to participants that respect for the network and reliable service to one's partners is enlightened self-interest. Then punish systems and their members publicly when failures are willful.

Are these measures sufficient when our ideology prizes competition more than cooperation? Systems—hence their members—are less concerned by threats to reciprocity when businesses, teams, schools, countries, and even families are encouraged to affirm themselves by competing and "winning." This attitude has practical limits, because competition is inimical to the purposes and well-being of many systems (friendships, for example), and because competition is a disease, not a benefit if it poisons reciprocities that make systems viable. Successful competitors don't swagger too much, lest they alienate the support that made them successful. There is a mean where cooperation mitigates competition, but it is hard to discern or achieve when the ideology of the market encourages belief that failed systems—those crushed by competition—should have failed. What was their flaw? We have no compelling reason but Spencer's précis of Darwin: the survival of the fittest. Walmart stores are profitable, hence fitter than their small, bankrupt competitors. Is it irrelevant that dense networks of family stores, town centers, and neighborhoods are eviscerated? Which is or was the greater benefit?

Conflict is moral when systems having mutual duties sabotage or frustrate one another. This may be a consequence of willful failure: one or the other is spiteful or indifferent. Or fulfilling duties is morally problematic, because time and resources are limited so that satisfying one precludes satisfying another. A company is duty bound to maximize profit for its shareholders, but obliged to spend its profits on burners that reduce pollutants vaporized through its smokestacks. A state is duty bound to secure and educate its citizens, though its resources are insufficient to do both. One knows systems that try scrupulously to honor all their duties. But many others regard their duties selectively. They are steered by members who understand their system's obligations in the narrow terms of its stated aims. They acknowledge clients and suppliers, but not collateral parties: meaning, those affected "incidentally" in the course of pursuing its aims. Mining may require that workers leave their villages to live in dormitories near the mine. Disrupted families and a plague of diseases are a consequence, but the company denies responsibility: it only mines gold.

How are conflicting duties weighed? Holism supposes that legitimate duties are reconcilable within a properly organized whole. Systems theory is either too abstract to supply a basis for ranking duties, or its humanistic version—communitarianism—resolves conflicted duties by favoring the core systems where character forms. Individualism is more direct: choose yourself. It resolves conflicts among secondary duties—those accruing when contractual obligations are undertaken voluntarily—by applying a simple imperative: rank duties in the order prescribed by self-interest. Systems, too, apply this rule. A state's duties to its citizens are greater than its duties to citizens of other states, and, equally, businesses that sacrifice other interests to profit reasonably choose self-interest over interest to others, whether customers, suppliers or the environment. But is this the right moral choice? One imagines various principles it offends: do unto others as you would have them do unto you; God created all humans (and systems?) equal, and has no preference for one before others. The first is good advice. The second is a social policy reformulated theistically to give it authority. Is there a justification that cuts both ways, one that mixes self-concern with concern for others?

Let Descartes be our point of reference. "I am, I exist, is necessarily true," he said, "each time that I pronounce it, or that I mentally conceive it."[53] Informed that Augustine had come to a similar conclusion, Descartes distinguished Augustine's intention from his own: Augustine

> goes on to show that there is a certain likeness of the Trinity in us, in that we exist, we know that we exist, and we love the existence and the knowledge we have. I, on the other hand, use the argument to show that this I which is thinking is an immaterial substance with no bodily element.[54]

But Descartes, too, supposed that self-love is a feature of self-discovery. Their tight relation is confirmed by each person's commitment to his or her well-being:

> But when we think of something as good with regard to us, i.e. as beneficial to us, this makes us have love for it; and when we think of it as evil or harmful, this arouses hatred in us.[55]

The desirability of the feelings and attitudes expressing this self-concern might be argued, but the feelings are spontaneous; we couldn't repress them if we tried. Existence and self-love are distinguishable. One might perceive one's existence without valorizing it, but Descartes like Augustine affirms the contrary: each person perceives and prizes him or herself in the moment of self-discovery. Accordingly, self-love doesn't have a principle to introduce it. The act and its recognition are as fundamental as one's self-discovered existence.

This genealogy subverts Hume's dictum: *is* doesn't entail *ought*. For the *ought* of self-concern emerges with and derives from the *is* of self-discovery. This is egoism, the undeflectable pursuit of self-interest. But egoism is not the moral disaster it is often thought to be, first because the passion of self-love makes one active and effective, second because self-love is extended to the other persons and systems that engage us. One may care so deeply for others that one sacrifices oneself for them. Parents, soldiers, and friends do it often. Others do it too in all the ways that people defer graciously to one another.

But this was to be a discussion of the moral conflicts focused by systems. Why is egoism pertinent to them? Because we unself-consciously extrapolate from the self-interest of persons to the self-interest of systems. Behavior approved in one is perceived as appropriate in the other, with this difference. Moral tension is usually less acute for systems than for persons, because systems are usually specialized—each is designed for one or a few principal functions—while each of us participates in many systems, including states, cities, neighborhoods, businesses, associations of many sorts, schools, friendships, and families. Add duties to oneself, and one has more obligations than time and resources to satisfy them. Human social systems typically have fewer roles, hence fewer duties. Schools teach; FedEx delivers packages. Every such system has a signature function, one that has priority when members responsible for the system rank its duties. Why call those decisions moral? Because they answer to duties, including a system's duties to itself, its members, or others to whom it has reciprocal relations (competitors or suppliers, for example). There is usually no ranking that satisfies every duty, but knowing this is sobering. Systems—and persons, too—choose more carefully, because they can't satisfy every legitimate interest or demand.

Systems also provoke moral tension because each electrifies a web of reciprocal relations and moral responsibilities. It isn't good enough that a system satisfies its "principal" function: profitable to shareholders, for example. Some other questions are also pertinent: does it satisfy its duties to members (its workers, for example), clients, and suppliers? What are its effects on bystanders and the environment? Systems exist because of the reciprocal relations of their members. They are sustained by these relations and by their reciprocities to other persons and systems. These relations are the foundations of duty and the links that propagate effects. Aristotelian essentialists restrict attention to a system's identifying function—raising children, generating power, making money. But there is more to consider: especially, a system's effects on others and its duties to them. Duties include the expectations of persons or other systems to which the system is reciprocally bound and the duty not to damage them or those others with which it shares no reciprocities. The environment is a special case, because duties are typically reciprocal, though nature has no duties to the systems existing in its midst. Duties to the environment may be construed as respect for the material conditions from which a system emerges and upon which it depends. Or this is deflected respect for persons and systems (itself included) that are unsustainable if the environment is degraded.

These various effects and duties are evidence that systems are nodes: they are richly consequential. This implies a particular responsibility: namely, the one of monitoring their effects in order to regulate themselves. Having many effects, they do or can make themselves responsible for altering or sustaining the actions that cause them. Is self-regulation a duty, less pressingly a responsibility, or merely a desirable effect? It is one or the other depending on the severity of the damage done by neglecting self-scrutiny. The urgency of the demand is a function of the same consequentialist calculus that justifies every moral virtue: life goes better when we mitigate or promote conditions that reduce or enhance it. Systems, as much as persons, are responsible for monitoring their effects.

ii. The conflicted duties of individual persons. Making normativity a function of law has the effect of making moral agents passive: we are virtuous if we do as we're told. But virtue is, or can be, active. We learn it in systems where others expect that we shall perform in ways appropriate to our roles. For education of every sort, moral education included, requires initiative. Our first experience is instructive: chewing, walking, talking are things one learns to do for oneself in contexts where others wait for and encourage us. First roles require little more, but the lesson is plain: learning is collaborative; it requires direction, but also our willing participation. Having a role in a social relationship is a tacit command: we're depending on you to learn and do it. The context is often benign. Our partners don't expect too much, and they gladly excuse our failures and distraction. But the expectation is plainly communicated: learn to respond in the differentiated ways appropriate to your situation. Others have their tasks; they expect that we shall master ours. But mastery is more than skill. It includes commitment to the task and to those others whose own work isn't done if we don't do ours. This is duty's inception: we learn to do what is expected of us. You expect it of me; I expect it of myself.

Is this story trivialized by its reliance on favorable examples? There are also pathological families, bad schools, punitive businesses, and abusive states. They, too, have corporate properties and an internal economy created by reciprocities that sustain them. Should we do—are we duty bound to do—what they teach and expect of us? Situations like this are troubling because they mix the teaching and expectation characteristic of systems with the pathology of particular systems. Their members are appropriately confused. They often perceive themselves in ways that confirm and justify their treatment, though their passivity bewilders observers. Why are they faithful to systems that harm them? Because they may have no perspective from which to see themselves differently and no power to alter their circumstances. But there is leverage that may save them. We typically have roles in several systems, not only one. The self-regard that flourishes in one system is a defense against those that abuse us. One may be unable to change such systems, but leaving them is victory enough. This is hard to do, if regret or guilt is confused with duty. But duty is an affirmation: this system is good, because good consequentially. It is good for others I value, or good for me. Abusive systems may be good for no one.

A member's relation to core systems is not always problematic. We affirm our loyalty and obligation to several, sometimes to many. Notice the critical word: *affirm*, not *chose*. We speak of choosing friends (though it is affinity, not will, that promotes friendship). Then, as mutual confidence and loyalty grow, we affirm duties to them within the friendships sustained by our reciprocal actions. This affirmation comes during or after the fact, not before it. For loyalty, gratitude, and respect are attitudes learned while participating in systems. Affirmation is all the more conspicuous when I discover myself within core systems that receive me as a member without my foreknowledge or choice. I may be unflaggingly loyal to a family, church, or nation, because I affirm its values as my own. But here, too, affirmation is not choice. Shaped by the system, I cannot easily distinguish its aims and practices from my own. Approving of systems as I participate in them, I also affirm myself.

Character forms when interactions with caretakers and others give nuance and shape to temperament, its inherited foundation. We learn to relate to others while relating to a few: our beliefs, attitudes, and skills are a function of the reciprocities in which we respond to those who respond to us. We are reliable and moral in our context, though being so doesn't preclude our fitting snugly within a gang of thieves. A woman and her children once surrounded me on a city street. Working like a team, they tried to steal my watch. The children were trained bandits, but they were doing the moral thing as family members. Their attitudes expressed the difference between *us* and *them*: the family and its targets. Fearing punishment might have deterred them, but it may not have altered their beliefs and attitudes. For the morality learned in core systems is the motor and keel of moral life. It is overlaid by the prudence acquired with our socialization in other systems, but prudence is defensive: it moderates inclination with habit and fear.

Moral freedom takes an odd turn, for it requires that one abstract oneself from the moral character acquired in core systems. One who acquires information, attitudes, and habits in his or her roles is sensitive to the interests and demands of core systems and their members. But now, limited time and resources oblige this earnest member to apportion his or her time and energy. Autonomy is the result. For one can't make these choices without stepping back to appraise these systems and one's interests: which do I prefer either because I endorse their aims or because they serve me better? This is a first step when autonomy consolidates, but not the last: I may turn on myself, scrutinizing and appraising the attitudes acquired in my core systems. Which of these attitudes can I reject without annihilating my moral identity? For these attitudes—and the habits, inclinations, and affirmations they express—are identity's content. How shall I bootstrap myself to moral freedom when that requires exemption from my moral roots? What new perspective could that be? Why trust its judgments? This is a paradox of moral character: grounded in attitudes acquired with our roles in core systems, we oblige ourselves to make moral judgments that are uncompromised by the conditioning that gives us moral traction. But there is no posture exempt from the attitudes that form us. Accordingly, we are never so free of bias as we may want to be, though we may have or acquire attitudes that enable us to suppress an established persuasion long enough to hear and consider other views.

One doesn't know all the details of another person's moral fingerprint. Each person has a mixed developmental history with the effect that his or her moral profile is hard to discern. Where is the balance between attitudes determined by his or her roles and the power to see beyond them to possibilities they preclude? Correctly estimating this balance requires that we know this person's history, or that we anticipate his or her responses to an indefinite array of possible circumstances. One thinks of inquiries that map a word's grammar: we know how to use the word in familiar contexts, but the map is forever incomplete. Perceptions of personal morality are similarly partial: someone well known may surprise us.

Things sometimes go wrong. People don't do what a system requires of them either because they are perverse, aren't paying attention, are badly organized, or don't know how to do it. Or people resist a task because they are provoked to rethink attitudes that once made them compliant. Failures that seem voluntary or willful (because of perversity or inattention) are deemed immoral. Even ignorance is a moral fault if one should have known what to do: the information was available, one's role required that one have and use it. Immorality is the Damoclean judgment that people (or systems) are culpable for errors they could and should have averted. Such judgments are graded: they are sometimes affirmed most intensely when deficient behavior occurs within core systems (abusive parents, faithless friends). We don't care as much that a salesman misses work to see a baseball game. Is he morally culpable? Deontology would declare every such failure immoral. Garden-variety moral sense is more generous. It stretches forgiveness to excuse the error, because backsliding is tolerable when systems are more peripheral or needs less urgent. But what shall we say of the moral traitor, the man or woman who repudiates attitudes that define us? There is revulsion, but few words.

The strangeness of another person's moral posture is complicated by a consideration not directly observed. Someone usually does what others expect, but he can't suppress a contrary inclination: the job pays well, but this competent employee doesn't like the work. His behavior is inconsistent because moral quandaries beset him. Responsibility for the task drives him one way; responsibility to himself has a different vector. Why call these considerations moral? Because morality is principally this three-part aspect of interpersonal behavior: one is respectful of partners in systems (core systems, especially) and responsive to their expectations; one appraises, then affirms or rejects the aims and effects of one's current or candidate systems; and one is responsible to and for oneself. These are duties to systems' other members, to systems, and to oneself.

Reliability is difficult if either duty opposes one or both of the others. For then, a private conflict disrupts the systems in which one participates. Other members satisfy their roles and expect me to do the same, though internal conflict makes me unreliable or ineffective. It would be better for all concerned were I to declare my commitments, rank my duties to this system and others, then act accordingly. But I can't leave a job that pays my bills, or stop thinking that it wastes my time and talents. So, I equivocate, annoying everyone. Is it my pathology, they wonder, or my immorality? It is neither in people whose duties are conflicted because of time or other resources. They affirm their roles and whip themselves to a froth trying to satisfy them. Such people—obsessed by duty—are vulnerable and exhausted, but not equivocal or immoral. Compare this moral posture—committed but overextended—to that of people who writhe in conflict, their every commitment qualified by doubt. One imagines their dreams: Who am I if I repudiate my duties to core or other systems? Will others approve my intention, if not my judgment? Shall I be a moral pariah?

iii. Relations between or among persons. Encounters with other people divide: some occur within systems where each is a member; others engage people incidentally in ways that form no systems. We are friends, fellow workers, members of competing teams, or merely passersby. The morality of personal encounters is nuanced appropriately.

A system's members have expectations that come with having roles: partners expect that other roles will be satisfied as the condition or consequence of their own role filling. There is also the chance—substantial in the case of core systems—that members value their systems: they rightly perceive that satisfying or neglecting a role is good or bad for a system they affirm. This triples moral praise or blame. Role filling supports other members, the valued system, and oneself; backsliding impairs all three. One requires cooperation; the other provokes conflict.

Much of learning conflates two tasks: acquiring skills and using them in coordination with others. For duties are founded on the assumption and trust that one's partners are willing and competent.[56] Conflict is evidence that teaching or organization were deficient, or that members have purposely or carelessly damaged their system. One hears the message of a system's frustrated fellow members: We can't afford to commit ourselves to people who will not reciprocate; don't tell us you'll do your part if you won't. Your irresponsibility violates duty, trust, and respect; it violates our freedom by encouraging us to make choices we would otherwise reject. The person addressed has few plausible rejoinders: he accepted a role for which he is, to his surprise, unqualified; he doesn't have the resources—tools or time, for example—that it requires; or he is ill. He is less likely to be excused for the honest response that he is ambivalent about the role, hence insufficiently motivated to fill it.

Encounters unmediated by systems don't benefit from the mutual forbearance or respect common to a system's willing members. What stops them from becoming antagonistic? Notice that such hostilities are less common than one imagines. Strangers passing on a street may be anxious, but usually without cause. For each willingly fulfills the other's expectation: the desire for safe passage is the tacit basis for the reciprocity of mutual recognition and safe conduct. Systems extend this far into civic life, without our noticing, even into neighborhoods crazed by civil war. Someone walking through them is lucky—no one notices—or people ignore him because of respecting a stranger. This respect, learned in the intimacy of core systems, would ideally pervade one's relations to all people. First recognizing it in the emotional and intellectual resonances of parents and friends, confirming it with others, one might look for or know how to provoke it in almost anyone. But this extrapolation is rare.

Is respect, nevertheless, a universal duty, one that each should have for all? This deontological view derives from an idealized abstraction—our common humanity—though regard for others is less sure the greater our distance from the core systems where respect and charity for others is learned. People often try as best they can when often they can't do very well. One may see this and respect them anyway, or one despairs of them but respects the trajectory that doesn't reach as far in them as one imagines it might. This is the teleology of human moral worth: we could be better than we are. Seeing the possibility in oneself and others, we may be careful not to damage it. Thugs who beat a helpless immigrant haven't made this extrapolation: their cruelty and bravado occlude the self-perception that conditions respect for him or themselves. The fault lies partly with our imperfect evolution: we are half ape, half more than that. Responding defensively to chance encounters with other people, we don't recover soon enough to stabilize ourselves or reassure them. We fight when there could have been civility or collaboration.

This sentiment reduces to piety when respect is dulled by contrary interests. Mutual alienation is common when a system's members compete for a scarce resource: think of children competing for parental love. It is all the more likely if no shared system mediates and mitigates their differences. Competition is a universal feature of human life. Physiology prepares us to fight. Situations provoke us. Conflict is the result. It invades systems like a virus and embitters human relations everywhere. There would likely be no way to reduce its effects if respect alone were the social lubricant. This is one of the extremities for which law is the urgent solution.

iv. Conflicts between legal and other duties. Which is the greater duty in the event of conflict, obedience to law or care for others or oneself?

Duty to law may be thought to supersede duty to persons, either because one is an expression of reason, the other of inclination, or because law serves many interests or persons, inclination only one or a few. But these are shallow reasons if the law at issue would hang me for stealing a baron's rabbits. The better justification is utilitarian, though more abstract: law, not inclination, is the best defense of social relations. This is plausible, but is it true? And, if true, does it always justify putting duty to law over duty to systems or persons?

These are easy questions for Kantian deontologists, because they start by discounting the moral value of inclinations and hypothetical imperatives (do this if you want that). But their order of priority ignores this complex truth: morality starts in the personal relations where the worth of other people shows itself in what they do and how they do it; law is the expedient when a complex society can no longer promote duty, reciprocity, and respect on the basis of personal knowledge. Law does regularize practice, but we conveniently ignore its deficiencies—the neglect of familiarity, local systems, and respect—to emphasize the difficulty, say, of controlling traffic without traffic laws. No systems are more rule bound than armies, but armies now institutionalize recognition that moral duties may have precedence over the rules of military command: enlisted men may refuse a commander's order to perform an "illegal" act. When is the order "illegal"? When it conspicuously violates certain human values, including the life and well-being of civilians or unarmed enemy troops. One imagines the anguish of soldiers who refuse such orders, knowing they could be shot for insubordination. But here is evidence of a conflict that is not solved, a priori, in favor of law.

v. Conflicting laws. Conflicting laws entail conflicted duties. Ideally, laws would never conflict, but they do: killing other people is bad, except in war where it may be obligatory. We could mitigate such conflicts by deriving uniform judgments from a calculus of mutually consistent laws. Or we supersede conflicts of law by sanctioning legal practices and judgments appropriate to the competing interests and urgencies of situations to which the laws apply. One law says you can't have something of value, another awards it to you after considering the histories, interests, and needs of the claimants. The judge makes a common law judgment: who deserves it? Legislators and lawyers often prefer the first option. They imagine a system of consistent and autonomous laws, one that supplies a deductive calculus for deciding contested issues: supply information

where the laws have variables, derive a conclusion. Special pleading—
your interests or mine—is unwelcome because extraneous: traffic laws
apply irrespective of a car's owner, color, or horsepower. These are laws
and judgments that satisfy a principle of the clothing trade: one size fits
all. Yet, we don't easily construct the logical calculi that would satisfy
this ascetic taste. Why is that so, given the ease with which logicians
axiomatize the theories of empirical sciences? Because social reality does-
n't fit the design of laws that ignore significant detail while applying
generically within a domain. Everyone is eligible to vote at eighteen,
though felons and resident aliens are excepted; we drive on the right
unless there are two or more lanes of traffic.

Duty is equivocal. Laws and the duties they create are a rational
stopgap—one that supplies order, efficiency, and transparency—when
the conflict, size, or complexity (hence, inefficiency) of human societies
precludes exclusive reliance on individual discretion (the judgment of
automobile drivers or airplane pilots, for example). Or law is the expedient to which governments turn when they need or want tax revenue.
Legal duties promise order or income; moral duties implicate the systems
and people to which one is joined for critical or merely shared aims. One
abstracts from the particularity that distinguishes the other. But there is a
middle ground. Laws often need a rationale additional to the efficiencies
they promote. Laws pertinent to this moral concern have distributive justice—fairness—as their principal motive. Fairness is a value that originates in the respect for others and oneself. It is learned in core systems,
then generalized. Laws that express and promote it are considered below.

✳

The foregoing five points of conflict are evidence that moral constraints
originate in the material conditions for socialization. Morality begins
when members are formed by systems they establish and sustain. Law
extends the application of moral values without annulling their origin.
For morality has neither vitality nor purpose without the systems where
people are reciprocally engaged. Laws facilitate action or proscribe it;
they create revenue, or distribute benefits and burdens. But laws do not
create the moral values they sometimes express.

The next two sections summarize these results: section 9 considers
domains where character and social relations are sufficient to generate
shoulds and *oughts*. Section 10 controverts the accepted view that laws
and regulative principles are the only secure basis for duty.

9. From Facts to Norms

Morality's context is established by several layered matters of fact, all of them apparent in the previous section. First—because ground for the rest—is the vulnerability that makes us interdependent. Incapable of securing or satisfying ourselves individually, we form core or other systems where members are defended or nourished.[57] Character forms within core systems as each member learns to do his or her work while cooperating with others. It deepens as we cooperate with them to make the laws that regulate relations among persons or systems. This persistent, socializing tide is resisted by the contrary force of psychic and moral autonomy. We experience their opposition as the contrast of intense core relationships versus the cooler stance of lawful behavior or membership in systems that are less psychically invasive. Or the opposition is simpler, but more extreme: how much to one's systems, how much to oneself?

There are four domains where *should* and *ought* derive from *is*: namely, i. human vulnerability and needs; ii. the core or other systems where members are defended or nourished; iii. the character that forms in each of us as we learn to do our work while cooperating with the other members of core systems, and iv. moral autonomy:

i. *Human vulnerability and needs.* Universal self-sufficiency would make core systems unnecessary. Protons don't need one another. Self-sufficient humans would be equally indifferent. But we aren't self-sufficient or indifferent. Needing help for the simplest tasks, we bond to those who provide it. Wanting sexual partners, we create families and tribes. Acquiring the goods that nourish and sustain us, we establish the laws and enforcers that protect property. Every elaboration of basic needs or interests further complicates the network of core systems. It also embellishes the characters of their members: we become more adept at filling roles within systems we create.

ii. *The core or other systems where members are defended or nourished.* Needs are satisfied in divers ways by core systems of two kinds mentioned previously. Organizations are distinguished by the specialized roles of their members, each situated in ways that make him or her more effective in relation to others. Associations don't have or need this structure because they are bound by the shared beliefs, doubts, or attitudes of their members. Each member confirms another's beliefs by avowing them: my doubts are reduced, my enthusiasm enforced when you model or mirror my attitudes. Some systems—families, for example—embody both forms: roles are differentiated, but members mirror beliefs and attitudes they share.

Systems endure, because of the cooperation, competence, and reliability of their members, and because of their relations to systems that supply resources, new members, or information. Cooperation is apparent when people crowd into a subway car or bus. People arrange themselves clumsily, until all withdraw as best they can so each may have sufficient space to sit or stand securely. The first moment is amoral; the second is moral. The first exhibits the mechanics of flow: people pushing or propelled through a small opening into a larger space. The second expresses the pervasive realization that filling the space with as little discomfort as possible is everyone's aim. Acknowledging the interests of a system's other members, coordinating our actions with theirs, we suffuse a material event with moral purpose.

This transformation marks the trajectory from mechanical reciprocity to reciprocities stabilized by cooperation. Members are responsible to a system in the respect that it dissolves in the absence of their reciprocal relations. But this value is practical, not moral, because every system—good or bad, loathed or approved—is conditioned in the same respect. Each is created and sustained by the reciprocal causal relations of its members: they are its existential conditions. Reciprocity is imposed but more than mechanical when intimidation explains the cooperation of prisoners who work effectively under duress. Habit supplies a different—internal—basis for reciprocity: it implicates the part of selfhood that emerges within systems, the part that cannot recognize or imagine itself alienated from them. The basis for participation is transformed again when habit is fortified by members who affirm their participation either because they perceive it as good for the system, good for its other members, or good for themselves. Appreciation for a system challenges its other members: work as I do, cooperate. Affirmation is sometimes mere zealotry, a posture calculated to make one member seem more ardent than others. But systems flourish when commitment is honest and infectious. For affirmation expresses dedication and an undertaking: I who affirm a system declare myself duty bound to sustain it.[58]

There is no alchemy in this transition from *is* to *ought*. It locates duty in the habits, perceptions, and volitions of those who accept or affirm their roles. No rule or law impels us: we do it for the good, practical reason that the consequences of cooperating in a system's work are favorable to ourselves or others we value. This progression—from mechanical compliance to willing cooperation—is apparent in the ways people work. Reciprocity cannot be established if a system's members are not competent and reliable. None can fill a role without resources appropriate to the work at hand, the cooperation of a system's other members, and the freedom to do his or her task. Participation may be careless and unconsidered; members may compete for tools and materials. But sometimes—more often when a system fills a mutual need—we acknowledge that our partners do critical work. This perception complicates duty: do the work that satisfies a role while allowing others the resources and opportunity to do theirs.

iii. *The character that forms in each of us as we learn to do our work while cooperating with the other members of core systems.* Systems and laws are two contexts for duty, but character is its foundation. Each of us acquires information, attitudes, and skills appropriate to our roles, however biased by idiosyncrasies of ability, taste, and need. Directives that bind us are the habits or intentions instilled as we participate in systems regularized by custom or law. Or they are provoked as we respond reflectively to our circumstances, contriving rules or procedures that would serve us better. Character is the formation that determines our responses. It may be rigid and dogmatic, or flexible and inventive. It is, more likely, a mix of both. One may think of character on analogy to trees bent by winds that swirl about them, but this analogy is much too passive. For people do more than accommodate to the systems in which they find themselves. We inherit families, but search for teachers and friends. We participate in core systems, learning their roles; but they are altered by accommodating us. Each has value for the other, because each is consequential for the other.

Theorists often look for the origin of moral values in obscure or exalted places, including a priori deductions, moral intuition, or God's firm voice. But this is window dressing. Habit, affirmation (hence inclination), and reflection are the moral drivers in our lives. Human needs, systems, and the individuals who do their work are their material conditions and context. Each of us has firm ideas about our interests, valued systems, and the loyalties owed them. Every effectively socialized adult learns what is expected of him or her, sees the advantage of doing it, and fears opprobrium as a backslider or punishment as a lawbreaker. Religious or secular rhetoric promises inflated reasons for doing such things as prudent good sense would have us do.

Can we be more precise about character's relation to systems? Is the family, school, or friendship good intrinsically, while members are good instrumentally? Or is it the reverse? Emphasis shifts back and forth as members consider their worth against the value of their systems. How dare I consider what is good for me when this system—family, business, or state—has dignity or worth that humbles my own? Social atomism—individualism—answers that each person perceives him or herself as an intrinsic good, other things being good or bad as they affect him or her. But this is too simple if personal identity is a function of one's roles in systems. For then, compromising core systems diminishes me. These apparently contrary perspectives may be complementary. There may be parity rather than priority: no esteem for one without esteem for the other.

This entanglement doesn't preclude separation. Both sides agree that we learn to differentiate ourselves from systems that engage and satisfy us, all the more from systems we dislike. Moving from family to friendships to school enforces the perception that I am distinguishable and separable from them, however firm my loyalty. This perceived separability is a principal feature of moral autonomy. It is critical to reflections that set us apart from any system that engages us, abusive systems especially. It also marks the transition from the habitual, unconsidered cooperation of children to cooperation one affirms. A reliable appliance is amoral: it works as designed. The reliability of a system's members is also explained by good breeding or education: they may have been genetically designed and instructed to behave as they do. Plato's *Republic* describes this ideal as it informs the lives of artisans and guardians. Yet, Plato knew that mechanical reliability is dangerous:

> He was one of those who had come down from heaven, a man who had lived in a well-ordered polity in his former existence, participating in virtue by habit and not by philosophy, and one may perhaps say that a majority of those who were thus caught were of the company that had come from heaven, inasmuch as they were unexercised in suffering. But the most of those who came up from the earth, since they had themselves suffered and seen the sufferings of others, did not make their choice precipitately.[59]

The child who learns reliability, skills, and cooperation within core systems is more than a well-designed cog in a machine. We know this is so, because he or she responds to incapacity (because of illness or a competing obligation) with anxiety or guilt: a role requires his presence, and now, despite his best intentions and effort, he cannot fill it. Character is moral when action is informed by respect for the aims of valued systems and other members. A member would be appreciated if his or her roles were filled efficiently, with none of this sensitivity. But this would be the regard appropriate to an effective robot, not the respect due a moral being.

Duties to others are fundamental for holist and communitarian views, because they suppose that character is partly a function of social relations. Atomists demur, saying that personal autonomy and distance from others is the actual and appropriate starting point for morality. They abstract idealized persons from the moral perspectives learned in core systems, all the while ignoring the psychic development and circumstances where integrity is achieved. Starting life within families, we are denied independence until we establish our ability to care for ourselves while working with others. The space of our autonomy is a shared space, or one that is virtually social because other people abide—in memory and anticipation—within it. Accordingly, the space that each reserves to him or herself is not freestanding: it is created with the help of a system's fellow members. Acknowledging their integrity, we claim our own. How do people communicate across the chasm of difference? By way of their mutual effects: one can't think of him or herself without remembering or anticipating one's relations to others. Atomists discount such memories and intentions as accidents, but they ignore both the effects others have on us and our commitments to them.

iv. Moral autonomy. A system's members may believe that their well-being is only the well-being of their system. Mutually hostile but stubborn members of a string quartet suffer together for the sake of their music. Others sacrifice themselves for no corporate effect they value and no personal benefit. But for how long? Things go smoothly—duty is unproblematic—if people behave as their fellows expect and approve. Moral scruples aren't roused, unless conflict or disorganization provoke questions about a system's effects: is this system good because of its effects on other things, is it good for me?

Moral autonomy is a developmental effect. A child gratified by his or her roles fills them without thinking what or why. Habit and approval are sufficient directives, until reflection is provoked by the contrary demands of one's caretakers. Language charges reflection exponentially, because words articulate the perception and implications of frustration or difference. The first relations to friends intensify it, because thoughtless reaction isn't sufficient when the friend's desires are weighed against one's own: What do you want of me? What do I want? And later: When and why should I defer to others? One turns aside, however briefly, to consider the merits of one's roles. These judgments—good or bad for others, good or bad for me—are findings. Assembling the relevant information, I choose and act. Sometimes, the action affirms a role; other times, one resists it or resigns.

Habit, affirmation, and reflection are phases in the evolution of duty. Habit is an accommodating response to circumstances; duties emerge when partners expect us to do what we habitually do. Or they expect it, because we affirm that we shall continue doing what we have learned to do. Reflection is an additional step, one provoked by conflict, anomaly—why are others more or less committed than I?—or merely by wonder: Why does a system work as it does? What is its aim? Is it good for others? Is it good for me? Reflection changes attitudes, and, thereby, the manner of filling one's roles. One continues as before, filling a role with the same degree of commitment promoted by habit or affirmation. Or dedication to a role is significantly altered by one's evaluation of a system or its members.

Positive judgments—we confirm that unconsidered habits or affirmations were appropriate—are less consequential than negative judgments. One justifies us in acting as we have done. The other requires that we behave differently, though doing so will likely disrupt a system and its other members. The positive judgment expresses approval, the other opens a gap between oneself and the circumstances judged disappointing. But criticism is socially dangerous, so we scrutinize our judgments, looking for errors. Or reflection turns self-critical: we examine ourselves, doubting the reasons or motives that would alienate us from systems once approved, systems we need or systems that need us to sustain them. One sometimes confirms that his appraisal was just, so that there is no way to avert this choice: suppress the finding or live with the consequences of alienating oneself from a system once prized. Self-criticism may endure through successive layers of self-serving attitudes, each seemingly final until a doubt or discrepancy carries reflection to the next. This is personal morality as inquisition: it subjects habit and affirmation to the demand that choices and roles be justified, not merely rationalized.

Autonomous attitudes are slow to form. Members are loyal to systems perceived as good for them. But just as often, they are loyal, because of misinformation, habit, or fear. The psychic identity that evolves with roles in core systems embodies the beliefs and inclinations dominant within them, however malign: think of abused children, still loyal to their parents. Self-regard accepts the material at hand. I affirm myself by affirming the system: I exhibit my identity and loyalty by doing its work. Character doesn't require reflection: one may have habits and intentions without it. Selfhood is a further step, one that isn't achieved without reflection.[60] For it has an effect contrary to habit: reflection distances us from our commitments, though we continue to fill our roles. Reflection is, nevertheless, empowering: it enables us to distinguish the pleasure and reassurance that come with roles in core systems from the power to judge them.

This practice is morally consequential. We mitigate habit and inclination with a soft imperative: don't do a system's work if it is inimical to favored people, systems, or interests. Kierkegaard imagined the knight of faith returning to everyday life, inconspicuously, as a tax collector.[61] The reflective man or woman may be equally discrete, though he or she firmly opposes systems and practices that others blandly affirm. The possibility of this interrogation exposes an opposition that is otherwise obscured. For individuals discover themselves within core systems. The possibility of autonomy, of standing apart from a system to criticize it, may be unthinkable to one whose identity is a function of the system. Reflection makes this dialectic reasonable, even incumbent, in three steps: it discerns an interest damaged by a problematic system, it makes the interest one's own, then infers a duty to defend the interest—hence one's integrity—by opposing the system.

Socrates exemplified, Nietzsche's *Genealogy of Morals* describes the irresolution this promotes: how can one be loyal to a system, but also its critic?[62] Duties of reflection are often adversarial: one or a few conscientious objectors oppose the others. They express attitudes that are mute or suppressed in anyone who lacks the stubbornness or courage to formulate or act upon them. For we hesitate to criticize core systems where values are first learned or laws that regularize social behavior. A private standpoint independent of these two social bases doesn't emerge until one has participated in systems whose aims and values are different or opposed. Even then, one hesitates amidst the volley of self-doubts: Is my appraisal more than a rationale for my interests; do I honestly speak for disinterested values, values that others should share? How could I validate my interests or attitudes? We stop the regress in either of two ways: by retreating, as Kant does, to the intrapsychic search for an a priori test that certifies the universal validity of moral principles, or we recover balance and confidence in our choices by asking what consequences will likely obtain if I or others (persons or systems) act in ways proposed or reasonably predicted.

Kant's solution is quick, decisive, and well known. This other procedure—thinking consequentially while scrutinizing particular actions or attachments, their context, and effects—is closer to everyday practice though much slower to achieve resolution. Attitudes that favor some answers, but deplore others are its fulcrum. Somewhat distinguishable, organized hierarchically, but hard to isolate by introspection, attitudes determine our appraisals of circumstances and effects, whether perceived or imagined. What are the likely consequences for others or myself if the system from which I distance myself (if only in reflection) acts as it normally does or would? Continued loyalty to the system may or may not be consistent with the answer, given the attitude or attitudes that determine my response. Suppose that the expected outcome would be good or bad for the system, but conversely that it offends or satisfies a dominant attitude. Reflection is determining, because this attitude imposes a duty that supersedes duty to the system.

This is a third notion of duty. The first concerns habits or inclinations acquired and affirmed as we participate in systems. Second are duties consequent on a society's constitutionally valid laws. Third are these self-imposed products of reflection. A system's members have duties of the first sort. Everyone falling within the domain of a law has duties of the second kind. But there is no social origin for duties of the third sort, because they are generated privately. One may explain the justification for his or her attitudes or judgments to others; but they may be unmoved. So, we speak of a "sense of duty," rather than of duty, itself, thereby implying the singularity of the obligation. Yet, duties and norms generated this third way alter duties of the first two kinds, first when personal conscience disrupts established systems or provokes the formation of revisionary laws, later when systems reform or when revised laws alter the organization of core or other systems and the self-perception of their members.

This process—achieving moral autonomy by way of reflection—is misdescribed if we confuse the distance reflection promotes with independence from the systems it considers. Systems that create our identity sometimes baffle or dismay us. But fundamental loyalties—duties—are firm. A child growing up happily in a sturdy, resilient family has no doubt that the family is good in itself and good for him or her. This family's unhappy child may be more thoughtful: What is this system's aim and value? Is it good for its other members? Is it good for me? He may separate more decisively from the context of his pain. But separation is slow, painful, and incomplete: one continues to embody some large part of the beliefs, attitudes, and inclinations learned in the system.

Abusive systems are all the more provocative. Their aims may be worthy, but they violate their members. This antithesis—good for the system, bad for me—incites reflection and requires a choice: subordinate self-interest to a valued system, or resist its demands and leave. One may choose to stay in the name of duty, as spouses accept the disappointment of their marriage for the sake of their children. The act of weighing duty to the family against duty to oneself is, nevertheless, tacit recognition that duty is a contingency: one duty or the other may be superseded by the judgment that a damaging relationship should be terminated. This judgment is, ideally, an appraisal of the facts: What are the circumstances, who profits, who is damaged? What do I need or want; what am I willing to do or accept?

Do we want the independent thinkers reflection creates? Social life would often be disrupted if every system's members behaved like the members of an anarchist debating society. But there would be benefits. Habit would yield to reflection. Knowing what we do and why would make it harder to turn or pervert us. Generals don't want privates who are too thoughtful, but work is usually done better by people whose loyalty to a task and fellow members is justified by reasons of their own. Having such reasons, or wanting and searching for them is the dialectical trajectory of moral development. It opposes circumstances and the habits learned there to thinking that differentiates and redirects us. But this thinking is not a priori or transcendental or alien to the selfhood that first emerges with habits and the attitudes that confirm them. For we must first acquire the duties and attitudes appropriate to our lives in systems before we can discern, judge, and revise our moral attitudes. Society, too, is altered by these personal disruptions. For the conflicted or merely different attitudes of disparate thinkers crystallize as shared norms under the pressure of having to deliberate about shared circumstances. Obliged to work together or merely to tolerate one another, we converge on attitudes that sanction mutually acceptable norms. These accommodations, perpetually adjusted to fit the specificities of a situation, are the inherent regulators of community life.

This developmental, pragmatic notion of duty is alien to Kantians, because it deprives reflection of a standpoint independent of and superior to the contingency of its roles and interests. Habits, affection, and inertia may preclude the harsh judgment that our systems and roles are perverse. They are admirable in the memory of contexts where every system and law was irreparably corrupted. But that is not always or even usually our situation. My duty to observe tax and traffic laws may satisfy the categorical imperative, but it is my role as citizen—not this logical test—that is the proximate and fully sufficient test of jejune obligations. Nor do we wait for or need the sanction of Kant's principle before acting on duties to children, spouses, workmates, or fellow citizens. Their moral force is circumstantial and social—in core systems, especially—not logical or a priori. Kant has reversed the order of priority, though his test would seem bizarre if duties to essential partners did not satisfy it.

Reserving morality to duties sanctioned by the categorical imperative is oddly doctrinaire. It has the rhetorical effect of making moral philosophers into moralizers: you think you're moral because you do your duty; but you're not sufficiently moral—or moral at all—if you aren't a citizen of the kingdom of ends. Earn your membership in that elite circle by rising to the level of individual, rational reflection. Test the plans and intentions that join you to other people by submitting them to the logic of the categorical imperative. Though the effect of doing this is isolating rather than socializing:

> Teleology considers nature as a kingdom of ends; Ethics regards a possible kingdom of ends as a kingdom of nature. In the first case, the kingdom of ends is a theoretical idea, adopted to explain what actually is. In the latter it is a practical idea, adopted to bring about that which is not yet; but which can be realized by our conduct, namely, if it conforms to this idea.[63]

Kant's formula is confounding in both the directions it prescribes. The theoretical idea is an idea of reason: it purports to signify "what actually is," but its reference—to a kingdom of ends—is merely ideal. The practical idea inspires no conduct but that of reflection—bringing one's will under the categorical imperative. Its "kingdom of nature," like the "kingdom of ends" is also ideal. Nothing on either side engages us with other people in the cherished or merely utilitarian relationships that sustain us. This is a morality for spectators, a morality of good intentions. One can satisfy it in reflection, confirm that this is done, and feel the pleasure of one's moral virtue without doing anything to satisfy the partners who expect us to sustain vital relationships.

This strategy for conferring morality is tendentious, because it devalues our relations to systems and other people, though they are committed, reciprocal, and beneficial. Kantians rightly respond that habits and passions binding us to others are sometimes an unreliable measure of morality: think of National Socialism and the Mafia. Bad systems and habits are dangerous; it is incumbent that we find them. Kant's cure is, nevertheless, excessive. For we need the categorical imperative or a principle of similar effect to test the morality of our practices, not usually to justify them. Satisfying the imperative validates duties of habit and affirmation, law, and private scruples when such duties have already satisfied one or another material criterion of worth. Duties that violate the principle can be reconsidered and amended, or disqualified.

Kant's test—universalize without contradiction—would eliminate any duty that fails the test. But his imperative—don't act on maxims that promote conflict—is tailored to egregious acts and their effects. It is too simple for everyday practices that have multiple effects, most of them benign. Raising children guarantees that parents will pass on some of their neuroses to their children. That isn't good, but it is unavoidable. Should no one have children, because no one can avert this effect? Should we do nothing until every proposed action is shown to satisfy the categorical imperative, or carry on, until challenged, with acts and systems whose morality is rooted in habit and inertia. We do the latter, risky though it is, because the business of life doesn't wait. Reflection comes later, not first. Where is morality in the meantime? In the habits and affirmations, laws, and scruples of people joined in core and other systems. Nietzsche called this "herd morality." He despised it. But this is principally the morality we have and usually all the morality we need.

Notice, too, that Kant's fail-safe moral test is psychologically wrong and ontologically consequential. It misrepresents our moral struggles, because it implies that moral reflection is cool and detached though we may be all but strangled by ties we struggle to appraise. It is ontologically consequential, because of its atomist core—the morally self-certifying ego—and because resolving moral doubt by applying the categorical imperative enforces personal isolation. For how shall the freestanding minds of atomist theory vindicate their morality? What resource do they have when their obligations are challenged? Such thinkers can only rely on justifications generated within themselves, for there is no alternative moral ground if we derogate systems and laws by saying that their morality is always suspect or flawed. Reflection is our only and final defense. It surveys the duties learned in systems and those sanctioned by law, approving some, superseding others from a perspective that is rational, sober, and disengaged for reasons that are categorical (detached), not hypothetical (situational and engaged). This is the fable of the disembodied conscience. It falsely implies a retreat into the void or an ascent to the transcendental ego, though we are neither transcendental, disconnected, nor alone. People reflecting are situated within systems, under laws. Aware of our circumstances, thinking of their effects, we reject the demands of deplorable relationships or laws. This response is not universal: some people are creatures of their circumstances; their judgments are only affirmations. Some others—usually a minority—take a dangerously schizoid step. In matters large or small, they judge the people and systems that nourish, form, and engage them. This is the paradox of Socrates and moral education: how to create thinkers whose loyalty to systems, laws, or other people is balanced by the courage to judge, admonish, or reject them.

10. Opposed Perspectives: Norms Founded in Material Systems or Rational Ideals

Should and *ought*'s relation to *is* is attenuated wherever laws and other regulative principles are the basis for duty. For these principles are introduced because of interests or values that are unsatisfied by ordinary practice alone: traffic laws are a jejune example. Moral maxims—"Help when you can," "Live and let live"—are more poignant, but also more abstruse. Both express our ambivalence. One considers people to whom we relate casually or adventitiously. Affiliating with them is incidental to our interests or needs: it may have utility; it doesn't breed loyalty. The other expresses our distance and want of interest. We imagine that people unknown have concerns like ours, and we may hope their lives are satisfactory and productive. But we aren't—can't be—responsible for their well-being. A small contribution to Oxfam or Amnesty International expresses our good intentions.

The cool reserve of these slogans offends many people. They locate morality's nerve in the obligation to see oneself in a stranger: if self-love prompts me to work in my own behalf, let me do as much for him or her. For distance is not indifference: there is no inverse square law in morality. Someone unknown would be as valued as people we engage were they our partners in valued systems. This claim seems justified whenever sympathy is roused by the good or bad luck of distant people reported on the evening news, with pictures to intensify feelings. But these experiences are too feeble a reed to support the claim generalized from them. Sympathy, affinity, and loyalty are first experienced as we participate in core systems, then generalized to people we don't know. The reverse doesn't happen: we don't start with love for all mankind before expressing it to those near us, hostile neighbors included. A priori arguments try to convince us that we are rationally obliged to consider others as we would ourselves, but they substitute an ideal world—Kant's kingdom of ends, for example—for the actual world, then demand that we transform the *is* of our circumstances to the *ought* of their ideals. Ideological arguments flourish as successive deontologists prescribe that we remake ourselves in one way or another.

This doesn't imply that every argument for distributive justice requires that we twist ourselves into a posture we can't or won't assume. Fairness requires a distribution of benefits and burdens, but this turns problematic when we specify the character of the distribution: Is it to be equal or proportionate to a measure of participation, contribution, talent, or need? Is it fair that everyone performing a service be paid the same amount or fair that they be paid in proportion to merit? The issue is unresolvable, because there are good reasons for coming down on both sides: should we emphasize equality, because all satisfy a least standard of competence or need, or merit, because of the additional effort it usually requires and because of the standard it sets for others?

We can avert this forced choice—either/or—by considering our relations to the other members of core systems. The distribution of rights and duties among them—parents and children, teachers and students, for example—is proportionate, not equal. But there is, or may be, equality of respect and recognition that no member can fill his or her role without the resources that make him or her a viable partner. We acknowledge, with only a little reflection to confirm it, that other people have material needs like our own and interests they pursue. We extrapolate easily to the conclusion that no member of any system can sustain his or her role without the least conditions for material well-being—food, clothing, shelter, and health—a qualifying education, and tools appropriate to the

task. Add respect for persons—generalized from self-esteem and respect
for one's partners—and we have the sufficient basis for willing a principle
of distributive justice: distribute resources so everyone may have the
means to sustain him or herself while satisfying his or her roles. We postulate that these systems are not malign. But now we concede that implementing this principle is incrementally more difficult as we move beyond
local systems and jurisdictions to the planet at large. Hence the lack of
vigor in efforts to extend distributive justice to deprived peoples. The
idea of justice is an extrapolation from local perceptions and feelings.
Lacking a compelling ideal firmly rooted in argument or a divine command, we settle for less charity, less fairness, than circumstances warrant.
For if fairness depends on generosity—an inclination—we aren't surprised that urgency falters when the identity of its beneficiaries is ever
more vague. Laws may enforce the practice, making it a legal duty, but
then distributive justice loses its moral impulse: we help others as we pay
our taxes.

There is a different solution, though it would likely fail to achieve
the universality required of distributive justice. Physicians and some
people in priestly or other roles accept the vocational duty to treat any
person who comes for help. Every such duty is an intention that requires
no particular response from those who are helped. Expressions of vocational duties, like moral duties, are particularized (doctors treat patients
individually), but they, like legal duties, are specific and abstract: parents
are duty bound to their children, but doctors will treat anyone needing
care. It is relevant, too, that parents anticipate having an intimate and
reciprocal moral relationship with their infant child. Doctors and priests
are all the more saintly for serving people who do not reciprocate. Legislators, policemen, pharmaceutical companies, meat markets, and taxi
drivers also have vocational duties, and they, too, are morally bound to
secure or enhance the well-being of those they affect. They inherit these
duties because of the work they do, and because laws or professional rules
specify the responsibilities of people doing it. Would distributive justice
be better served if it were vocationalized? Professionals would need moral
and financial support from those who acknowledge that fairness is a principal value, but they could do practically what others merely encourage.
The World Bank is evidence that this is already our policy.

Vocational duties are transitional and precarious: they mark the
change from duties founded in systems—morality's material basis—to
those invoked or imposed by laws or the rules of professional associa-

tions. We emphasize this distinction—pushing vocational duties one way or the other—by contrasting nature and convention, but that difference is too often exaggerated. Fashion is conventional, but clothing is designed for human bodies, not for dragons or princes with six arms. The dialectic of philosophic argument nevertheless forces the issue in either of two opposed directions. The view defended here supposes that laws are scaled to our material circumstances and revised until cogent, because they express our biological capacity for adaptation and self-regulation. The other side fights with brimstone, theology, or a priori arguments to establish the authority of moral absolutes. Plato, Descartes, and Kant argued that mind is removed from nature or the flux, and that immateriality liberates it from having to address circumstances it cannot know or control. Forms, clear and distinct ideas, or universalizable maxims: these are the proper objects of reflection. But this story is a myth. No human animal escapes either his or her materiality, the systems where selfhood forms and needs are satisfied, or circumstances that are facilitating or confounding. The morality appropriate to beings like us bends ideality to the needs and resources of practicality. Reflection is the middle term: thinking about our circumstances, testing alternative plans, we alter them and regulate ourselves to create viable, life-sustaining systems. Neurath's boat—every plank and beam changed at sea—suits morality as well as belief.

Norms are variable, because communities acquire different styles when each has consolidated its idiosyncratic responses to situations that are common across communities (family or fire protection, for example). Noticing the difference—because members visit other communities, or because of conflict between them—we reasonably ask if there might be norms that apply everywhere. Kant and Hegel answered that reason prescribes norms that apply necessarily, hence universally. Neither of them believed that tribal loyalties are more than a crude beginning to moral development. Kant, especially, exaggerated the virtue of reflection while condemning moral choices made solely on the basis of fidelity, need, or interest: they, with the habits and inclinations that express them, were said to have no moral status. But reflection, too, has diminished stature for Kant: its self-declared duties are subordinate to those confirmed when will submits to the finding that a maxim does or does not satisfy the categorical imperative. Lose your idiosyncrasy, suppress the vanity of thinking that your measured judgments are or could be universal laws. Will only those maxims that are worthy because they are universalizable without contradiction. Hegel was more balanced, but he, too, believed that local relations and loyalties should be superseded by an orderly, rational plan. Inclination is tribal and self-interested; duty should affirm the universal. This is good advice when blinkered emphasis on one's place and loyalties obscures a system's context and harmful effects on others. Traffic laws and street signs seem intrusive and annoying, until one considers the problem of routing traffic through the maze of city streets. But the cure is deadlier than the disease, if morality is denatured by its rational ideals. Reality, not only politics, is essentially local. Core systems and the duties they promote are justified when they satisfy basic needs. We cannot discount the moral force of these systems or the duties they generate without sacrificing moral passion to legal duties owed to no one in particular. Egoism and tribalism promote conflict; but the legalism of Kant and Hegel discounts personal, situated morality for an abstract dedication to law. There is more cynicism than moral principle when people don't bond to others until they have consulted the lawyers who would defend them for breaking contracts.

We may suppose with Hegel that these two considerations—dedication to core systems and respect for law—are moments in the natural history of morality: it evolves from local affiliations to respect for the principles of a universal code.[64] But this narrative begs the question. It avers that loyalty to core systems is hardly more or better than moral superstition. This is a shallow reading of our circumstances. For these two bases for morality are sometimes mutually independent and opposed. What provokes the greater anger, seeing tax laws broken or affronts to core systems? The systems one values may be replaced several times over the course of a lifetime. But there is, at every moment, the network of systems called *home*. They, not reason, are the incubators of obligation. For Kant was mistaken: one couldn't teach duty to someone who did not know it in the first instance as duty to friends, a tribe, or oneself. Would friends be grateful if we remembered their birthdays because law requires it?

The thinking that locates us and our systems in larger contexts is critical if we are to regularize benefits while averting harm. We try to minimize damage and waste. We hope to establish the material conditions for fairness, a value generalized from the respect for the other members of core systems. These are critical values, but neither implies that reflection's trajectory is always or usually the one of Hegelian reason rising irrepressibly to the noble vacuity of universal laws. Modifying or affirming local practices, solving local problems are also its domain. Reflection and legislation are practical responses to the need for the common understandings and procedures required if we are to square our interests with those of the people with whom we work.

We discover that our loyalties are parochial and self-concerned when we confront people whose moral convictions and loyalties are equally entrenched, but different. The first evidence of alienation and difference was earlier still, in the moment when a child noticed that a parent was distracted by other interests. Distance and difference are all the more apparent as we search for common ground with partners as near as spouses, as remote as the French. The outcome is fluid, and unresolved. For there is no algorithm for finding or cooperating with partners. Each person or system has priorities and commitments peculiar to him, her, or itself. Reflection responds by inventing rules of thumb for deciding which interest has priority, one that is local or another more distant but urgent. Do unto others as you would have them do unto you is a fair précis of thought's discovery: we are not alone; others have needs like ours. Life goes better if we acknowledge them. Do I need this expensive ticket more than the thousand starving people who could be fed for less than it costs? I weigh the respective benefits and make my choices. Usually, I choose to benefit my systems—core systems especially—their members, and myself. But I realize that I am also a member of larger systems, so I vote to raise my taxes for benefits I can only surmise. Or photographs show me the need, and I give money or blood to people whose names I can't pronounce. Distributive justice—fairness—and the complexity that exceeds local solutions (requiring traffic laws, for example) is a counterweight to parochial loyalties.

What is law's relation to local morality? Is this difference graded or oppositional? Their relation is obscured by the altruistic, but naïve rendering of otherwise reasonable slogans: "The greatest good for the greatest number," "Treat everyone as an end, not as a means." The first is universally inclusive in principle but not in practice, because legislators have insufficient power to redistribute resources in the way prescribed. The second is plainly false: we often encounter other people in the terms fixed by our respective roles. We may treat them respectfully; but our transactions have aims determined by the instrumental value that one has for the other: dentist and patient, passenger and driver, student and teacher. The duties generated within such relationships are principally situational and instrumental. Criteria used to appraise them are practical rather than legal. What are a system's effects? Are they good or bad for their members and others? We sometimes express ourselves imperiously and abstractly—"Residential traffic only, no trucks"—but this is a crude way of avoiding the material and significant facts of the matter, local practice and circumstances, for example. We suspend the law, without a judicial hearing, if this truck is an ambulance. "Give each his due" is more apposite than other slogans, because it is usefully vague: each may signify all or merely everyone encountered. The first sense is appropriate to law, the second to one's personal, communal relations. But the second stands against the first. Most people have very limited opportunities to engage others: the locality of persons and their systems is an obstacle and reproof to law's universalist aspirations.

The Enlightenment dream foundered, because Kant and Hegel were unable to demonstrate the necessary truth of assertions about such norms (by showing that their negations are contradictions). Truth telling and promise keeping are not necessary rules of conduct; one can lie or act in bad faith without creating havoc in logic or social practice, because most people tell the truth most of the time. Still, the failure of their grand project is properly charged to bloated hopes for reason, not to reflection. Questioning, probing thought is private and situated, not public and cosmic. It sometimes discovers universal principles when its topic is logic. But Aristotle was thinking metaphorically when he wrote that man is most like God when making laws. Reflection's aim—usually personal, local, and modest—first expresses itself as unease. A system doesn't work, or works in ways that are inimical to one's aims or values. Thought suggests ad hoc, practical responses. Reflection recedes, and duty remains comfortably habitual if they succeed. Or the disruption endures, because relations are altered in ways not easily repaired: a once favored system no longer justifies this member's loyalty.

Duties founded in habit and inclination grow like dendrites as people couple themselves to one another. Legal duties are legislated and imposed. Lawmakers—whether parents, teachers, or congressmen—set priorities and manage conflicts. They are responsible for enhancing the efficiency of a tribe's social relations by giving perspicuous, consistent expression to its regulative values: literacy, health, and fairness, for example. But legislators are not gods making rules for the Apocalypse. Laws of every sort, from constitutions to petty regulations, are expedients: they usually refine arrangements already in place. Laws prescribing practices or relations for systems that are newly organized (transport to the Moon) are less common. They articulate an abstract possibility by creating rules to police it. The work is admirable, but the abstractions for which they legislate are, so far, morally bloodless. The possibility may eventuate, but then unforeseen complications will oblige us to amend its rules because local practice is always a check on theory.

Hegel supposed that reason should prevail over social contingencies: they may be obliged to satisfy our rules. Think of biblical prophets hurling thunderbolts into the miasma of lapsed hope and bile. The image is false, because it distances prophets from the targets of their scorn and lawmakers from the practices they regulate. Tradition is a mix of the habits and rules formulated when others made life viable in circumstances they couldn't entirely control. Legislators inherit their solutions, and some of their attitudes. Responding to a current difficulty with a judgment about relevant empirical findings (traffic accidents are bad) they formulate rules (revised traffic laws) to alter the effect. But rules have no traction without the cooperative activity that installs them in public practice. The norm is not imposed from afar: it is the regularizing rule introduced into troubled circumstances by thinkers who extend self-control into situations that engage them. Other animals react; we regulate, living all the while in circumstances that alter us as we alter them.

This opposition—morality that is local and tribal versus morality based on reason's universalizing ideals—seems exaggerated when regulation often solves local problems in ways that are easily generalized: traffic lights at this crossing imply a solution for every crossing. The opposition persists—law dominates our thinking—because we believe the rationalist myth (a perfect solution, once and for all), because the displacements of contemporary life make tribal loyalties hard to sustain or dangerous (40 percent of all New York City residents were born abroad), and because the preference for a morality based on laws is reinforced by the dominant ideology of American life. We make right and duty devolve upon law when atomist—individualist—scruples have so blinded us to the reality of systems that we acknowledge no duties but those to law. This perception reduces families, friendships, schools, neighborhoods, businesses, and governments to whatever utility they have for their members. None requires or deserves respect for its corporate value; none binds its members to one another in relations of mutual loyalty. For duty reduces to the enforceability of contracts when relations are merely businesslike: one

sues a partner who ignores his legal obligations. We become more liti-
gious than loyal.

This effect is mitigated, because law's value is only instrumental.
Social life everywhere is complicated and contentious: law regularizes our
practices, supplying a standard for behavior and a criterion for adjudicat-
ing conflicts. But law cannot settle every difference of opinion about
issues that are altogether local: reproduction and sexual conduct, for
example. Each side may want its attitudes justified and enforced by law,
but these are moral conflicts that law cannot resolve. Which has priority:
a woman's loyalty to her self or loyalty to her fetus? How compelling will
morality be if either side finds itself obliged to behave in the detestable,
"immoral" way the other requires? Legislators are confounded. Should
they solve by decree what is only negotiable or negotiate endlessly to
soften antagonism? Law makes no progress in dilemmas such as this. But
the failure is telling: it implies that the energy for morality comes from
the bottom up—from local systems and practice—not the contrary.

The passions that mobilize these conflicts are often intensified by
factors extraneous to the matters at issue, religious doctrine, for example.
But absolutism is not only religious: secular, ethical theorists are also dogmatic. Their reflections—still dominated by the rationalist dream—are
deontological and convinced, not tentative and pragmatic. They interpret morality's trajectory after the example of reason's liberation from
Plato's cave: forsake the biased habits and beliefs learned at home for
reason's universalizing prescriptions. Ordinary people congratulate themselves for the "moral" life of core systems, because they don't see or can't
acknowledge the moral ugliness of tribalism or self-interest. They are
oblivious to the scope of the moral principles known to reason, though
nothing else can justify believing that me or mine should be subordinated
to the interests of all.

This tension animates political discussions wherever a universalist or
statist perspective collides with communitarian interests: France is a current example. The *loi Chapelier* resonates in the partisans of a unitary
state, one that speaks for the universal rights of man, not for the
parochial interests or practices of its constituent communities. Anxiety is
palpable and appropriate, because a low birth rate and need for immigrant labor mixes pride in the accomplishments of a unitary state and
culture with fear that France will be divided within itself by religion, language, and no shared understanding of elementary rights and obligations.

America prides itself on being a melting pot. It tolerates diversity, while unified by its Constitution and economy. We celebrate individualism but accept communitarian differences, because they usually seem incidental to our political processes and procedures. But we are, self-consciously, a country of immigrants. France perceives itself as homogeneous. Communitarian differences seem threatening and explosive.

Is there a "natural" response, one appropriate to the reality of communitarian differences? Acknowledge disparate religions or other systems, for example, but deliberate about common interests within a political framework that ignores communitarian differences when it legislates for the common interest. This is the (idealized) American model: diversity rounded and made congenial by a powerful economy and a viable constitution. But one may challenge communitarian differences as dentists oppose cavities, if defending them subverts other values. What is it reasonable to do when opinions differ: acknowledge communitarian differences within the practices of the state (representing them proportionately among the state's officers, for example), suppress the differences in the name of universal ideals (no head scarves in schools), or separate the social domain of communities from the public domain of the state? The answers are practical and pragmatic. And probably, there is no best answer, none that guarantees mutual tolerance and an efficient public authority.

Reason, even reasonableness, doesn't promote a single outcome, because reason speaks in different voices, usually in ways that propose to override communitarian differences in the name of law. Some would reshape moral practices, as traffic laws rationalize traffic. Others would transform social relations and behavior to satisfy a personal point of view: acknowledge, for example, no difference in the interests or desires of men and women. There are also the politicians, business or military men who anticipate a time when engineers can alter or "tune" public morals by manipulating the thoughts, desires, or genes that affect social behavior. Imagine a society as efficient as a garrison state or well-managed business, Sparta or a company town.

Which of these four is best for human welfare: i. moral attitudes and behaviors that are locally effective, but less coordinated as one moves beyond each center of moral practice; ii. these same practices, sometimes rationalized by laws that regularize moral attitudes and behavior throughout a domain; iii. universal, a priori regulation that suppresses or ignores

local differences; or iv. the effective redesign of moral attitudes and practices motivated by an ulterior interest (profit or efficiency, for example)?
Morality is local, because individuals learn it in the context of core systems. Conflict, reflection, and familiarity with other systems, societies,
and cultures extend the domain of moral concern beyond core systems
and oneself. But live choices may soon reduce to versions of the second
and fourth alternatives: the morality learned in systems, then reshaped by
law will oppose the morality programmed into humans by engineers
directed, more likely, by efficiencies congenial to businessmen, politicians, or generals.

What would be the last line of moral defense if this second alternative were to prevail? It wouldn't be laws, because they would be corrupted
by the special interests that promote or enforce them. It wouldn't be our
duties to core systems, because these systems would be remade to satisfy
the interests of social engineers. Reflection would arm us to resist, so it,
too, would likely be eliminated. One thinks of Rousseau: "Man was born
free, and he is everywhere in chains. Those who think themselves the
masters of others are indeed greater slaves than they."[65] This is the posture of every thinker who stares down a coercive power. But this dictum
is no obstacle to clever engineers. They would eliminate all the bases for
resistance; there might be no last line of defense. The rationalist ideal
would have its perverted victory: reason, but now the practical reason of
the manipulators, would determine what we are and do.

There is also a different way to anticipate this prospect. Human self-
regulation works optimally in negative feedback loops where nature—the
context of our evolution—also regulates our behavior. Excessive human
power—especially the technological power driven by human intellect—
minimizes nature's regulative force: we are more and more masters of our
environment (given its current relative stability). Negative feedback is,
thereby, transformed. It becomes positive feedback if we modify our
genetic endowment without the constraining effects of having to adapt
to our natural circumstances. Before, selective resistance promoted
cogency in our acquired responses: the human cycle of wakefulness and
sleep is tuned to the cycles of day and night. Now, adaptation is less relevant, and we approach a time when molecular biologists may produce
whatever human variations they or others can use and control. Like a fire
we may consume our substance, transforming human freedom and
responsibility into a charred version of itself. We may be one of the last
generations able to defy such rational ideals.

11. Norms of Several Kinds

System formation generates norms of several kinds. One useful distinction—norms distinguished as *maximal* or *minimal*[66]—emphasizes the difference between local practices and universal principles. Minimal norms are least conditions for morality, conditions that cannot be breached without violating other persons or their systems. The Ten Commandments are a précis; "Do unto others as you would have them do unto you" is an example. Some are wronged, all are threatened, if these norms are contravened. Maximal norms are local and contingent: responsibility for one's clients or children doesn't extend to people having other clients or children. Contingency is all the plainer when people fall in and out of relationships that make them responsible for their partners in systems. Hence the opposition of local practices and universal norms: everyone is owed the consideration specified by minimal duties, though one may have no responsibilities to last year's patients or students.

Minimal norms are the residue of ancient theological views about the worth of human souls: no one should harm, everyone should respect God's handiwork. But there is no evidence to support this belief—faith aside—and none to justify secular reformulations that derive imperatives from alleged features of human nature: Kant's emphasis on rationality, for example. There is, however, this alternative way of justifying them: reversing the order of priority, we extrapolate the minimal from the maximal. Caring for partners in core systems, we do or can learn to think sympathetically of people to whom we are unrelated. For we plausibly suppose that every person has needs or interests, and wants them satisfied. This is not a deontological demand for respect, but rather the natural history of attitudes that emerge when one recognizes in others a vulnerability, need, and courage that are like one's own. The emphasis is pragmatic: What do we need? What works? Distinctions among our norms divide accordingly. Three are conspicuous: i. norms particularized by a system's distinguishing task; ii. procedural norms; and iii. moral norms.

i. Norms particularized by a system's distinguishing task or style. These are norms distinguished by the specificities of a system's task—family or friendship, for example—and by the organizational style chosen to satisfy it: democracy is common to Britain and America, though their constitutional styles differ. We often say that an end doesn't justify the means used to achieve it, but this slogan is refuted by the cases at hand. A system's aim always justifies its implementing organizational style, in the respect that the aim limits what may count as an appropriate means. This is not a justification for the aim: it may have no redeeming value. But Machiavelli didn't argue that the princes for whom he wrote were good men doing good things, merely that certain practices and norms would serve their interests.[67]

ii. *Procedural norms.* Procedural norms are enabling. They avert harm or facilitate action. Traffic laws do both: they bend social behavior into forms that are viable, fruitful, and safe. Norms of this sort apply to systems everywhere, irrespective of a system's membership or aims. Two sorts are familiar. Proscriptive norms—don't interfere; let others do their work—specify behaviors that are barred or discouraged because of their malign effects. Prescriptive norms—coordinate roles, cooperate while filling them—facilitate productive activity by making us effective. Norms of this sort seem to have a mechanical purpose only—facilitate cooperation, or don't impair it—but each is infused with moral purpose: norms that make schools or hospitals effective enhance the well-being of people they serve. The moral value of procedural norms is, to be sure, qualified by the aims and organization of the system at issue: a system may be scrupulous procedurally, but vicious.

Habermas's discourse ethics describes procedures and constraints for achieving cooperation and resolving disputes.[68] But there are prior questions: What information must people exchange if they are to organize effectively? What norms—truth telling and impulse control, for example—make it likely that the information is reliable? There are several or many styles of marriage and family life. But a few procedural norms—including cooperation, freedom, respect, prudence, and reliability—apply wherever people meet to solve shared problems. These are norms that emerge from the trial and error of practice; nothing transcendental certifies them. They spread from their many points of inception—in every viable system. Traffic and tax laws supersede the competing jurisdictions of counties and towns, because their conflicts and anomalies impede effective organization. Nothing comparable is required to guarantee the uniformity of these procedural norms, because the conditions for and expressions of cooperation and coordination are largely the same everywhere.

Mutual dependence makes cooperation the necessary condition for well-being, but cooperation evades us if it is not voluntary, hence free. Nor do we achieve it if self-concern makes us oblivious to others. Respect for them implies recognition of their vulnerability, skills, and good will. Prudence is two things: thoughtful regard for the possibility of error or contingency (what shall we save or repair if things do not go as planned) and forethought regarding the conditions for sustainable systems. Democratic politics is prudent for both reasons: it is a procedure for correcting errors and a context congenial to system formation. Reliability is a universal demand, though the specific demands of a submarine or piano factory are focused by the mechanics and tasks of those systems: what do they do; what practices would enable them to do it better? One may object that this paragraph lists procedural virtues, not norms, but these virtues are norms. Cooperation, freedom, respect, prudence, and reliability are directives to action, criteria for appraising actions done, and norms that are immanent within systems when their members work effectively together. Cooperation is a fulcrum for the other four: there is freedom to cooperate, trust and respect for those with whom one cooperates, and prudence in respect to tasks that are unachieved without cooperation. But cooperation, too, has a normative context, one that includes mutual interest, need, and commitment. Commitment is the resolve of a character formed in core systems. Its normativity is task-specific, moral, and procedural. Commitment is each member's response to the expectation—the tacit demand—of other members that his or her role be filled.

iii. Moral norms. We can't universalize moral norms, if we lack the information and sensibility learned in circumstances that are particular and local. Children learn moral virtues in families and schools where they are taught what to respect, and when and how to be reliable or free. This is the inversion promised above: the parochial is ground of the universal.

Having needs and interests, wanting help that won't be forthcoming if we don't give it in return, we become moral partners. Yet, it isn't apparent to anyone learning moral norms within a core or other system that these virtues apply universally. For virtue is known by its specific expressions in the grain and form of social and private lives. What clothes shall I wear today? There are questions to answer before I decide: am I male or female, what age, in which season? The answers are pertinent, because my choice will be appropriate to considerations such as sex, climate, and public morals. Boys and men won't wear skirts; girls and women will be careful not to seem mannish. We know and keep our place, lest our identity be misconstrued or lest we offend. For these constitutive principles are also regulative: others know how to navigate among us when they see the norms applied. Yet, moral norms generalize; they exceed the local circumstances of their learning to become minimal—universal—norms. What explains their generalization? Probably several things: there is

sympathy and respect for the failures and successes of people otherwise
unknown; there are the many people known more or less because one
participates in several or many systems; and the realization that our systems affect others—for better or worse—though they have no interest in
what we are or do.

We respond by extrapolating from local practices to these strangers:
treat them as family. This generous response isn't sufficient, because we
can't often rely on it to mitigate or avert conflict. Those are the occasions when morality requires something more than good will: namely,
laws—minimal norms—that establish common understandings among
people and systems that are otherwise mutually incomprehensible and
hostile. The relative weight given norms that emerge within a practice
versus those introduced as laws is not well established. Local practices are
often ragged, but self-sufficient and satisfactory: they don't need legal tinkering. Or the local norms are problematic (they fail to regulate disputes
among neighbors, for example), but law's intrusion would be clumsy.
There is also uncertainty about priority: which are preeminent, the regulative principles of local practices or laws? We could never replace the
supple, evolving tissue of local norms with equally supple laws, so legislators tread carefully when local practice has established its moral authority. The tension between local norms and legislative design is,
nevertheless, unremitting. Many laws—drive on the right, pay your
taxes—apply unproblematically, but the American experiment with Pro-
hibition exemplifies law's opposition to local moral practice. A subtle
sociology would likely confirm that the great majority of universalizing
moral rules have no origin apart from the nuanced practices of systems
and their members. Norms that restrict established practices—those pro-
hibiting popular sexual behaviors, for example—are ignored if their
enforcement is not rigorous and punitive.

Fairness is a conspicuous example of tension between local interests
and universalizing altruism. One favors one's partners in core systems,
though the partnerships one makes are a contingency: one could have
been coupled satisfactorily to any number of other people, all or most
unknown. The respect we have and show to other members of current
core systems could as well have been felt for strangers. Knowing nothing
of them, we may nevertheless wish that their opportunities and well-
being were equal to those of our partners. We don't and won't know
those others, but we can find specific ways to equalize their chances: vital
drugs or education, for example.[69] These sentiments intellectualize a

motivation that is more primitive, a desire impelled by observing our partners. Discerning their frailty, aspirations, and needs, even as we rely on them, we reciprocate: let them have what they need.

We somewhat resolve the clutter of these distinctions by saying that norms enabling systems to form or function may be construed in either of two consequentialist ways. Considered from the perspective of those they regulate, norms are standards that frame the context of choice and action: I perform as my systems and their other members expect that I shall. Norms considered instrumentally have two effects: systems perform their signature tasks; their members exhibit and augment their talents, virtues, and satisfactions. Both perspectives illustrate the mix of maximal and minimal norms. Traffic laws have this double effect: we observe them because this is a condition for using local streets, and because the welfare of all is better served when transportation is safe. This two-sided, consequentialist justification is the only one required by any norm.

12. Rights

Rights, not duties, are the point of reference for most contemporary accounts of morality, but here, where constraint is the issue, rights are secondary. A clarifying distinction is, nevertheless, close at hand. Duties and rights are mutually implicative. Citizens are obliged to pay taxes, but they have a constitutionally defended right to vote. Drivers need a license, but they have a right to drive. These legal rights and duties have a correlative in one's duties to systems. For the acquired duty to a friend or workmate is the right to receive the situationally appropriate response from him or her. Loyalty to a system's other members is a presumptive basis for the right to be treated in kind.

Natural law theory supposes that acquired rights are founded in rights that are acknowledged but not created by practices or legislation. Those are, allegedly, rights that come with being a person or rational agent. But this is an unverifiable dogma, one that inflates the idea of a person or rational agent in order to derive a list of natural rights from the idea. Why is it less plausible to say that rights are better described as interests? For one may have an interest in a person or property, but have no right to either until or unless the right is created by the reciprocity—the friendship—established with him or her, or affirmed by the legislative authority of a state able to enforce it. This seems harsh, but consider: how do human animals acquire rights if they are not negotiated or legislated?

Popular discourse has no patience for the alleged contingency of rights. We want our rights affirmed by a higher authority: let legality be civil recognition of that transcendental sanction. But there is no evidence that it is, and therefore no appeal to any authority but law or public conscience when interests are trampled. For there is this essential difference between claims of these two sorts: legally acquired rights are defended by the power of the state; rights correlative to the duties that come with participation in systems, core systems especially, are not usually affirmed by supporting laws. There is little or no risk of a legal penalty if one disappoints a friend. Hence, this weaker correlation: duties incurred by participating in systems promote expectations that a system's other members will respond in kind, but these expectations—however reasonable—are not usually supported by legally enforceable rights.

This account of rights may seem threadbare. But the responsibility for a richer story lies with those who propose it: how would they verify—rhetoric aside—that one has the inflated list of "inalienable" rights often claimed? Attention to specific claims invariably confirms the elision of rights with interests. Some are legally sanctioned, most are not. None are innate.

13. Layered Publics

Rights and duties merge—in the respect that either may be invoked—when a system's members organize as a public. Its public is a system's forum. Members appraise the system's effects on others or themselves in order to meliorate them. Or they articulate its aims and priorities. Formation of a public is evidence that a system is self-stabilizing. It has a corporate identity and trajectory. Its members are responsible for what it is, does, will be, or will do. They oversee and regulate its effects on themselves or others.

Every human system of whatever scale needs a public, because there are corporate effects and interests, or because committed members reasonably want and claim the attention of other participants for whatever problems encumber their roles. Each system's public does or can sensitize members to the effects of actions past, and each does or can promote the corporate and individual deliberations that enable members to anticipate and justify the consequences of actions done in its name. The system achieves a corporate voice, and a general will. Or it stalls when deliberation exposes discord or grievances that are better heard than suppressed. Communal assent is not our only aim. Prudence requires that every public—whatever the scale of the system—be unflinchingly critical in its self-analysis. Nothing less is prudent for systems that are unviable if their effects, organization, circumstances, and prospects are misperceived.

Many large communities and states find themselves roiled by conflict. Members are divided by their disparate communitarian loyalties and morals:

> Our country [France] has continued, for ten years at least, to aggravate its enfeebled political situation in the face of federalisms of the right and left; communitarianisms based on ethnicity, religion, and [other forms of] identity; [and] a renascent corporatism worthy of the Ancien Regime. It has not ceased to nourish—in its seats of government, schools, courts of justice and administrative buildings—the appetites of minorities, each of which sees the world from its own perspective, and which are all the more formidable because they blackmail democracy in the name of tolerance and human rights. . . . [T]hese minorities become a majority when no obstacle opposes them, for to them are added the voices of those disappointed with government policy. It is obvious that the breaches opened by particularism should be healed by reestablishing, little by little, the republican foundations of law, education, and [human] rights. We must concede that the principal cause of these breaches, contrary to Marxist rhetoric, is ideological rather than purely economic and social. . . . Multiply social expenditures as much as you like, . . . [but] you cannot prevent ghettos from being built first in people's minds. The same perverse logic tends to fix in space and time a separatism that pervades all levels of society.[70]

Law, education, and rights are emphasized—each a focus of struggle—because their advantages don't flow magically to those who think, like Hegel, that moral enlightenment is our *telos*, an aim realized immediately in the minds of all who perceive it and in those who hear incantation and command in the voices of a right-thinking elite. These benefits have two foundations. First are local systems where every person learns his or her moral identity. Second are rules and laws that facilitate the work and defuse the conflicts of local systems and their members. These rules, more or less amended, are rechristened "universal principles," when a society regulates itself by constructing the public that revises, generalizes, and negotiates solutions that were previously local and ad hoc. A society that neglects its local communities—its schismatic tribes—while invoking universals discovers, sooner or later, that its people haven't been listening.

The idea of layered, overlapping publics—a public for every system—may seem a recipe for suffocating their overworked members. How are they to participate responsibly in the many systems that engage them: how many meetings, how much discussion can one tolerate? What difference does it make that someone else decides the conditions of one's work, the space of one's life? The fatigue of satisfying several or many roles reduces one's interest in publics to a minimum. But freedom—the freedom to choose the trajectories of one's systems and the terms of one's affiliations—isn't cheap. Autocrats, bureaucracies, or machines will do for us what we decline to do for ourselves.

The opportunity to participate in a system's public is a right acquired with membership. Members have a claim against their system and its other members for the resources required by their roles. Participating in the deliberations and decisions of the public they do or could establish is one condition for optimally filling a role. Participation is also a duty. For a system's tasks cannot be done well or done at all without deliberations that affirm the system's responsibility for overseeing the reciprocities that sustain it, its effects on members and others, and the direction it will go. Generals, surgeons, teachers, and airline pilots may demur, because their roles require that they make choices for others. But there is a difference between authority and self-sufficiency: the most autocratic ruler is foolish if he makes decisions without consulting subordinates who will implement them. Their knowledge of the circumstances is vital information for him and them. The prudent leader—whatever his or her authority— wants their freely given advice.

The need is plainer still in systems steered by the good will of its several or many members. Families, friendships, teams, businesses, neighborhoods, and states are unsustainable or unnecessarily vulnerable without the forums where members affirm their responsibility for the system's priorities, efficacy, and effects. For duty to a system and its other members is impaired in the absence of a public. Imagine the contrary: each member thrashes about, isolated and angry, filling a role while oblivious to the corporate aim or the difficulties of other members. But no system functions optimally if all or most members work in the dark, unable to communicate with their fellows, unable to see what the system does or where it goes. This has pernicious effects on members, because their personal identity is consequent to some degree on both the roles they fill and the degree of their responsibility for either the system or a modular part. Their intellectual and moral strengths are wasted or impaired if membership fails to earn them a voice in deliberations that make the system responsible for its effects and prospects.

The risk is plainer if we imagine alternatives to the formation of a responsive, deliberating public. Intra-systemic relations are reduced to habit. Or bureaucracy displaces a public in systems of larger scale, killing initiative, efficiency, and imagination. But even a bored clerk is more likely to be responsive than the computer program designed to coordinate the members of complex systems. Pilots are reduced to monitoring automatic systems in advanced airplanes. How long before surgeons monitor robots? This is desirable, if the robots are better surgeons, but the difference between authority and self-sufficiency has its parallel in the difference between efficacy and responsibility. We grant the authority of generals and the efficacy of machines. It doesn't follow that machines or computer programs are morally self-sufficient or morally responsible. Elected presidents consult with legislators while limiting themselves to actions that satisfy judicial review. These are roles in an array of constitutionally prescribed offices. People occupying them may fail to establish a public, preferring confrontation and gridlock. But government goes better if discord is openly declared in the forum where disagreement is mitigated by deliberation and a desire to compromise for the good of the state. The need for a public is all the more apparent in smaller systems—friendships and amateur teams, for example—where no one has autocratic authority. Every such system is decorticated—irresponsible and maladaptive—for want of a public established by its members.

Publics have an additional benefit: bridging the gap between duties founded in a system's roles and duties ascribed to those who fall within the domain of a law, they mitigate the anomie of organizations and aggregates by transforming them into communities. There is usually no less than a proto-public in families, friendships, or teams: members speak regularly of their common hopes and interests. But there is less talk and less deliberation in a large company or state. Members typically accept the rules or laws that determine relations among them without discussion. History is relevant. The modern idea of the public was the invention of atomist thinkers who needed a device to create order in the ranks of autonomous moral agents. For if every thinker is self-directed, there is no basis for social cohesion or coordination. Hobbes solved the problem by supposing that a prince would impose order on subjects who would otherwise be stubbornly hostile and recalcitrant. Locke, Rousseau, and Kant acknowledged conflict, but argued that it results from contingencies such as crowding, scarcity, and mutual misunderstanding. Rational agents supersede their differences by creating an assembly of the whole: each person temporarily ignores his or her private aims and grudges for the opportunity to participate in the forum where laws are made. But this is the design for a formal practice: one participates in the forum as a socially responsible, rational agent, not as a situated person having particular allegiances, interests, and antipathies.

Dewey distinguished this task from the additional one of creating a Great Community, meaning the assembly of persons whose mutual regard and affinity is the firmest guarantee of their peaceable lives together.[71] Citizens should bootstrap themselves to community, so that people who share responsibility for the state—by way of the organized, self-regulating public—may come to respect, then to like one another. Duties that seemed alien and onerous are reconstrued when citizens perceive the order created by the public and its laws as conditions for community. No one likes paying taxes, but all may agree that taxes well spent serve the greater good. The imperious, law-making state is hereby transformed. Atomism yields to community where personal affinity supersedes abstract, formalist notions of contract. The difference between duties founded in habit, acquiescence, or affirmation and those prescribed by laws is diminished accordingly: duties of both sorts are the consequence of one's participation in a community.

How is this effect to be achieved in states larger than Holland or Luxembourg? By decentralizing government wherever possible. Encourage responsibility by returning it to neighborhoods, cities, and regions. The organizational and budgetary problems this implies are prodigious, but they are justified by the intensification of personal and communal responsibility.

14. Truth and Error

What is the status of the thoughts and sentences signifying norms? Are they descriptive, prescriptive, or expressive? Deontologists and emotivists affirm that sentences using *must*, *should*, and *ought* are prescriptions, recommendations, or expressions of feeling. Neither, they say, is true or false. But this is contestable. Prescriptions very often embody descriptions: "Take aspirin to cure your pain." "Did it work?" we ask, wanting confirmation that the implicit, descriptive claim is true. For we don't usually prescribe an instrument's use if we don't reasonably assume that it will have the effect specified or implied. It is all the plainer that talk of stipulated norms is true or false when thought or language is explicitly descriptive ("We drive on the right"), but implicitly prescriptive ("Obey our rules"). A policeman, judge, or other driver can truly say that one is at fault if a law was breached. Or the charge is false, because the covering law has been changed. Error of another sort is also possible: one may be charged for violating a norm, though he or she is not a member of its domain. You should have voted, we say, to one who responds that, no, he couldn't vote because he isn't a citizen or resident.

Truth and error are germane wherever there are states of affairs and thoughts or sentences specifying them. The duties and norms binding people in systems are states of affairs, with the difference that they—unlike domains established by law—result from the causal reciprocities binding people in systems. The duties of family or friendship, school, business, worship, or citizenship are learned and embodied as habits, inclinations, attitudes, and self-directed imperatives. It is true or false that one satisfies them, though the margin for ambiguity and misunderstanding surpasses that of laws because the duties and norms of systems are more susceptible to dispute. One partner believes herself bound by friendship, the other misses appointments and feels no guilt for doing it. Such duties are situational—someone casual in friendship is careful at work or home—and they exhibit perspectival differences. He explains that lunch was suggested casually; nothing was agreed. She—who waited—is angry; he, thinking himself misperceived, is annoyed. Such norms and duties often lack the clarity and force of law, but evidence is relevant: did they agree? If yes, one has erred by ignoring an obligation; if not, the other is mistaken: there was no duty.

Reciprocities are often unbalanced. Misunderstanding flourishes because bonding of every sort is a process, one that intensifies a relation or fails over time. Duties form as individuals establish reliable bonds. Amorphous at first, they don't gel without the reciprocity of mutual response and expectation: hoping for reciprocity, we know that we may not have it as systems form. Careful not to demand more than we shall likely receive, we indicate, rather than command, the desired response. But we want moral clarity: What are our duties? What principles regulate the organization of our systems and the reciprocities that sustain them? Truth and error are equally uncertain, until the vagaries of context and differences of perspective are successfully reduced. Clarity is achieved when systems are stabilized, for then mutual expectations are also stabilized and mutually known.

There is less caution or ambiguity when relationships have formed, hence less reluctance to supplement description with prescription. We say truly that parents have duties to their children, and we add, imperiously, that they should satisfy them. Assertions about duties and norms are both true (or false) and directive: we declare that participants in systems—core systems, especially—ought to acknowledge and satisfy their duties. Why add this higher-order duty to fulfill a duty? For several reasons: because having a duty, we feel duty bound to satisfy it, because observers in parallel situations generalize and project their sense of obligation, because of sympathy for the victims, and because they may become a burden to those who were not otherwise directly engaged if the duty is not satisfied. It is a matter of fact in every such case, hence a truth, that a duty created by the reciprocal relations of a system's parts is or is not satisfied. But truth ramifies, for two norms are violated. One is restricted to the system where duties are generated by the reciprocities of the members. This norm typically has no foundation beyond the habits, inclinations, and expectations of one or more members. The societal norm is a rule expressed as a shared expectation, or as a law. Consideration would rarely or never exceed the first domain if local norms were rarely or never broken. Societal norms intrude when the effects of ignoring duties local to systems require penalties and a cure, because they are pernicious and costly. Here, too, prescription has a descriptive base: do this or that to avoid an effect that will be more costly to fix.

Prescriptions often presuppose descriptive truths; descriptions sometimes imply prescriptions. Yet, truths about duties and norms can be distinguished and separated from the same thoughts or locutions used prescriptively: you, a member of the mob, have an obligation to defend it, but I, your attorney, am not recommending that you do so. Still, this decoupling and inhibition are uncommon. Truths about duties and norms are more often elided with directives to satisfy them. For we are joined in a tide of expectation: we say what is true and say it prescriptively—"We pay our taxes; you should too"—in order to remind others or ourselves of the societal interest in having duties fulfilled. We do this without invoking anything mysterious or other-worldly: the duties, norms, and expectations that bind people in human systems are as objective and natural as habits, inclinations, affirmations, systems, and the reciprocities that create them.

There are meta-ethical—"irrealist"—views that emphasize the use of moral language to guide action, but deny that moral attributes such as duty are generated in material states of affairs specified by descriptive moral language.[72] Irrealists favor a minimalist, deflationary theory of truth, one denying that sentences are true if satisfied by extra-linguistic states of affairs. Deflationists say that the predicate *true* is incidental, for example, when applied to sentences derived from a well-confirmed scientific theory. But this is moot. Why ignore truth when we cannot ignore error and the possibility that sentences so derived are false because the theory is false though apparently confirmed (belief that the Sun orbits Earth, for example).

Morality is practical: we organize, then make ourselves responsible for actions that serve our individual and corporate aims. We sometimes lard moral views with grandiose ideas—Plato's Good or God's will, for example—because they seem to provide transcendental authority for everyday norms. Irrealists distrust these speculations and apply the deflationary theory of truth to suppress them. They emphasize the many ways to describe, encourage, and prescribe moral behavior without making substantive claims about states of affairs of any sort, be it moral agents, their circumstances and practices, or these mythological powers. But we could also have tax laws and a litany of complaints and jokes about them without money, businesses, or taxpayers, though one is parasitic on the other.

Why should we import this philosophic oddity into a theory of morals? Because of an answer implicit in the prefix *meta*: irrealism is motivated by concerns incidental to the material basis for morality: namely, the deflationary theory of truth, and by Wittgenstein's emphasis on the autonomy of language games. People, their relations, and actions are incidental. But irrealism would be consequential were it taken seriously, because decoupling moral talk from moral reality would cripple moral practice and education. Imagine alternative versions of an imaginary game, one played alone or by exchanging moral stories with other players. Imagining scenarios where moral action is required, each player tells what he or she would do. Logical laws and the Ten Commandments are the only rules. Only taste or social custom justifies a preference for any response when each story is coherent and diverting in its way. Should we extrapolate, saying that morality, too, is an autonomous language game, one indifferent to circumstances where the game is played? Could it be an idiopathic game, one played differently by every moral agent?

These are bizarre inferences, motivated by concerns that are incidental to morality, but current among philosophers concerned to avoid skeptical traps: the reality of an extra-mental, extra-linguistic world, for example. Moral discourse would be a rootless style or fad—incapable of truth or error—incidental to human needs and circumstances if moral ascriptions did not apply to actual people as they act and relate to one another. Having no grip on human character, actions, and relations, moral talk would be uncorrectable, but for the possibility that the moral language currently favored might be displaced by others that are equally groundless. No one annoyed by careless partners is satisfied by this metaethical conceit.

The materiality of our context and the practicality of our aims does not imply that there is an agreed morality waiting asymptotically at the end of inquiry and moral reflection. There are matters of fact—persons, systems, interests, and needs—and truths about the conditions for their stability, efficacy, and satisfaction, but there are moral cleavages within societies and variations among cultures that tolerate disparate outcomes to similar interests or needs: all cultures favor children, but one may encourage polyandry, another polygamy. Some moral truths—the importance of cooperation, for example—are universal. Others—concerning generational or gender relations—are local and variable. There are truths about moral character, norms, and behaviors in each, but moral certainties in one context are heresies in another.

15. *Should* and *Ought* from *Is*

The ideas proposed here locate moral norms in the habits, attitudes and affirmations, regulative principles, and laws that shape human practice. The investigation is ontological, because factual. Discover what we are and do; observe the ways we cooperate with one another, while controlling ourselves. The origin and use of norms is a function of human nature, need, and activity. This is material for sociology, anthropology, and ontology. Yet, social ontologies are properly challenged, because their descriptions are so often distorted by ideology. People and their relations can be molded to satisfy each of the three theories—atomism, communitarianism, and holism—if we generalize about the character of social reality from the restricted domain used to confirm the applicability and adequacy of a favored theory. The reality thereby fashioned justifies saying that the theory is true in the conventional respect that the states of affairs signified satisfy the differentiations and relations ascribed to them by the theory. But this correspondence is easily explained: social relations have this character, because the theory has been used as a recipe to create them (as a cake is true to its recipe).

This result is a trap, one we avert by again distinguishing ideas, ideals, and ideologies. Health is an idea: it signifies the condition and processes of a self-equilibrating system. Health is also an ideal: be healthy. And health may be the focus—the aim—of a plan, a recipe, or ideology for remaking oneself to achieve the condition signified by the idea. Conflate these three notions, and we wrongly elide the difference between representation and prescription. Thoughts or sentences may be true or false: they represent or misrepresent things as they are. Prescriptions are neither: they tell us how to make or remake some feature or region of things. All three of the ontologies mooted here may be construed in either way. Yet, there is this limit: the three hypotheses are contraries. No two can be true of the same phenomena at the same time in the same respect. Their mutual exclusion is disguised when the same relationships are remade (if only in imagination) to satisfy each theory.

Does reality have a decided form—one or another of those signified by the three theories—so one is true, the others false? Is it so, instead, that social relations are determinable—malleable—and that they may acquire the form prefigured by either of the theories if molded in ways it prescribes? This would imply that the intrinsic form of human relations is generic and determinable, so ideologists may prescribe either of the three forms. This second alternative is favored by romantics who believe that reality is the product of imagination, understanding (theory), or will— Kant, Fichte, Nietzsche, James, Carnap, and Quine, for example—but their interpretation misconstrues our circumstances. Neither practical life nor science is a game, neither is a version of literature. Both test and confirm the hypothesis that reality has a decided form: it is malleable, but not formless. Atomism and holism are empirically false, because they misrepresent its form, one because it ignores systems or misconstrues them as aggregates, the other because it postulates a single system of comprehensively binding internal relations, though there are no systems of this description. Young adults are sometimes close to the dream of atomist autonomy. The behaviors of families and clans are sometimes holistic. But these are limiting cases that fall altogether within the communitarian model.

Isn't this claim precluded by our social malleability? Why acknowledge that society can be molded to atomist or holist designs, only to imply that they are empirically false? Atomists and holists succeed by generalizing from favorable examples—fiercely competitive men in the case of atomism, teams or organisms in that of holism—then by acquiring political power that enables them to remake social relations in ways their theories prescribe. But no individual is autonomous in the comprehensive way that atomism requires; no holist example—discovered or contrived—justifies its claim that all reality is a many-in-one. Communitarianism doesn't need to establish its cogency by remaking human society in its image. Its truth is confirmed by the same evidence that falsifies atomism and holism: namely, the array of nested and overlapping or mutually independent human systems. Communitarianism is also tested when its claims about the norms intrinsic to interactions that create or sustain systems are shown to be true or false. It alleges—with considerable evidence confirming it—that duties acquired as habits, then affirmed are a principal condition for the reciprocities that establish or sustain core and other systems.

How does communitarianism generate *shoulds* and *oughts* from the *is* of systems? The answer proposed here has the three parts cited earlier. First, systems are established and sustained by the reciprocal causal relations of their members. So, atoms have existential value for molecules—the bonding of one creates the other—though the responsibility of one for the other is normative because causal, not because we wish, will, or commend it. Friendship, too, is normative, though it has no resource but the habits and loyalties of the friends. Second, people who participate in a core system typically accept their responsibility to it. This is partly habit, partly the inclination that comes with acquiring aspects of psychic identity in a role. But participation is morally ambiguous. Does it express approval or merely acquiescence? Habit made rigid by fear doesn't imply acceptance, though habit can be a force resisting or reproving change. There is, for example, the agitated defense that people habituated to slavery don't want freedom, because they are disinclined to accept it and because they affirm their duties to the slavers. This would be a quandary if habit and affirmation were the only bases for duty; but they are not. For, third, a system is appraised by its reflecting members or others: it is good or bad, given its practical value for them. Effects that are seen to be adverse for oneself, valued systems, or other members may override habit and inclination. Good effects reinforce them: we affirm beneficent systems, especially the core systems—families and friendships—where self-hood emerges. These are the natural bases for *should* and *ought*. Like health, another practical norm, they confirm that morality doesn't need a deontological or theistic justification.

There is, however, this pertinent difference among *oughts*. Some derive all their prescriptive force from *is*: some particular thing ought to be done, given a system's interest in having it done, and given the expectation of other members that a partner is trained and primed to do it. These are *oughts* by momentum or inertia. Ideals are *oughts* of another kind. They may not obtain, though they should, because they would benefit us or useful systems, given the character of our needs, interests, or circumstances. But even these ideals derive from an *is*: namely, the material state of affairs to which they are appropriate. A piano ought to be tuned if it is to work as pianos do. For this is to be a tuning appropriate to pianos, not to radios or motors. Imagine that the tuning is required by a pianist for whom the ideal is situational, not abstract. Playing is a way of life for him, a way he can't pursue if the piano is not restored. This *ought* is implicit in what he is and does.

Instantiated ideals—tuned pianos—are the easier cases. Ideals are more likely to be confounding when they are not, and have never been instantiated: inequities perceived versus the justice imagined, for example. Here, too, the gap between the real and ideal is no obstacle to joining *should* or *ought* with *is*. Reflection is the decisive middle term. It works with the material at hand by conjuring ideals, and revising norms in ways appropriate to our nature and circumstances. For anyone redesigning relations between persons or systems must consider what we can do or be, given what we are. Architects provide stairs, elevators, or escalators: no one requires that we levitate or fly between floors. Reflection enhances the work of core and other systems by invoking ideals that are near or achievable extrapolations from current states of affairs—

health or civil order, for example. Imagination sometimes embroiders objectives that are currently unachievable, but these are ways of prefiguring possibility: they don't count as norms.

The reality of ideals is nevertheless construed as a decisive counterexample to the hypothesis that actual states of affairs are shaped and directed by inherent norms. One hears the contrary thesis in slogans such as this amended version of one mooted by William James: "Mind engenders truths upon reality."[73] Nietzsche sometimes averred that nature is a blank slate, one that would be void of norms if minds did not prescribe them.[74] But systems are pervasive in nature, with norms inhering in their sustaining efficient and formal causes. Current circumstances may not satisfy us, if, for example, we could be healthier than we are. Or we have health and want to keep it. Either way, health is a condition for the stability of organic life: it is a material and inherent touchstone for *ought*.

The materiality of norms is fiercely contested since Descartes argued that there is a categorial difference between mind and nature. Mind is the artist that introduces form into malleable, otherwise inert and indeterminate matter, or mind is free to create a world congenial to itself, given that it cannot know things in themselves. But this story is a delusion, if thought is an activity of human bodies, not a substance somehow distinct from them. Bodies are organic systems. They are unsustainable if they cannot equilibrate and stabilize the relations of their parts. Thought extends this power by controlling some of the external factors on which the body's steady state depends. *Engendering truths* is, more exactly, accommodating ourselves to who and where we are. It requires wearing clothes, eating apples, or carrying an umbrella. Nature is often amenable, but it is not void of norms.

Chapter 1 argued that *is* constrains *ought*. Is there also warrant for the stronger claim that *is* is sometimes necessary and sufficient to entail *should* or *ought*? There is no disputing that many values are introduced by tradition or fiat, manners for example. Who opens the door? Who is first to walk through it? Actions that satisfy values often express our aims or power relations, not significant, justifying differences in the things valued. But many others norms, especially those promoted in core systems, have their basis in affiliative human relations and the systems thereby formed. Those norms stabilize families, conversations, friendships, and every other system where *is* requires satisfaction of one's duties. *Requires*, in this context, is the material surrogate for the logical *entails*.

How do we find relationships that meet this high standard? Proceeding like geologists, we use surface appearances to locate systems that satisfy human needs or wants while causing minimal friction among their members and minimal cost to other systems or persons. Think again of children who learn their duties by participating in a family's work. They wouldn't perceive the difference between *is* and *ought*—the *do* and *ought to do*—of family life if Hume's dictum were explained to them. Are such children brainwashed, because learning a task has been conflated with thinking well of it? No, the work may be unpleasant, but they do it because chores identify the child with others whose work sustains the family: the *is* of their lives instantiates an *ought*.

Hume supposed that *is* and *ought* are separable because distinguishable (implying the separability of fact from value, not the removal of a member from his or her system). His principle creates the mistaken impression that we must somehow couple factors that are otherwise independent. But separating them is incomprehensible or scandalous to parents, friends, soldiers, and workers of all sorts. Hume's distinction carries no weight with them, because they do not separate the imperative from the act: we learn what we ought to do by doing it in core systems we accept or affirm. Deontological lightning isn't required: most people willingly do what they ought to do. Backsliders typically respond when reminded. Relatively few need the more severe penalties sanctioned by laws that backstop such duties.

Affirming a practice, or merely acting as it prescribes, is better described as *living a role*. Think of the ease with which one converses in a native language. We can abstract its semantic or syntactic norms, listing them in a catalogue of linguistic rules, but the act of speaking coherently isn't separable from norms it instantiates. Equally, we can speak of duties as if they were disembodied or imposed, though the efficacy of our roles—their causal, existential value—is inherent in the dynamic of systems. Attitudes toward these systems vary with the work they do, and the satisfaction of their members. Many members of many systems act from inertia, fear, or insensibility. Others experience the work as torture. But some affirm the systems that engage them. These are people for whom *is* and *ought* are merged. Hume's dictum—*is* doesn't entail *ought*—generalizes falsely from examples where fact and value are indisputably distinct: it often happens that circumstances imply no directive, so that people act because they hear the legitimacy of an extrinsic command, or because they fear that resistance will be punished. But obligation is not always imposed. One who is satisfied by the system that engages him reliably does what he ought to do given his role, though no one ever tells him that he ought to do what he does. Duty and dedication are two sides of the same inclination and practice.

Hume would say that these last sentences concede his point: *ought* is joined to *is* by psychological states—habits, inclinations, acceptance, or affirmation—not by logic. This is true, but not, therefore, discountable. Hume's procedure is Descartes': attend to each idea, rendering it clear and distinct; then observe that neither *is* nor *ought* is implicated in (entails) the other.[75] Facts in themselves are value-neutral (or valueless). Norms are ideal, or merely the expressions of sympathy or desire: there may be no facts that satisfy them. This argument has carried the day since Descartes implied and Hume proposed it.[76] But why is a priori meaning analysis decisive for the relation of facts and values? Why does it follow that no human practice embodies norms merely because ideas can be "clarified" and reduced to a compass where neither implies nor entails another?

This is a confusion of fact and idea, one that could not flourish if we had not already convinced ourselves that materiality reduces to ideas. The muddle is confirmed when a priori, essentialist definitions mutilate meanings by abstracting them from the richer senses successfully tested against experience. Who will say that space and time are distinguishable and separable in our world merely because the ideas of them are divisible? Separating ideas of fact and value also fails as a proof that facts and values are everywhere separable. There is no friendship without trust, though friendship and trust are distinguishable and separable ideas. No one tells a disappointed friend that he makes the simple error of conflating them.

Other moral norms also have their inception in our circumstances. They, too, are misconceived, because of the assumption that clarifying ideas—of freedom or respect, for example—confirms their essential exemption from corrupting material influences. We inherit this intellectualist myth from Plato and Descartes, though freedom to act is only the freedom to organize one's commitments in ways that are suitable to oneself and one's circumstances. We sometimes extend freedom by altering our circumstances, but freedom in the moment is contextual. We are free to choose our roles if character and circumstances empower us and free to fill them if freed from the interference of others. Freedom is situated. Every man or woman of ordinary initiative moves among various roles—

parent, worker, spouse, neighbor, or citizen—while deciding the order and degree of his or her commitment. Freedom out of context is a fantasy.

Respect, too, is situated, and it, too, is critical if systems are to thrive. That is so, because systems don't thrive unless we perceive the value of roles complementary to one's own. Respect for a role is extended to the person filling it when we realize that any role may be filled poorly: someone doing better earns our esteem. The person receiving it responds to recognition by trying all the harder to do this job, but also to fill his or her roles in other systems. There, too, effective work is rewarded with respect so that the esteem of others enhances self-esteem, then the additional effort that provokes more esteem. People who receive no respect and have no freedom never conflate *is* with *ought*. Those who have both may be unable to perceive the difference: *ought*, for them, is the propitious outcome of their circumstances. This is a naïve elision given the many people who have neither, yet, the juncture of *is* and *ought* is predictable in circumstances where *ought* is grounded in the mechanical *is* of the preferred, sustainable systems we inherit or create.

Construing freedom and respect honorifically (as we typically do) wrongly abstracts them from contexts where they have decisive instrumental value within and among systems. Yet, making this claim introduces a further dimension in the characterization of systems. Before, it was sufficient to remark that systems are created and sustained by the reciprocities of their parts. Talk of negative feedback adds specificity to this account without extending it. But now, we do extend it by considering the alterations required if a system is to embody norms or other values it currently lacks. For systems have or may have an inherent telos, one that enables them to intensify their realization of moral norms such as freedom and respect.

The attractor states, described in chapter 3, are created by assembling materials in ways that are stabilizable. This implies stability in the reciprocities of their constituents and stability in a system's relations to its circumstances. Some systems—human bodies, families, businesses, and states, for example—satisfy these conditions. The reciprocal causal relations of their members are sustainable, because they are competent, because they command sufficient resources to do their work, and because they are efficiently organized. So, human cells, tissues, and organs are not stabilizable until organized within human bodies. Why? Because, these subsystems cannot acquire or store energy sufficient to maintain them. Stabilizable bodies have this capacity: they are attractor states.

This hypothesis—that entelechies drive or draw natural conditions to inherent aims—is the obscure but tantalizing idea in Aristotle's notion of final cause.[77] The processes seem mysterious, until we add that natural systems are self-equilibrating for reasons that are strictly mechanical: thermodynamic reasons, for example. These considerations are obscured by our preferred examples of mechanical processes: people pushed and bumped as they move forward through a crowded door, for example. This is behavior in a moving aggregate, and here, too, energy satisfies thermodynamical constraints, though no stable system is created because the aggregate has no internal organization to sustain it. Compare systems. They evolve in either of two ways: they dissipate because sustaining conditions are absent, or they stabilize because those conditions are achieved.

The stabilizing mechanisms in human systems (whether single bodies or human social systems) are negative feedback loops. Establishing the loops is often complicated, because several conditions must be satisfied before they are complete. Freedom and respect are two such conditions in human social systems: a system's members cannot do their work if they are not free to do it; they won't likely work as well as they could if a system's other members fail to show respect for their effort.

Attractors are nodes. Think of businesses that support clients and suppliers or states that stabilize their neighbors. Often slow to form, but viable and consequential when stabilized, they support both their parts and other systems. How should we characterize the attractor state for which freedom and respect are facilitating conditions? Let health be the directing example. An ecosystem is healthy when its niches are mutually sustaining within specifiable parameters. The members of a team play well together, sacrificing personal vanity for teamwork. Every such example implicates the steady-state conditions for viable systems, though nothing in this sense of the word implies the worth of a healthy—viable and consequential—system, al-Qaieda for instance.

Health, once achieved, is stubborn, because it facilitates the reciprocities of a system's members. The energy-efficient relations of its parts are hard to disrupt, because the energy required to disturb them is typically greater than the energy that sustains them. This suggests that relations among a system's members have an inherent economy, one that restricts them to a variable range of differences. Stable and sustainable within those limits, they are inefficient and unsustainable when the limits are exceeded. Conversation succeeds when each party hears and responds to the other. The exchange is disrupted if emotions such as anger prevent one from responding.

Morality is one of the factors that discipline the economies of human social systems. Duty, respect, trust, and freedom are nuanced accordingly: members who act in a system's behalf, by habit or choice, are obliged to know and observe its steady-state conditions as they accommodate to one another. The conditions for a sustainable conversation vary with the participants and their degree of mutual tolerance: some tolerate a greater range of emotion than others. Still, there are limits to the range of variation for sustainable systems, hence the practical—moral—imperative that participants know and observe those limits.

The internal economies of systems may differ radically, even when they are apparently similar. Similarities facilitate learning a norm of conduct appropriate to systems of a kind. Yet, morality isn't satisfied by rules applied mechanically. The idiosyncrasies of the members and their relations assure that each system's range of sustainable variations is peculiar to itself. This increases the moral burden, because participants in a system they affirm need to know its range of tolerable variations. The members of large systems may not have the information or perspective this requires. But members are or can be sensitive to the economy of the subsystem in which they work—managing their relations to near partners—and they may be aware that smaller wheels must be coordinated if the large wheel is to turn.

The attractor state prefigured by these considerations—justice—is everywhere familiar but mostly unrealized because of the complexity of its conditions, including freedom and mutual respect. Justice is social health: the steady-state relation of a society's members when its opportunities, benefits, and responsibilities are equitably distributed. Plato described its details, emphasizing the reciprocity of society's structural and functional parts and the preparations required if each person is to fill a role. But what is equitable? Are opportunities, responsibilities, and benefits to be shared evenly or proportionately? Justice is stymied—for this and a myriad other reasons—because we can't decide and organize accordingly. But the problem, hence the continuing disparity between *is* and *ought,* is not unique: organizing complex circumstances for any large-scale effect is confounding. Nature often achieves such effects without the benefit of directing, human intelligence: many things are healthy. But justice doesn't happen without intelligent intervention. Achieving it requires the self-regulation of the people and systems to be organized, though we can't achieve it without an agreed aim or as long as we prefer the short-term advantages of personal striving to the long-term benefits of collaboration. Justice, the attractor state, presumably requires some mix of the two. We aren't clear about the proportions. Worse, eliding *ought* with *is* seems fatuous when freedom and respect are more often ideal than real. But is it? Imagine that cars don't work: motors break down, carburetors misfire, tires oversteer, until someone builds a car that does all these things properly. Before, we had reason to suppose that *ought* always exceeds *is*, so an appeal to what ought to be was always perceived as a derogation of what is. The working car is evidence to the contrary: now, *is* instantiates *ought*. Its every subsequent invocation is no longer a gesture in the direction of the unachievable. We point to its realization, saying "Do or be like this."

Such vignettes seem cute rather than cogent, until we consider that ideals for us humans could not plausibly be unrealizable states or conditions. The ideal is commentary on the real. Specify the attractor state that would stabilize social relations while satisfying human wants and needs. Make the standard high, but attainable. Project an ideal informed by our actual talents, then raise the bar when any lower level is achieved. The four-minute mile was ideal, until it became the standard that every serious miler ought to achieve. And then achieving it became jejune, and the ideal was an ever faster mile. Should—could—anyone run a three-minute mile? Here is a test of the assumption that *ought* must always exceed *is*. For no physiologist believes that any human could do this on Earth: human lungs aren't big enough; human bodies running at or near sea level can't metabolize oxygen fast enough. Physical *oughts* necessarily track the physiological *is*. Moral *oughts* are constrained by the social, psychological, ecological *is*: we ought to do such things as enhance human flourishing, given the limits of cooperation and coordination and conflicts that are ineliminable when systems compete for scarce resources. *Is* and *ought* cannot come unstuck because their cycles of difference and elision drive human hope and imagination, and because there is no plausible *ought* that is oblivious to *is* or *can*.

How far can we advance through the hierarchy of more and more complex systems, using self-regulation to subordinate both ourselves and our circumstances? Is there an indefinite sequence of attractor states, each an *ought*, each an ideal that would stabilize more and more complex systems? There may be thermodynamic or other limits to complexity (limits on the possibility of communication or the distribution of resources, for example). Practical limits damp speculation about ideals, but they have solutions. Solve them, and the next sequence of attractors is less remote.

Is *attractor state* merely a neologism introduced to neutralize the contentious ring of ideals and ideology? There may be accord about the stabilizing conditions for protons and molecules, but there is no consensus about social ideals. How are we to choose among them? We do it by identifying reliable, empirically grounded rubrics: sickness and health, for example. One may object that every alleged expression of social or psychic "health" is a rhetorically disguised pathology. But is this cynicism accurate? Plato didn't doubt that Polemarchus, Thrasymachus, and Glaucon described familiar circumstances.[78] But each characterized justice in ways that subvert the formation of core systems and effective people, their members. Plato taught us that sickness is the privation of health, not its point of reference. Social and psychic health, not pathology, is the basis for reflections that identify human norms.

We recognize personal vitality. Is it equally sure that we know the signs of social health? The communitarian ontology describes it. We look for those viable, productive relationships that do the work required for human well-being. We find them where reciprocal, causal relations generate and sustain systems critical for nourishment, reproduction, protection, education, work, and self-regulation. What kinds of people emerge from systems that do these things? Capable and reliable, they satisfy their obligations. Consciously free, they choose many of their systems and rank the degree and timing of their participation in some or all of them. Humean inhibitions—don't mix facts and values—make us hesitate, though our grandparents, more self-convinced than we, would have described these systems and their members as morally healthy. Weren't they mistaken, because health is a variable appraisal, not an immanent norm? No, health is a condition for the sustained well-being of systems. It is both fact and norm. We prize it because of its effects, though health is critical to the well-being of systems, whether or not its effects are acknowledged.

Consider that individually and socially, we humans may lie within a nested hierarchy or separate hierarchies of attractor states. Call them *ideals*, and they seem desirable but remote. Think of them mechanically as states that stabilize complexity, and *ideal* means *unachieved*. These states are, speculatively, the *shoulds* and *oughts* pertinent to human life and systems. But not all are speculative. There are stable systems, healthy people for example. They are what they should be.

16. Support from Principal Moral Theorists

Moral theorists invoke Hume's dictum—*is* doesn't entail *ought*—as though no responsible thinker could oppose it. Yet, some notable moralists—this survey is cursory—have said that the character of things is decisive for moral imperatives. I distinguish naturalists (thinkers who found moral norms in material states of affairs) from deontologists (those who invoke norms without regard for their material basis). There are very few pure deontologists.

Plato's account of moral character in the *Republic* is framed by the succession of contexts described by Cephalus, Polemarchus, Thrasymachus, and Glaucon. The latter three promote, and try to justify, moral pathologies including: factionalism (Polemarchus), tyranny (Thrasymachus), and a social contract where everyone who can cheats (Glaucon). But we repair broken machinery and cure sickness; we don't use them as baselines for generalizations about effective machines or human well-being. Plato would have us repair moral failure, and its effects. He described a society sustained by the reciprocal (mutually supporting) relations of its parts (artisans, guardians, and philosopher-kings). The virtues, he cited—specialization, cooperation, and self-control—are conditions for this complex social arrangement. They are achieved by a society that bootstraps itself to justice using only the material means at its disposal, especially the talents and inclinations of its members (though philosopher-kings also have access to the Forms, especially the idea of the Good).

Aristotle also discerned norms in matters of fact. He proposed that we locate the mean for principal values, then the habits and actions that stabilize character by instantiating them. So, courage is a proper goal, because systems are destabilized by cowardice and bravado. He described the chronic disputes of oligarchs and democrats, but emphasized the stabilizing talents and self-control of a middle class.[79] Aristotle would have liked traffic laws. Troubled by gridlock and accidents, we make laws that facilitate traffic flow. They have a regulative effect, but a wholly material ground in the habits of people who observe them. No moral virtue has any other condition. For what is the difference between good and bad people, or good and bad states? Only the material arrangements—the internal ordering principles—of individuals and their systems.

All the values Spinoza commended are implicit in our material capacities and relevant to our circumstances. Desires should be appropriate to our nature and situation.[80] Declining to swim a river that teams with snakes, I save myself, thereby expressing the self-love that needs no justification beyond my having it. Vanity would be evidence that we mistake our importance and the scale of the stage on which we move. Spinoza emphasized humility, courage, and reverence, all of them virtues appropriate to people who acknowledge that reality is infinite and necessary though we are finite and contingent. Hobbes despaired of human character, but supposed that corporate acts of self-regulation, enforced by a prince, make social life viable.[81] Hume, too, commended values that have human character and our capacity for self-organization as their only basis. Seeing mutual care in the relations of family and friends, he inferred that sympathy is the engine of moral sentiment: we bootstrap ourselves to interpersonal ideals by regularizing social relations as it directs.[82]

Kant is the premier deontologist, but he, too, believed that morality issues from what is. The categorical imperative is said to be implicit in our rational nature: reason universalizes its ideas or rules, while abhorring contradiction.[83] Kant was, nevertheless, hostile to my proposals in this respect. His aim is stable, social reciprocity.[84] But the means for achieving it are reason and will: they legislate for all rational creatures. Kant would have us abstract from the specificity of our circumstances, including the reciprocal causal relationships where duty, respect, trust, and freedom are learned. Actions undertaken to satisfy desire have no authority, unless the hypothetical imperatives promoting them are tested to confirm that they satisfy the categorical imperative: could they be universalized, could everyone apply them without contradiction?

Kant's apriorist purity is compromised in two ways, at the beginning of reflection and at the end. Maxims—the generalized formulations of actions considered—are generated by desire and interest: the actions proposed have no other motive. But wait, Kant tells us: abstract from material interests. Translate—elevate—material considerations into the language of logic. Don't act, until it is confirmed that everyone could do such things without contradiction (don't make promises while sabotaging the practice by willing that no one should keep them). But this shift, from the material to the logical and transcendental, has no substance but the shift from one set of words to another. The cash value for contradiction, the evidence of reason's violation, is the social conflict generated by acting on maxims that are not universalizable. Conduct is right or wrong because of its effects. This deontologist is a consequentialist.

The logical mechanics of Kant's argument obscure his primary concern: harmonize the multitude of wills. Create a test such that each person can determine before causing damage that actions he or she proposes reconcile personal interest (expressed by the maxims chosen to direct one's behavior) and social cohesion (trust doesn't survive—no one accepts the word of others—if all break promises). Harmonization is more critical than the particular maxims chosen or the desires they are calculated to satisfy. For we would survive if desires were different, though we sabotage the possibility of both cooperation and freedom from harm if we ignore this least condition for social coherence. This effect is a warning, especially to people living in mixed societies where cohesion is precarious. It is also tacit recognition of regulative principles that are essential to a social world having the two aspects emphasized by systems theory. One is the requirement that actions should not subvert the cooperation required if core and other systems are to form. The other is respect for an open playing field: do nothing that would preclude other people from forming systems independent of one's own.

Kant's minimalist, a priori solution is, nevertheless, faulty in two respects. Its use of logical talk—contradictions—gives a falsely abstract turn to an essentially practical motive: avert social conflict. More arcane, but equally telling, is a missing piece in Kant's argument for universalization. His categorical imperative requires that no rational agent should will a rule of action—a maxim—unless every rational agent could will it without contradiction (to avert circumstances that preclude the action prescribed by the rule). Suppose we test Kant's imperative. You will that everyone drive on the right, as they could without conflict. Now it's my turn, and I will that everyone drive on the left. Which rational test eliminates one of the rules in order to avert the disasters sure to happen if both rules are enacted on the same road? An authority—presumably political and installed with universal suffrage—will need to intervene, choosing one practice or the other. What criterion shall the authority apply when deciding? For there is no purely rational calculus that discerns an advantage in one or the other: both rules satisfy Kant's criterion. One can will either without contradiction. Authority ends the stalemate with a stipulation: drive on the right. Imagine now that drivers who wanted to drive on the left are stopped by policemen who remind them that the duty prescribed by law requires driving on the right. What is the basis for this duty, they ask? One part is reason (in the form of a rule that satisfies the categorical imperative), another is the interest of all, a third is caprice. We do one thing or the other—after tossing a coin to decide— because the effects of doing both would be destructive. But Kant can never justify, in his terms, duties that derive from arbitrary choices. For reason and the will it shapes are the sole basis for the morality he describes. The choice made by tossing a coin is arbitrary, hence irrational. But this is a reasonable basis for choosing among contraries having equal weight: an *ought* derives from an *is*, the result of tossing the coin. Practical intelligence knows no better way.

All the thinkers considered give some weight to our circumstances, nature, interests, or practices when telling how we should behave. Some others never concede that we do or could take moral lessons from prevailing behavior, however well regulated by plans and laws revised in the light of experience. These are the prophetic moralizers. Their scalding views about other people's behavior compare to their vision of standards that should obtain. The most confident among them are moral intuitionists. They know what is right or wrong, good or bad, without having to observe what people do or why they do it. Information acquired in this way would be local, contingent, and fallible. Intuitionists disdain it. Like Plato describing knowledge of the Forms, they suppose that we perceive moral virtues, rules, and principles with a clarity and conviction that preclude error or equivocation.[85] But their persuasion is flawed. Intuitionist conviction is not probative if one or more of the people having it are mistaken, as some must be mistaken and all may be mistaken because their dicta—about contending religious truths—are contraries. There is also this prior question: does mind have intuitive powers? No brain has them, so intuitionism embodies a material error, if—as seems likely— mind is the activity of body. But intuitionists are canny: they never affirm virtues or principles of the sort we humans could not apply. So, perfect virtue—even the virtue ascribed to a god who is never tempted by evil— is described by extrapolating from human experience and abilities. Why temper claims in this way? Because intuitionist virtues would have no cogency for us humans if intuitionists did not make assumptions about our nature and context. Moralists who ignore what is would have no chance of speaking relevantly of what we ought to do or be. There is no difference between naturalists and deontologists—no difference critical to this discussion—if both discover what we should do by considering what and where we are.

17. Resolving the Diversity of Moral Theories

The aim of moral theory is simple enough: describe what people are and do, our circumstances, and the least conditions for human flourishing, then consider the practices and virtues appropriate to us and our conditions. Theories differ in respect to their views of human nature and our circumstances, or because agreement about them is consistent with different, even contrary recommendations for human practice. Still, the diversity of ethical theories is odd: how could a single topic provoke such diverse responses? Like the four blind men trying to identify an elephant—trunk, flanks, tail, and feet—we produce theories that seem to have no obvious link. But there are generic similarities. Each point of view has the same three constituents, though each of the three—practicality, interpretation, and idealization—is variable. Practicality is efficacy as regards the nuts and bolts of life. Rooted in circumstances where needs may be urgent, we are impelled to form the relationships—families and work crews—where they are satisfied. People have different notions of what is practical—what family and work arrangements are appropriate—because there are alternative interpretations of one's self, circumstances, and interests. Am I rich or poor, adult or child, man or woman, vulnerable or secure? Idealization conceptualizes moral practice as a shortlist of prescriptions or perfections. In a respect neutral to theoretical differences, idealization is the transition from the description of character or practice to its prescription: habits, inclinations, or affirmations become duties; reliability is reconstrued as responsibility, a moral virtue. Moral and social theory is a late moment in the trajectory from the practical to the ideal: starting in the experience of successful or failed social relations, it conceptualizes the arrangements and obligations appropriate to its assumptions about human well-being. Folk morality—the vaguely articulated beliefs we affirm but rarely justify—is practical value interpreted, idealized, and institutionalized.

Moral practice, too, is lived and appraised at the intersection of these three variables. Parents care for children, because children are unable to care for themselves (practicality), because parental duties are experienced as commands (interpretation), and because we believe a story that sanctifies parental responsibility (idealization). But some parents guiltlessly abandon children because they are inconvenient (practicality), because parental duties are construed as choices (interpretation), and because self-regard is thought to be the highest value (idealization). Every moral theory or point of view provides for all three factors, though interpretation and idealization dominate theories that emphasize the prescriptive force of a priori reflection. Their authors hope to perfect moral lives by transforming moral perceptions and intentions. They discount accommodations to our circumstances and one another either because of doubting, like Kant, that will can intervene in the material world, or merely because they believe that practical life is less significant morally than an informed and directed conscience.

Principal idealizations emphasize these seven preoccupations: i. Reciprocities that create systems (communitarianism), ii. Individual character (virtue ethics), iii. Agreements (contract theory), iv. The benefit of all (utilitarianism), v. Universal prescription (deontology), vi. Moral insight (intuitionism), and vii. Moral feeling (emotivism). Egoism and conflict (Hobbes) seem to be additional emphases, but the first is a version of character, while the other is the contrary to agreement. Each of these idealizations subsumes a congenial interpretation of the relevant facts, and each promises to clarify or perfect them.

i. *Reciprocities that create systems.* Communitarianism avers that systems created by the causal reciprocities of their members are the factual basis for moral theory.[86] This is so because we humans are needy but not self-sufficient. Needs and wants are satisfied as we cooperate in behalf of shared or complementary aims. Character is shaped by these transactions, so that beliefs, attitudes, and skills constitutive of character are products of our successive engagements with partners in core or other systems. Here, as always, idealization emphasizes features made prominent by theory. Systems theory idealizes the achievements and virtues of the systems it describes, including character, cooperation, duty, freedom, trust, and respect.

ii. *Individual character.* What are the desirable features of character? Virtue ethicists mention intelligence, temperance, honesty, reliability, courage, empathy, and generosity. They sometimes emphasize autonomy, though none suggests that this bars or limits a capacity for cooperation with other people. Hobbes is impatient of "desirable" features, preferring to start from evidence that we are surly, grasping, and hostile. Does he imply that Aristotle's virtue ethics misrepresents us, preferring an idealization to our actual behavior? There is a different explanation: Hobbes describes frustrated, hostile people who fail to achieve sustainable core systems[87]; Aristotle describes the willing, trusting, optimistic members of successful families, estates, friendships, and states.[88]

This difference among ethical theorists resonates in psychoanalysts. Freud looked for a self in the midst of its disoriented functions. Feelings, memories, and drives are said to be isolated by repression, but patients don't know or acknowledge these causes of their behavior and unhappiness.[89] Heinz Kohut objected that the self is an "encompassing superordinated configuration." It includes ambitions, skills, and ideals, each related to the others by way of the "energic tension arc (from nuclear ambitions via nuclear talents and skills to nuclear idealized goals)" that persists throughout a person's lifetime. The result is a "'nuclear self' . . . an independent center of initiative and perception" where repression and isolation vary inversely with the quality of one's integration into vital affective relationships. The process unifying the self is not fully specified, though Kohut supposed that self-objects, one's remembered and idealized caretakers, have a principal role in making the self forceful and coherent. Their love and demands nourish its self-esteem and standards: "The child that is to survive psychologically is born into an empathic responsive human milieu . . . just as he is born into an atmosphere that contains an optimal amount of oxygen." A cohesive self is the product of its roles in systems where interdependence—reciprocity—is idealized and encouraged. For the self is created as it acquires the habits and inclinations that make it socially responsive.[90] Compare the fractured selves that Hobbes described.

Hobbes, no less than Kohut, described real people; but he wrongly supposed that everyone satisfies his description. Kohut didn't make this error. He acknowledged the fragmentation and demoralization of people who lack the developmental advantage of living in stable, core systems. This difference is critical for moral theory: should it generalize from the experiences of people whose systems fail, or from people who have or had the advantage of Winnicott's "good enough mother"?[91] One can argue about the human condition from the perspective of sickness or health:

both are facts of life. But which is the appropriate baseline for idealizing ethical theory? Expect the worse, and defend yourself. Or acknowledge the possibilities for despair, but describe the conditions for doing better. One who insists that we acknowledge and start from the less propitious scenario will favor Hobbes, but countervailing evidence favors the other side: successful core systems are a feature in many lives. And notice: this is a factual basis for idealizing moral theory, not the airily utopian vision of what might be but is not.

iii. Agreements. The emphasis on contracts expresses two interests: facilitate the union of people having shared or complementary interests; protect each party against the possibility of the other's nonfeasance or abuse. Imagine a vise that holds wood blocks until the glue that binds has dried. People who join to create a system don't typically need this external force; they are often primed for reciprocity and qualified for their roles. Theorists may respond that contracts protect the innocent against opportunists. But this doesn't justify saying that individuals are essentially disconnected, so that nothing short of contracts sanctioned by law and the threat of punishment protects us from the nonfeasance of partners. Stable, core systems are incubators of reliable character: we are protected if companions have experienced their benefits. Finding such partners is safer than relying on contract law, though one is sometimes grateful for its protection.

iv. The benefit of all. Every member of every system pursues his interest or that of his allies. Utilitarians suppose that value is optimized when the activity of the many systems creates the greatest good for the greatest number. This is or ought to be our corporate goal.[92] But this aim is hard to calculate, and harder to achieve, because of disparities that preclude a common measure for "goods," because conflict is perpetual when systems having opposed but legitimate aims compete for resources, and because every system creates noise or pollution that obstructs others. Indeed, we can't aim for the greatest good for the greatest number without suffering the demoralization that comes with constant failure. Hayek rightly argued that the social world is too complex to be managed comprehensively from a center of power.[93] This precludes Mill's objective, but not its close alternative: we may hope to discover and exploit those principles and procedures that enhance satisfaction and reduce conflicts, all the while acknowledging that the poor author, musician, or saint may think himself better off than the illiterate mogul. Mill acknowledged as much when he distinguished animal from moral and intellectual pleasure.[94] This, with Hayek's point, is death to simplistic applications of Mill's greatest happiness principle.

Locke's dream of America was the hope that each might live his or her life to the fullest in a space of one's own, with resources to match. Leibniz's theodicy is the accurate riposte—the best of all possible worlds is a mix of goods and evils—though he mistakenly implied that they have a single, optimal distribution.[95] There are, it seems, myriad possible "greatest goods." We may disagree about the one preferred, while agreeing that many others are greater evils.

v. Universal prescription. Deontology abstracts from practical processes and procedures to a crystalline structure of universal, a priori commandments: reason or God would have us do always and everywhere what we struggle to do locally.[96] "Local deontology" looks to be a pleonasm, one that mixes rational imperatives with the behaviors appropriate to a tribe or faction. But this is odd, because one imagines imperatives that apply selectively—to men or women, students or teachers—and because there may be no rules that are appropriate always to everyone. Murder is unthinkable, except for occasions (war or self-defense) when it is legitimate because useful.

The history of deontology suggests that moral imperatives must apply universally, because their source is a priori or divine. But imperatives also have an alternative source: namely, practical experience. Traffic laws evolve with the means of transport. They are unequivocal and they do have force, but they are local. Drive on the right, except where other peoples with others histories drive on the left.

vi. Moral insight. Having learned to behave morally as children, more because of our experiences in families and other local systems, less because of thumping deontological lessons, we know good from bad, right from wrong. Intuitionism makes practical experience incidental. It inherits the claim of Plato and Descartes that ideas or rules are inscribed in thought, either because finite minds are shards of nous or because God imprinted them.[97] A mind so formed perceives its moral truths merely by turning on itself. Such minds have a luminous certainty: they know what is good and right. No matter that their moral beliefs entail contradictions (no to abortions, yes to the death penalty). Or that the complexity of practical life precludes universal directives: never steal. Intuitionists disagree about what shall count as an unexceptional principle—self-love or self-sacrifice—but inconsistency never diminishes their clarity and assurance.

vii. Moral feeling. Emotion is often an immediate reaction to things perceived: victory excites us, injustice and inefficiency make us angry. These emotional responses are often reliable information about our circumstances or our interpretation of them, because they are coupled so directly to their provocations. Yet, this is not the focus of the emotivist bias in morals. Its primary concern is the truth value of propositions. Their truth is decidable, either empirically or formally (as in mathematical proof). Yet, moral claims are not decidable in either way, for the reason that emotion is said to be the expression of favor or disfavor: I like it, or not.[98] Nothing more is to be learned from anyone's moral or aesthetic responses, but for the addendum that willful people sometimes convert their feelings into rules that others learn and apply.

Hume distinguished states of affairs cognized from the feelings and preferences with which we respond to them:

[T]he distinction of vice and virtue is not founded merely on the relations of objects, nor is perceived by reason."[99]

An action, or sentiment, or character is virtuous or vicious; why? Because its view causes a pleasure or uneasiness of a particular kind.[100]

These remarks imply that the distinction between cognition and affect is unproblematic: the first includes perceptions of external states of affairs and reasonings about them (whether deductive or probabilistic and causal); the second comprises feelings aroused by the "contemplation of a character."[101] We are to suppose that feelings are a reaction to matters perceived. They may be appropriate, given the person contemplated, but they are states of arousal, not cognitions.

This is another instance of Hume's procedure for treating and emphasizing difference: distinguish percepts or ideas, clarify the difference, then insist that one cannot be the other. The categorical division of cognition and feeling is an example, though Hume misconstrued the difference, given the empirically confirmed hypothesis that *some* emotions are the cognitive states of primitive regions in the human brain (the amygdala, principally).[102] Pleasure and pain are cognitions, the one of things good for us, the other of things that are and feel inimical. What do pleasure or pain provoke us to do, or avoid? The primitive brain doesn't formulate sentences or thoughts. Registering our encounters with other people or things perceived as good or bad, pleasurable or painful, it construes *ought* and *should* as natural imperatives of animal life.

The mechanism is simple but effective. Things that give us pleasure—food, sleep, and sex—are life enhancing: seek them. Violence, hunger, and sickness are painful and malign: avoid them. This aspect of brain's evolution has a limited effect: some feelings of pleasure and pain are good evidence of what we should or shouldn't do—lift your hand when you feel the burning stove—but feeling, like every cognitive modality, is fallible. The modern brain informs us better, though just one of its many functions is critical here: namely, the consequentialist deliberation that enables us to calculate the effects of acting in ways that enhance or diminish well-being. What gives pleasure, what causes pain? Is it sometimes true that pain is good for us, and pleasure bad? The cortex registers and elaborates information supplied by the primitive brain before formulating the maps and plans that enable us to appraise the conditions and effects of pleasure or pain, then to take advantage of our circumstances and this information. The possibilities for error are magnified, because thought and language liberate imagination from the immediacy of our encounters with other things: self-correction is often slow when thought-directed action is pleasing but harmful. Still, Hume's dictum—sensibility and desire are distinct from cognition; the imperatives of the first are not derivable from truths of the second—is falsified by the cognitive role of many feelings. Those pleasures, pains, and desires are evidence of what we are, where we are, and what we should do to benefit or sustain ourselves.

Hume might have agreed that *oughts* mediated by these pleasures and pains derive from *is*, because some emotions are appropriate to their circumstances. I am aroused and angry if the key doesn't open my front door, then calmed but embarrassed to realize that I am trying to open someone else's door. Each of the two feelings is the obscure, but still cognitive, response to my situation. The moral and aesthetic implications are apparent: one is morally satisfied or aesthetically pleased by acts or conditions, performances or objects seen as well done or made. Mill would have agreed: connoisseurs rightly trust the cogency of their feelings.[103]

Remember that these remarks were prefaced by the acknowledgment that they apply to *some* emotions only: those said to be cognitive states of primitive regions in the brain. Emotivists can save the distinction between cognitions and feelings by specifying feelings for which this is not a plausible account. But what are these other feelings? Is the emotivist distinction vindicated, for example, by feelings that express attitudes?

Attitudes are cognitive-affective postures. They are orientations, ways of regarding and responding to particular things or things of a kind. Feeling disposed or hostile is evidence that the thing or things favored or deplored by an attitude are close enough to rouse us. But attitudes are not true or false. They combine orientation and appraisal, without purporting to make truth-claims. Imagine the panic of a child about to have his first haircut: it is his fear, not its validity that moves him. Attitudes sometimes evolve, so that the man he becomes doesn't like haircuts but isn't afraid of them. The child's fear would be inappropriate in the man, but this trivial point is critical to the thought that attitudes might be sources of the feelings emotivists seek. For attitudes are rightly challenged: do circumstances justify your bias and feelings? This question demands a cognitive answer of just the sort that couldn't be required of moral judgments if emotivism were correct.

Emotivists have a choice: concede that some feelings—pleasures and pains—are cognitive, propose that feelings are cognitive in the way of attitudes—they are likes and dislikes focused by beliefs, biased by expectations, and subject to the demand that they be justified—or identify feelings of a third sort, feelings that have no cognitive content. This third alternative isn't derisory: there are other feelings. Some moods are internally generated states that have no exogenous causes: they are, for example, hormonal. It might be true that all moral judgments are expressions of just these feelings. But saying so requires emotivists to make a much closer study of feelings than typically they do.

※

Theorists who emphasize one or another of these seven topics would have us agree that theirs is the core of ethical theory, every other consideration being subsidiary. Utilitarians sometimes affirm that the greater good justifies sacrificing the life or well-being of a society's few virtuous members. Some deontologists argue that lying is never right, whatever the cost. There are intuitionists on both sides of arguments regarding abortion and contractarians who will not concede that some relationships—those of parents and children or friends—are misdescribed or sabotaged when warped to satisfy their ideas of mutual consent. The blind men pawing an elephant have nothing to learn from theorists who scupper opponents while ignoring the insularity they share.

A better theory acknowledges and integrates all seven points. It can't be formulated until we gather empirical information. For human circumstances and practices are the point of reference for moral values. Who are we? What do we need? Getting this information is vexing, because people disagree about matters germane to moral practice (health of the mother, or health of the fetus), and because they are inclined to distort descriptions in ways that favor their bias. Yet, disagreements are not significant for moral theory, until they have passed three gates. First, we want to describe our situation and practical interests without the warp of unacknowledged beliefs about good and bad, right and wrong. Is poverty a result of laziness, scarce resources, or social organization? This is a factual, practical question. We need to purge our answers of extraneous values and attitudes if we are to address it without a distorting bias. Second, what is the question to be answered? Is it a practical question? Or is that question proxy for other, more or less disguised interests? For it often happens that contrary moral judgments express the conflicted interests of systems that compete for resources and personnel. Those disputes raise moral questions, but the responses of the belligerents obscure the practical issues that divide them: rancor isn't moral merely because we use moral language to express it. Third, we need remember that a moral theory's idealizations embody an ontology: meaning, its conception of human nature and circumstances. Hence this question: Is the ontology empirically tested? Does evidence confirm that things are as the theory says they are? A theory's idealizations are unlikely to be pertinent, if it is contravened by empirical data. This third point is decisive for moral theory, because many of its idealizations are formed against the backdrop of atomistic or holistic assumptions. That can't be good, because those theories are empirically false. People are neither atoms in a void nor soldered together by pervasive internal relations. We are neither free to do anything we like, free of all constraints, nor immobile because of obligations that bind us to one and all. These two theories dominate thinking about morals, but they misrepresent us.

Communitarianism—systems theory—is the one ontology standing: reality, human society included, is an array of systems. Moral theory responds by requiring that its idealizations track communitarian emphases. They explain the formation of moral attributes that virtue ethics can only cite. They provide for character by explaining its inception and development, for contracts by specifying the conditions for forming new systems, and for deontology by describing the idealizations of those virtues and practices that enhance personal and communal life. They anticipate moral intuitionism by explaining that people know the behavior expected of them. They prefigure emotivism by observing that we feel confirmed or affronted by the behavior of others, because of attitudes formed in systems where such actions were approved or discouraged. Morality is local because core systems are local, though we extend it and them incrementally.

Communitarianism suffers for being underdeveloped and invisible in the philosophic culture that stipulates atomist principles, then regards them as solemn truths. But this is ironic, given that atomism and holism are limiting cases of the communitarian account. It acknowledges systems that are mutually independent (young adults and ambitious entrepreneurs), loosely integrated (neighborhoods and cities), or wholes (IBM and the National Basketball Association). It is comprehensive, where they are partial and skewed.

An empirically confirmed ontology, like a good map, orients us correctly while making our circumstances intelligible. Abetting action, it generates additional, confirming perceptions. Compare most ethical theories. They are typically supported by scattered observations about people and their circumstances. Writing enthusiastically of freedom or solidarity, they say little or nothing of systems where freedom is constrained or initiative encouraged. Tend only to theory, and one ignores the people who vibrate under the tension of the opposed claims made of them. They have substance and effects, though ideas of character, wants, collaboration, and virtue are static and abstract when isolated from contexts where a system's members engage one another for shared or complementary aims. Can I be true to myself while responsible to others? How much effort here, how much there? A moral theory misses these tensions, if there is no empirically grounded ontology to acknowledge them.

Ordinary people—most of them moral most of the time—ignore disputes among moral theories for the simpler morality learned at home, in church, or on television. One version tells them to resist the demands of core systems or other people, because power is the only justifier: do as your interests require without concern for any benefit but your own. A different story imagines a creator God who makes moral demands, endows each of us with the capacity to satisfy them, and rewards or punishes those who satisfy or ignore his laws. Its God is a utilitarian who would save all of us at once. Narratives of either sort appease us. Internal anomalies are papered over or ignored, because they make life meaningful, moral, and safe. But there are many appeasing narratives. Anyone noticing their contrariety could infer that all may be false.

Grounding moral theory in an empirically accurate ontology doesn't guarantee that it will have no alternatives. There will be many, because the properties and relations cited by the ontology are generic and determinable: they may have several or many, more determinate forms (talk of color doesn't differentiate yellow from blue). Every human society has the same basic needs and vulnerabilities, hence equivalent (if different) core systems. But this shared nucleus tolerates the idiosyncrasies of each culture's moral code, and the meanings it ascribes to life. Moral theory is gerrymandered and shaded as we distinguish figure and ground while elaborating one or another of these interests. Shall we emphasize systems that are mutually independent (young adults), integrated systems (neighborhoods and cities), or wholes (nation-states)? Do we idealize single systems—persons, for example—or arrays of systems, nesting, or overlap? There is and will be discord galore—even granting that communitarianism is better than atomism or holism—because of disagreements about the priority rightly accorded to one system or another and because some will argue that conflict, not cooperation, is the baseline for describing systems. But these are details. Communitarianism locates moral norms in circumstances that are stubbornly factual and practical.

CHAPTER FIVE

Aesthetic Norms

Systems established by the causal relations of their parts are dynamic: motion is routed through the reciprocities, but not stopped. Most of the systems emphasized in this chapter are static rather than dynamic: there is no interaction between or among their ordered parts. Static systems are complementarities: the fit of their terms replaces the causal reciprocities of dynamic systems. Examples include the notes of a chord or melody, the lines and planes of a building, the distribution of shapes, colors, and textures in a painting, and the sentences of a logical proof. (Music is odd: sequences of notes are static—notes don't interact— though their progression and rhythm suggest motion to the brain.) Every such thing embodies one or more schemas, its form. Notes, lines, shapes, or sentences are its variables. Schemas are constraining: the roof line of a building is controlled by its other planes; the last line in a proof derives from higher-order sentences. Relationships of both sorts—static or dynamic, calligraphy or dance—may also have aesthetic qualities. Some—dappled water, clouds moving across the face of the moon—carry beauty to the sublime. This chapter describes material norms for static and dynamic, created and natural beauty.

Is beauty created from the whole cloth of sensuous or ascetic imagination, be it the imagination of artists or those who enjoy nature or things artists make? Or does the experience of beauty require that we appreciate constraints in the particular things or states of affairs to which beauty is ascribed? I shall be saying that aesthetic qualities are relational: they engage thinkers or perceivers to things that have properties compelling to thought or perception. Acuity is intensified and focused by the materials, design, contrast, and proportion constitutive of such things. We, in turn, see them as though they were suffused with beauty. As *though* is critical: aesthetic objects are passive; we who think and perceive them are active. The experience of beauty is our reaction to them.

1. The Conditions for Aesthetic Value in Created Works

The aesthetic value of created works is a function of seven variables: i. a provocation, ii. an idea, iii. the materials used, iv. organizing schemas or rules, v. artistic innovation, vi. their product's accessibility to human thought and sensibility, and vii. the cultivation or idiosyncrasy of the perceivers. Each of these variables is a constraint on both artistic production and the aesthetic experience of the work created.

  i. Provocation. Most of us who live or work in buildings are oblivious to the contingency of their designs. But architects know that every space could have been organized in several ways, and they may wonder about the motives or intentions that are expressed in the materials and form of particular buildings. Painters are stirred by colors, perspectives, feelings, forms, incongruities, or ideas: anything that may be interpreted as color and shape. Composers awash in the folk songs and dances of their people have a mine of possible ideas. But each of these is a specialized resource. Provocative experiences also include random perceptions, memories, or stubborn thoughts. Everyone has them, but most of us lack the sensibility, discipline, or skill to make viable ideas, and then art of these beginnings. There is also this other incitement: the artist with a history of trial and achievement is his or her own provocateur. Knowing what one has done, knowing what could have been different is often sufficient to impel more work.

  The factors provoking art may seem incidental to its aesthetic value, as often they are. But it is not incidental that provocation includes both the artistic and the political or religious traditions of the ambient society or culture. Most every Turkish caliph built a mosque in which to be buried, or to honor others. Because mosques took years to build, a village of workers and artists grew and prospered around a building site. But then the caliph died. His successor assured work for a new generation of artists by planning another mosque. Craftsmen responded to needs of the caliph's household and to artistic imperatives: use sumptuous materials to express an established motif, but make it elegant.

ii. Ideas. The idea provoked in the mind of an artist is a web of associations focused by the inciting percept, thought, or memory. It will be developed and may be transformed from the moment of inspiration to the time when the work is done. Aspects that were conspicuous in its first expression may be superseded in the finished work by elements that were penumbral or suppressed. The observer, too, is provoked, but his or her provocation is the work, itself. And here, as well, comprehension is better focused and extended with time. One doesn't perceive all the form and nuance of a painting or sonata at first sight or hearing. Even a short poem can be read many times before its structure, contrasts, rhythm, and effects are collected and resolved.

Philosophers were once confident that they could isolate and identify ideas: we need only perceive them as they stand before the mind's eye. But this is mistaken, if thinking is not the analogue to examining sensory data. Fascination with language helped to make the analogy plausible by identifying ideas with words or sentences seen or heard. Yet, this emphasis—ideas perceived when set before the mind—perpetuates an error. We do have percepts, memories, and dreams, and some of them—the imagined benzene ring—are good representations of thought's extra-mental objects. But figurative imagining, dreaming, or remembering is not thinking. The ideas of novelists, composers, dramatists, and choreographers are more or less elaborated and focused webs of association. They direct thought or imagination without supplying an object or content for an act that resembles perceiving. Think of two writers conversing. Ideas flow as each responds to the other by developing suggestions in ways that neither could anticipate. Both withdraw, their heads swimming with associations and excitement, and both write for hours or days, with focus but without a distinct idea of what any next sentence will be. What and where are the themes they elaborate? They are carried and disciplined, in ways introspection doesn't describe or explain, by the association of ideas.

iii. Materials. Things of beauty display ordinary qualities—ordered colors, shapes, or sounds—produced with ordinary materials: paints and brushes, brick and stone, sentences, or the metal and wood of musical instruments. Why are colors, shapes, and sounds the proximate material of aesthetic quality? Because these qualities are accessible to human thought and sensibility. Angels—pure spirits—intuit the beauty of the Forms, though beauty is invisible to us unless expressed in materials we can think or perceive.

iv. Organizing schemas or rules. Aesthetic objects are shaped or integrated—informed—by schemas or rules. Melody is a sequence of organized notes. Its score is a rule for ordering notes. More complicated music is produced by sequencing or overlaying melody on melody, form on form: harmony with development or tolerable dissonance, for example. One may achieve a dimly aesthetic result by using standard forms—the generic rules—that express the tradition in which the artist works: popular ballads and the photographs used to illustrate fashion magazines, for example. But art wants more. For there is no excitement and release, no consummatory experience, if the artist doesn't exploit the common rule in an idiosyncratic and compelling way. How radical should artists be? One may be an innovator without predecessors; but this guarantees that a work will baffle others who see or hear it, for a while or always. Styles evolve with the inspiration or idiosyncrasies of the contributors, but, usually, each learns the rules current in his or her time. They guide the development and realization of the manifest form: the line of notes played and heard, for example.

The rule-driven control of things is often external, as when policemen direct traffic. Compare works perceived as graceful or beautiful, because of immanent constraints. We see or hear their perceptual content—colors, shapes, or sounds—before perceiving the schemas that give them form. Author, composer, architect, or painter: each has one or more ideas expressed as an organizing schema, and each creates an object having aesthetic qualities by applying schemas altered subtly or radically to ordinary materials. The result is a manifest idea: the building through which one walks, the poem one reads.

Experts know the generic rules that shape the forms of particular works, but most of us can only recognize their effects: principally order, complexity rendered with economy, contrast, and resolution. Rhythm exhibits all four. *Order*—coherence—is created by introducing or exploiting connection (by way of logic, narrative, or merely space or time), proportion (symmetry, for example), or development. *Complexity-with-economy* is order that reduces distracting dross, while challenging the eye, ear, or thought: logicians and poets are especially adroit. *Contrast*—the resistance and tension created by difference—averts the blandness of homogeneity. We achieve it by mixing orientations, geometries, tempi, colors, musical keys, or tones. These are contrasts within a work; though there is contrast of a different sort when a painting or story is seen against the backdrop of others. Think of works that evoke classical styles they alternately express and defy. *Resolution* is the effect of superseding the strains introduced when an idea is subjected to the competing demands of order, complexity, and contrast, the strain created, for example, by joining complexity to coherence. The process is conspicuously temporal and developmental in music and literature, but in painting and architecture, too, tension is created, then resolved. Dewey rightly says that, "esthetic objects depend upon a progressively enacted experience."[1] "No work of art can be instantaneously perceived because there is then no opportunity for conservation and increase of tension, and hence none for that release and unfolding which give volume to a work of art."[2] There is, nevertheless, this difference. Musical tension is usually resolved diachronically, because tension formed by a previous phrase is resolved by later ones. Resolution in painting and architecture is synchronic. Perception evolves as one perceives the weights and design of a painting or building, but then, as one comprehends the whole, tension is seen and resolved at once. Even musical resolution is sometimes synchronic, as when harmony offsets dissonance in a chord of three notes.

v. Innovation. Where is genius or beauty in things made by reworking materials in accord with a schematized idea? One answer is the freedom, the inventiveness of the maker as he or she applies accepted forms. Bach used accepted rules in standard ways, but usually with a fluidity that transformed his materials. The music is orderly in the ways required by the schemas he used, but the results are as fresh as the cakes of chefs who don't use recipes. Schemas are malleable: they are alterable as circumstances, ideas, and materials require. The goodness credited to innovation is the measure of an artist's skill with analogy or extrapolation: originality exploits the unexpected plasticity of old materials or forms.

The effect is surprise: eye and ear are led in familiar ways, until something anomalous forces the observer to reorient and reintegrate the material perceived. Disrupting coherence, surprise adds freedom to form. Broken symmetry and the cats of Egyptian sculpture—human irony and cunning in a cat's face—are examples. We recognize the form, but excitement mixes with repose: we shiver with the unexpected turn. Dismayed by formulaic art, one soup can like every other, we prefer work that is biased but not entailed by the assumptions and procedures used to create it. Even deductive proofs are variable: there are several ways to axiomatize a theory or prove a theorem: leeway for the inventive logician. We look for, and want, form with freedom, regularity with surprise. Though we shouldn't exaggerate our enthusiasm for difference: we like artists who disrupt old forms without making them unrecognizable.

Some aesthetic objects seem to lack surprise: simple tools, for example. But here, too, we see anomaly: they are delicate, but bold. Surprise is a forceful awakening: we are all but slapped, obliged to rouse ourselves from our normal torpor. Morality is unsettled by novelty; art wants it. Like bugs moving their antennae, we enjoy the present only long enough to infer its successor. Surprise alerts us to pay attention, here and now. Objects that provoke it are parasitic on everyday, perceptual experience, with the difference that surprise obliges us to see or hear the irony or intelligence of the artist. Is everyday experience coherent and predictable? Let the artist seduce us with apparent regularity before introducing anomalies that disrupt us. Or let us know from the first sentence, bar, or door that standard expectations are inappropriate. Then set us at ease: use resolution to mitigate disorientation. Let the work evolve from the bias of its starting point to a form its audience comprehends, however unfamiliar the recovered ground.

vi. Accessibility to human sensibility. An artist is accessible to his or her audience because of using schemas that are similar or complementary to those applied when the work is seen or heard, and by working with materials—colors, shapes, and sounds—for which the audience has a natural affinity. Sounds that resonate in us—human voices, for example— are sequenced, then reworked and reprised as schemas for development and symmetry are applied. Compare the mix of rhythms, timbres, and harmonies in art songs to a noisy subway train. One seduces the ear, the other assaults it; one is raw, the other supple; but both are heard. Aesthetic experience doesn't require novel faculties; it cultivates those we have.

Consider that human physiology is an adaptation to our circumstances, and that it is only our everyday cognitive and perceptual faculties that are sensitized to aesthetic qualities. Don't paint in colors of wavelengths I can't see; don't play at frequencies I can't hear. Be careful within the parameters of human sensibility and understanding. Orchestrators are careful using brass with strings, because no one hears the strings when the horns play too loudly. A drawing that violates perspective may be uninterpretable, however dramatic. Aesthetic experience is parasitic on faculties whose ordinary uses are practical. Very few artists dare to use forms or materials for which there is little perceptual affinity: none write music for chalk and blackboard.

Aesthetic experience is the complement to practical life. We are dazzled, intimidated, moved, or elated because the artist manipulates a restricted medium—words, shapes, colors, or sounds—to evoke emotions that are less restrained because there is no cost to expressing them. Aesthetic experience is safer than ordinary experience, because it is stripped of collateral and distracting effects, especially, cues to action. This is aesthetic distance: we luxuriate in the feelings evoked, but no one rises to assault the blackguard on stage. (Children sometimes do rise; but only because they don't distinguish aesthetic from practical experience.) Relieved of having to perceive things as utilities or obstacles, we see the mix of order and difference in façades lining a street, or form and color, not food, in a bowl of fruit. Bioaesthetics will locate the processes activated when aesthetic objects are perceived and enjoyed, but decoupled from action.

vii. *The cultivation or idiosyncrasy of the artist or perceiver.* Theorists disagree about the generating conditions for aesthetic qualities. Subjectivists say that the goodness of aesthetic objects is in the eye or ear of the observer; people don't enjoy the same things. But this response ignores a cognitive issue: do artists or observers see or hear—look or listen—the same ways, or equally well? Recognizing a good pot is easier than hearing a sonata or poem. The subjectivist tolerance for conflicting aesthetic judgments ignores the possibility that some or all the disputants may be in error: they don't know the relevant criteria, or they misperceive the relevant features of the things appraised. We are reluctant to acknowledge these failures, because we don't want to offend people of faulty judgment. But it isn't news that judgment varies with information and sensibility, and that people have more or less of it. Not everyone is a connoisseur of fly-fishing. Familiarity with tapestries or part-singing isn't more common.

This has an implication reminiscent of moral virtue. Someone drafted into a position, without affiliation to a system's other members or skill at the task, has none of the information, inclinations, or habits required for doing its work. Aesthetic experience makes comparable demands. One can't expect a neophyte to perceive the aesthetic properties of a painting, sonata, or poem because he or she lacks the preparation that would sensitize him or her to its relevant properties. The experience of beauty is relational. It requires objects capable of provoking a response and people formed for this possibility.

Is the objective beauty of things compromised, because beauty is in the seeing or hearing? Does this imply that goodness is ascribed to things because of the interpretation or pleasure they provoke in us, implying that aesthetic value is ultimately subjective? This is the aesthetic version of Plato's question to Euthyphro: are aesthetic objects good because we are pleased; or are we pleased because they are good?[3] If these are antitheses, the answer is a synthesis. Beauty is a function of two things: the material and formal (organizational) properties of objects and the sensibility that enables us to perceive them as beautiful. Beauty emerges as the experience of beauty when the first engages the second.

These two are refined as three if we distinguish the effects things have on us from the sensibility that enables us to experience them as beautiful. Someone tone-deaf doesn't hear music. One who hears the notes as different may not hear their beauty. Are they beautiful, anyway? We answer by assimilating the experience of beauty to that of secondary properties. Something is seen as red, because it reflects light of certain wavelengths into eyes having a particular structure. Redness is in the eye, so to speak, but only because of the character of the eye and object seen, and because of the relationship created by the light that passes from one to the other. Beauty, too, is a quality that emerges in the interaction of perceiver and perceived. The objective pole is satisfied by objects that have the attributes described under the rubrics just cited: an idea realized in materials organized by the deft application of schemas is accessible to human perception and understanding. Like the redness seen, beauty is in the eye of one who discerns the properties that provoke the experience of beauty.[4]

What is the singular aspect of aesthetic experience? Beauty is experienced when materials are so well joined that they evoke visceral and intellectual, even moral pleasure in cultivated perceivers. Cultivation is all but universal for sunsets, but more demanding for string quartets. Either way, *beauty* is used indexically. We can specify some of its conditions, as above. We can point to things provoking it and exclaim as pleasure rushes through us; but the experience—acute and focused, a mix of thought and feeling, calm and excitement—is all but inarticulable.[5] There are paintings that leave us staring into a revelation and buildings that exalt us as we walk through them. The quiet intensity of a piano splendidly played makes people weep. Beauty is in the weeping; but not everyone weeps.

2. Objections

Objectivists will protest that a proof doesn't lose form merely because someone ignorant of logic doesn't see that its last sentence is entailed by those above: the beauty of the proof is inherent, however invisible to him. There are two ideas here, ideas better separated than merged. First is the notion of essence or kind: there are properties necessary and sufficient to distinguish sonnets from sonatas. Something is good as an instance of its kind when it has all the relevant properties rightly joined. The proper way of joining properties depends on the kind of thing being made, and the relevant creative tradition. A building or dance is adequate or good in ways appropriate to its kind—"workmanlike," we say— because of the ways these properties are assembled. Familiarity with things of a kind—pots, paintings, symphonies, or stories—supplies criteria for judging that they are well made. A Mozart or Giotto does more, but the words used to characterize the difference—"genius," "inspiration"—are an exuberant but metaphorical homage to consummate skill. Second is the experience of beauty. More or less complex and subtle, it varies with those who have it. So, the tidiness of a deduction is apparent to many. Its elegance and cleverness are enjoyed—as beauty—by the few who know that logic is a kind of play, and that a conclusion may be derived in several ways. These two—object and perceiver—are jointly necessary and sufficient: there is no beauty without both.

Objectivists respond that emergent properties—metabolism, triangularity, and grace—are commonplace. Beauty, too, may supervene on the other, constitutive properties of things perceived as beautiful. But where does beauty emerge? Is it the property of things perceived as beautiful or an aspect of our experiential response to them? Suppose that works of music, literature, logic, or art are well made. Each exhibits the virtues of its kind: harmonies and contrasts, for example. The objectivist must say that beauty is the emergent effect created by assembling these properties, an effect seen or heard by properly educated observers. Yet, observers may listen to the finest music or stand rapt before the finest building while perceiving nothing but their well-organized materials.

Where is beauty? Its proper sites are thinkers and perceivers: beauty is the ecstatic experience that emerges in agents primed to think or perceive the attributes of things divers as ballads and bridges.

The relational conditions for aesthetic experience explain the radically different responses to a thing or event. Listening as people talk during intermission, I hear their delight in a performance I don't enjoy. They experience the performance as beautiful; I am disappointed and annoyed. They have their reasons; they wouldn't care for mine. This is so far a difference of sensibility: one side likes what it sees; the other doesn't see what it's looking for. One might regard this as a dispute about the intrinsic beauty of the performance; but that would misconstrue it. For the experience of beauty implicates the relationship in which something is perceived as beautiful. We sometimes say that Greek temples are beautiful in themselves. But this is the false conflation scored above. We may use *beauty* to signify the properties that provoke the experience of beauty, but this use of the word is a misleading abstraction from beauty's two conditions: those properties and the perceiver's response to matters thought or perceived.

My formulation is, nevertheless, incomplete: it doesn't specify the properties rightly experienced as beautiful. Failure to do this—indeed, inability to do it—satisfies relativists, because they deny that certain properties are the only ones qualified to provoke the experience. A properly belligerent response avers that certain properties—order, complexity, economy, contrast and resolution, for example—are rightly perceived as beautiful, and that the experience of beauty is delusory if it occurs in one who is insensible to them. But there is no way to make this point by argument alone. Experience is a better arbiter. Which are the more pleasant conditions for walking: sunny, breezy days or violent squalls? And equally, listen to or look at works well made. Discern the properties significant for aesthetic experience, and discriminate among works of a kind: poetry or music, instrumental music or song. Ask someone acquainted with both. Wine has its connoisseurs. Beauty has them, too. Attentive experience is the best and only preparation for both.

Our democratic culture doesn't like this answer, because it implies that experience is cognitive, and that some people analyze and integrate things perceived better than others. This is the elitist belief that connoisseurs are more qualified than the rest of us to specify the properties that provoke the experience of beauty, or to distinguish its degrees. It doesn't follow that these experts can't be mistaken, disagree, or change their

views. But who is more likely to make informed judgments: people uninformed about art, literature, or music, or those who know it better. It is
chastening or encouraging that the judgments of connoisseurs typically
converge on properties and objects much smaller than the available alternatives. The local barbershop quartet is good, but the Beach Boys are
better. This is a judgment others can test.

My formulation is still ambiguous, if it implies or allows that the
beauty ascribed to things may be the function of nothing more than a
perceiver's ideas, attitudes, or feelings. Someone feels the elation of
beauty while standing in a dark, airless closet: should he infer that his
experience is a response to darkness or isolation? This is a question about
the complexity of the relationship in which beauty is perceived: could
the experience be generated by the perceiver alone? Could a properly
stimulated brain-in-a-vat experience beauty? Perhaps, it could, though
doing so wouldn't nullify the relational account proposed here. For now
as before, the perceiver's response would implicate something additional
to itself: namely, the stimulation that substitutes for the properties of the
thing perceived as beautiful.

Subjectivists will say that such examples fail to prove that the experience of beauty is not self-generated. Perhaps mind embellishes what it
thinks or perceives, unconstrained by objective conditions. Again, the
cogent response is empirical evidence, not argument. Is it true that there
is no correlation between the experience of beauty and certain properties
that mind does not manufacture? Are there people who find beauty in
abattoirs and garbage dumps? Suppose none do, for then subjectivists need
to explain the absence of this response, given their claim that beauty has
subjective conditions only. They should also explain the converse effect:
what is it about some things thought or perceived that evokes this experience? Subjectivists are mistaken: the correlation of aesthetic experience
with objective circumstances is strong, not weak or even doubtful.

This relational account of aesthetic experience has two forms. One
emphasizes cognition, the other cognition and affect: we experience
things as beautiful if we think or perceive that they have certain properties, or we think or perceive them as beautiful when our experience of
them is intensified by attitudes or feelings. One declares that beauty is a
cognitive response to objective properties (complexity and resolution,
for example) whose expressions vary among domains (music, painting,
or dance); the other affirms that beauty is an affective response to objective properties thought or perceived. This difference opposes asceticism

to romanticism, logic to opera and gardens. It implies that emotions, too, can be disciplined and cogent, rather than merely effusive. There is no decisive claim against either proposal, because each has many confirming experiences: logical proofs, some music, art, architecture, and poetry for ascetics; drama, opera, and examples from all the other modalities for romantics.

Emotion is, nevertheless, problematic, because hard to discipline. We often sentimentalize some person or thing. Children look ordinary to others, but beautiful to their parents. Are parents deluded? They are if beauty is in the cognitive response to certain properties thought or perceived, and if the belief is false because those properties are absent. But parents are undeceived, if sensibility is one of three critical variables: objective properties (a family resemblance), thinking or perceiving these properties, and the affective response to this information. Parents or friends could be taught to discount extraneous associations (my child) and to focus on the actual features of the thing perceived. But why teach them? Objectivity has all the respect it deserves when the experience of beauty is a response moored in the perception of constraining properties: the face that looks like her mother's.

People differ in their ability to discern relevant constraining properties, because of the complexity of things perceived, because of having or lacking relevant perceptual skills or information, or because of their attitudes or emotional states. But there is no way to trump someone's claim that he or she is suffused with pleasure when seeing the beauty of someone loved. The connoisseur (or other parents) may respond, soto voce: I don't see it that way. He knows what to look for, and—minimizing the expectation and excitement that would mislead—he finds it or not. Yet, hauteur and the cognitivism it expresses are excessive outside the university, museum, or concert hall. The experience of beauty is familiar to all, though few of us are connoisseurs. No harm is done when the emotional response to objective constraints—the properties of things perceived— overrides the scruples of the expert.

This has a useful result: it extends the domain of personal experiences relevant to aesthetics. For notice this difference between aesthetics and moral theory. References to family and friendship locate us immediately in terrain we know: duty's origin in the reciprocities that bind a core system's members is familiar. Talk of beauty's seven conditions is abstract by comparison: one might learn its conditions without being able to name a single beautiful thing. The appeal to individual sensibility closes this gap: we acknowledge personal experiences of beauty, even though we are unable to specify or remember features that provoked the experience. Would it be better to legislate in the name of taste? Discount the experiences of uninformed perceivers: they don't know the proper use of aesthetic words, because they don't know the properties that justify their attribution. This would trample the experiences people have and find elating. Why bother? We do justice to the relational character of beauty by acknowledging that it requires the presence of relevant attributes in things seen as beautiful, and that people vary in their ability to discern those properties. Is the experience the same, whatever a perceiver's ability to discern and appraise the thing perceived? No, there is a difference. Wine tasters do more than discriminate properties that most of us ignore; their enjoyment is also different. What empirical data justify this surmise? The experience of tracking the evolution of one's own discriminations, from Thunderbird to burgundy. This is the subjective side of the connoisseur's learning. Cognition, verbally articulate or not, refines the emotional experiences it promotes.

3. Natural Beauty

Many things in nature are seen as beautiful. Dandelions and clover suffocate the grass in my garden. Weeds in the eyes of careful gardeners, they are beautiful to me. There is more accord about the beauty of thistles and roses, or morning surf on an ocean beach. Is their beauty like or unlike that of things artists make?

One similarity confirms a suspicion provoked by the beauty ascribed to things made: we see their aesthetic qualities when the demands of practical life are least pressing. We hear music better when nothing distracts us. Someone afraid of the coming storm doesn't notice the beauty of the clouds; mist and rain are beautiful if one isn't shivering cold. Liberated from needs and preoccupations, we see and hear things as they are, not as we prefer or fear them. There is similarity, too, in nature's materials, complexity, and surprise. But many things surprise us, not all of them perceived as beautiful. What distinguishes those having aesthetic qualities? Things called *beautiful* are often merely pleasant or pretty. Or we use the word as a compliment, without regard for justifying qualities in the person flattered. But some things shake our complacency. They are perceived as beautiful, because of what is: their properties. The pertinent *should* derives from it, too, because we should see things as they are.

What if we look for natural beauty: what are we looking for? No single feature is common to every thing experienced as beautiful. Some are sensual (the deep yellow in sunflowers or gorse). Others have form (a sliver of the rising moon) or fluidity (fish of different colors, moving randomly about a reef or in a tank). Some—undulating water or lights in the sky—have few properties, as though informed by a single idea. Many seem unthinkably complex. Some are immense, others small; some—sky and sea—are exempt from anything we can do to sustain or alter them; others—abandoned towns—are human products. Contrasts—light and darkness, fore- and background—are everywhere. Yet, something vital to the arts is usually missing in natural beauty: namely, the ideas and schemas—the organizing principles—that artists exploit as they work. There are conspicuous exceptions: crystals and snowflakes, for example. But there is usually no awareness of the organizing, directing plan that is ever more apparent as one sees what an artist does.

Religious romantics disagree: seeing nature as God's product, they look for his organizing plan. But God's ideas exceed human understanding, so we postulate, but cannot discern them. Imagine the closest human analogue to an omniscient God, the physicist who has learned his unified field theory so well that he sees every state of affairs as one of its applications: understanding the organizing conditions of things thought or perceived informs his every experience of natural beauty. Physicists or chemists who know a little less may share some part of this illumination, but most of us do not. Our experience of natural beauty differs from the one of looking for and finding the organizing form of a structure or painting. We see difference, but not a resolving form. We are awed, but passive.

Another difference is also critical. Nature's beauty is exhilarating, but calming. No one applauds a sunset, but people can barely contain themselves when hearing extraordinary music. We manage our feelings until the end, and then erupt with pleasure. Why? Perhaps, because we experiences art's beauty as an expression of intelligence driven by emotion. Artists often achieve their effects by joining recalcitrant materials, whether they be conflicting ideas or characters in a play. We look for and find the organizing idea; we see or hear and feel a resolving emotion. Tension passes; we are purged or elated. These are effects in us; but they are aroused by the informing affect and intelligence of the artist. Nature is awesome, but its beauty lacks the tension created by a master who has struggled to resolve all that is problematic in his materials, ideas, and the feelings they provoke in him and us. Music and art are made by people like us, people who challenge us to track their thoughts and feelings with our own. Nature doesn't have thoughts or feelings. Kant may have had this difference in mind when he distinguished beauty from the sublime.[6] For natural beauty surpasses understanding and empathy, too, not because of its scale or complexity, rather because it is sensuous without passion, orderly but not planned. Awe is the surrogate for affect and understanding.

4. Virtual Form

Talk of nature, schemas, materials, and the craft of artists leaves one factor unconsidered. What of space and time: what do they contribute to the experience of beauty?

Consider a temporal schema. How many beats establish a rhythm? One isn't sure that two beats and the interval between them—the phrase, beat + beat—are sufficient. But four beats, two that are louder, then two softer and faster are sufficient. Beethoven may have agreed: he repeated the first four notes of his Fifth Symphony, perhaps because of believing that a phrase isn't heard as rhythmic, unless repeated: so, (beat + beat +beat + *beat*) + (beat + beat + beat + *beat*) + ... There is also this other question: what is the objective ground for rhythms heard? Is it only the beats of the rhythm-maker, or the combination of beats and the time they measure? Does time tolerate every rhythm—making it altogether the function of a musician's timing or our hearing—or is there an additional constraint immanent within time itself?

Time may be a formless medium, one that exhibits whatever rhythms are inscribed in it. Or rhythms are established and heard, but this is incidental to the way time is intrinsically marked. Verificationists respond that there is no marking, or none that can be alleged, if it is not observable. But observation is incidental to the question at issue, if we consider the possibility that this, like many features of reality—the shape of spacetime, for example—are unobservable. Hence, the surmise that time may embody innumerable rhythms, each virtual, until it is marked—played. But rhythms are contraries. Shouldn't each bar the others, thereby precluding the possibility that all may be present at once? No, rhythms don't displace or preclude one another if all are virtual. This is problematic, to be sure. Properties differentiating the many virtual rhythms would be virtual beats, and virtual durations. Disqualify them, and the verificationist alternative stands: time, in itself, is formless; rhythms are not established until actual beats mark intervals. This is the preferred alternative from the standpoint of evidence. It may not be the deeper truth about time.

There is a parallel dispute regarding space. A figure articulates the otherwise empty backdrop of space; or it realizes one of the myriad, virtual forms that qualify it. Think of a tile inscribed with a succession of designs: same region, different forms. Do the designs express—realize—virtual forms, or are they inscribed in a medium indifferent to them? The arguments appropriate to time are also appropriate here, though evidence of virtual forms in space is more familiar. Left and right hands are isomorphic, but neither is translatable into the other: there is no transformation in three dimensions that smoothly turns a left hand into a right one. Is this a fact about the difference between right and left hands or a fact about regions of space that embody contrary forms? For the issue has nothing to do with the materiality of hands, but only with the untranslatability of spatial forms. Are forms inscribed in a space that is indifferent to them, or does space accept no form that is not already contained virtually within it? Verificationists respond that "virtual form" is meaningless in every context. Spatial regions may be defined by boundaries; intervals may be established by the beats that mark them, but space and time are otherwise formless. The burden falls to those who infer that forms of any sort—shapes or rhythms—may be virtual in space, time, or spacetime.

Two alternatives frame the issue. One hypothesis affirms that spacetime is a formless receptacle. Or the idea of virtual forms is reformulated to make virtual forms more palatable: rather than say that certain forms are *virtual* in a space, time, or spacetime; we say that a particular spacetime *tolerates* the inscription of some forms only. The untranslatability of left and right hands is our clue, and *tolerate* is the critical word. For spacetime does not tolerate forms inconsistent with its structure. The virtuality of forms is just the dispositional character of spacetime, given its topology, geometry, and kinematics: spacetime can be formed in all the ways consistent with them. This is more apparent when we imagine living on a torus: spacetime is distinctively disposed where every straight line is an arc or curve.

This reformulation gives verificationists the cash value of virtual form: meaning, the structurally based possibility of manifest forms. But it must strike them as equally mysterious and compromised. For how can it happen that space, time, or spacetime resists—does not tolerate—the inscription of some forms? They will say that spacetime's structure is another meaningless idea if we are asked to imagine it virtual and empty. Yet, spacetime is one of very few primary realities. It is a contingency that our spacetime has one or another structure: others are possible (they embody no contradiction). But this spacetime is not formless. Its topological, geometrical, and kinematic properties are the basis for its virtual forms, some of them realized as virtual lines of force. Virtual forms constrain and prefigure every manifest form: meaning the distribution and organization of individual masses, down to and including the rhythmic beats of a drum.

The structure of our spacetime is less conspicuous than that of a torus, but we have an intimation of its form when topology identifies structures that cannot be transformed into one another because of spacetime's distinctive structure. And decisively, this is not mere lack of imagination or know-how: translation would be possible were space to have one or more additional dimensions. Nor is it incidental that general relativity theory supports these speculations. Denying that spacetime is a tabula rasa, passive to forms inscribed in it, general relativity affirms that spacetime has a particular structure, one that determines the range of realizable forms. Every thing perceived, including every thing experienced as beautiful, satisfies this immanent constraint.

5. Must, Should, and Ought in the Context of Is

Aesthetic objects are made and perceived in contexts established by successive orders of *must, should,* and *ought.* First are the laws of logic: these are *musts* inhering in all that is, *musts* we can't violate. Space and time are also constraining. Think of painters whose narratives are frustrated by having to present successive times as concurrent. Writers use flashbacks, or narratives that are signposted, before and after. Painters can only allude to times previous or subsequent to the matters presented; or they make several paintings, displaying them left to right to indicate temporal succession. Music would have the complementary problem were it to mimic a still life: all form and content, no change. Physical laws are a third order of constraint: top-heavy buildings don't stand. The capacities of one's audience are fourth: composers write music for the human ear and constructible instruments; no one composes for dog whistles. There are also *must nots* that limit the effects materiality can achieve. Choreographers mustn't ask dancers to fly; painters mustn't suppose that red paint is more than evocative of blood.

Other constraints are looser, but still controlling: these are *shoulds* and *oughts*. An artist should use the established materials and forms of his or her culture, because tradition is a laboratory and record of initiatives that succeeded or failed, and because one creates for an audience that perceives current work in light of forms already used and learned. Why work as I should? Because I have learned some variant of my culture's style, because I am wary of violating our conventions and sensibilities, and (perhaps) because I want to sell what I make. People usually speak to one another in the local language. The *ought* they observe is normative as well as practical: their behavior expresses their culture's expectations. It is a condition for the understanding they want from others. Foreigners are tolerated—they may be treated generously—but natives tire of permanent residents who don't learn their language. *Should* or *ought* in these circumstances is indistinguishable from what is done. Artists exploit the local style, while transforming it. Picasso painted in a classical style when it suited him, though he was more concerned to challenge and alter it. The *ought* was an homage, one he honored even as he remade its norms. Transforming effects were innovations applied from within. This was the tightwire act Nietzsche described: be one of them, speak to them in their language, and do nothing memorable; or go one's way, risking the possibility that the artist shall be incomprehensible to them and himself.[7] The saving, middle way is narrow and precarious: learn the style of one's people or locale, make it one's own, then remake it in ways that will be intelligible to the few who dare consider its mutations.

Artistic freedom is a slogan, one taken too literally when we construe it as disregard for established conventions. What can be changed without bringing the structure down? What is left if every classical schema is rejected? The artist is most liberated when established styles are mastered to the point that he or she distinguishes what is necessary and contingent within them. Artists and critics, too, know that Nietzsche's dictum—"God is dead, and everything is permitted"—is facile and wrong.[8] Many things are not permitted. Much of the rest isn't worth doing. Artists solve a focused problem: how to transform the given in ways that exploit its promise without being formulaic. Their solutions join freedom to constraint.

CHAPTER SIX

Cultural Variation

Needs and interests are generic and determinable. Hunger is a need, and satisfying it is a value, though cultures differ in the means they prescribe: their rice, our wheat. This chapter describes both the variability of norms across societies and cultures and the generic constraints that limit these differences. It locates norms in two considerations: determinable needs or interests and the particular satisfiers that cultures or societies provide.

1. Generic Needs and Their Determinate Expressions

Nothing would be valuable to us if we had no needs or interests. Forever complete and self-possessed, we wouldn't look beyond ourselves for company or support. We would also be simple (like Leibnizian monads[1]), because complexity implies parts and the need to stabilize their relations in a dynamic world. Autonomy would also require that all things needed to maintain us—energy, materials, and information—be present and accessible within us. But they are not. We need regular inputs of all three. We sometimes replenish these resources by foraging for ourselves, but more often, we get them by communicating and cooperating with other people within systems that satisfy mutual needs and interests. And tellingly, we usually satisfy them in terms prescribed by these systems: the goods we seek—energy, materials, and information—are socially created and approved.

Normativity has two expressions that exhibit the difference between generic needs and their culturally or socially sanctioned satisfiers. One is determinable; the other is its situationally appropriate, determinate expression. The generic norm is a biological or social need, a need one would have irrespective of his or her culture, or a need that is consequent on living in circumstances or societies of a kind: as a fisherman or farmer, for example. Wanting nourishment is normative and common: it regulates behavior, requiring particular successes and satisfactions if a person is to live. But cultures use different materials, styles of preparation, and techniques to satisfy the need. Using a knife and fork is a norm in Western cultures; chopsticks or a spoon are the rule in the East. The implements have the same purpose: both respond to the need that there be something with which to feed oneself when eating with one's hands is a clumsier alternative. Needs become interests when, for example, the need for food becomes the refined taste for foods prepared and presented in a culture's style. But refinement, too, satisfies the generic need: good restaurants nourish their clients, even when this isn't their principal aim.

Determinables can be represented graphically. Imagine a blackboard covered with sixty-seven random marks. Each mark represents one of the sixty-seven cultural universals acknowledged by anthropologists.[2] (I ignore questions about the accuracy of their count.) Each is a generic practice—a norm—that satisfies needs divers as food, cooperation, protection, and information. Suppose, too, that we connect all the marks in ten or a thousand different ways. Each pattern of marks and connecting lines signifies that a culture has a distinct expression for each of the determinables, and that each expression is related normatively to the sixty-six others, directly or by way of intermediaries. Dance may have few significant relations to other practices within one culture, but many direct and vital relations in others.[3]

The idiosyncrasies of a pattern—diagonals, swirls, or a lattice of squares—obscure the identity of determinables across cultures. A culture's members are mystified by another's ways, or confused because they can't discern its style of relating the determinables. Yet, the determinables and their relations are discernible amidst the welter of idiosyncratic detail. So, friendship is a determinable, and Aristotle described three of its variations: friendships of pleasure, utility, or mutual esteem.[4] Other kinds of friendship are also conceivable: those based on kinship, shared belief, or partnership in a system, for example. Each style implicates different, companion determinables. Utilitarian friendships implicate work; those of pleasure promote marriage. But there is a constant. Friendship is mutual reliance in personal affairs. It invokes the duty of mutual loyalty and assistance, irrespective of cultural or social differences. Why are there variations that couple it to any of several other determinables? Because of circumstantial reasons that include the disparate environments where practical life evolved, hence each culture's distinctive ways of managing its affairs. Could there be cultures where friendship is always chilly and utilitarian? One imagines businesses where there is no other kind.

Our response to cultural differences is schismatic. Speaking as relativists we say that there is no way to judge fairly between or among a determinable's variable expressions: one spouse or many, for example. Or we despise cultural relativism for justifying immoral lives, often meaning lives different from our own. Is tolerance prescribed, because every such judgment wrongly implies that other people and their cultures should be judged by local standards? This would imply no judgments about the food, clothing, and morals of other cultures, and none they could make of us. An anthropology teacher once told me that he first experienced comfort in the tribe he was studying when he saw the beauty of ritual scars on the faces of the men. Critics of cultural relativism will respond that respect for a culture's decorative style needn't extend to tolerance for its morals: we don't excuse Hitler and Stalin as products of alien cultures.

How could we defend these critical judgments? One may respond that the superiority of our culture makes it an appropriate perspective for judging others. A better answer differentiates cultural determinables and their culture-specific expressions. Every culture satisfies generic interests that none can evade (including birth, death, nutrition, property, education, child rearing, sex, security, and social regulation), but each satisfies the determinables in ways peculiar to itself. Distinguishing the culturally specific style from the determinable thereby expressed, we can appraise behavior from either of two perspectives. Deferring to a determinable's culturally specific expression, we accept its norms, and judge accordingly: is it successful in its own terms. Judging a matter from the standpoint of the determinable, we take a position external to, and independent of the determinable's several or many expressions. We differentiate, for example, between the generic requirement for nourishment and its culturally specific variations. Emphasizing cultural differences, we describe recipes and preferred ingredients. Emphasizing the determinable, we ask if people are well fed. Doctors or physiologists can testify that they are or are not without respect to these stylistic differences. Social control requires that authority be vested in a state's officers, be they all its members, one, or a few. But the authority to regulate is a necessary social function, not an excuse for authoritarian abuse.

Seeing these two sides undercuts the tolerance for barbarism: distinguish cultural determinables from their expressions, then appraise those practices by considering their contribution to a people's viability and welfare. This distinction implies a cascade of questions, all of them presupposing that there is or can be a valid, culturally neutral criterion of human flourishing. We often affirm the contrary: that well-being is only and always culturally particular and determinate. We thrive as Greeks or Romans, not as generic humans. But this is a subtle error. Food is always particular; it has a specific content and form, but that is incidental. It is nourishment, not the idiosyncrasies of its cultural expression, that sustains us.

Flourishing is complex. It requires health, participation in core and other systems, and conditions that favor the expression of higher-order faculties, attitudes, and skills: books and schools, for example. The least conditions for bodily mainenance—so many hours of sleep, so many calories of food—are apparent across cultures. Determinate expressions for higher-order determinables—aesthetics, for example—are more contentious, because of our divers circumstances and because of cultural variations that favor wood carving or couture to poetry or song. There is also this uncertainty: flourishing is problematic, because the range of variation is unspecifiable. Its lower limit is firmly grounded in physical health, core systems, and the efficacies of practical life, but higher-order possibilities—including literacy, music, and scientific theorizing—are unknown until achieved. Our Stone Age ancestors couldn't imagine the tastes and talents that we count as essential to well-being. There may be talents and activities vital to our descendents that are unthinkable to us.

We often measure flourishing sequentially, determinable by determinable—first nourishment, then mental acuity, for example—though the integration of satisfiers is as critical as their character. This complicates cross-cultural comparison of flourishing, because there are many possible integrations—sixty-seven factorial for the sixty-seven determinables. Add that each determinable has several or many possible determinate expressions so that every integration may have an indefinite number of variations. Many integrations will be mutually anomalous, so that neither maps onto one or many others. (Which is preferable, a shorter, vital life or one that is longer but dull?) These considerations preclude both a single measure for flourishing and the comparison of individual integrations (one culture versus another). But we aren't reduced to silence, or obliged to stipulate what flourishing must be. For this is an empirical question, one answered by identifying its least conditions among the determinables, determinate values, and alternate integrations. Societies flourish, for example, when their constitutive, need-fulfilling systems—including government, businesses, and farms—are effectively managed. Individuals flourish when their talents are used in ways that are personally gratifying and socially useful. These effects have conditions that include love and work, health, friendship, peace, and factors that vary with the time of one's life: teachers in childhood, nurses later.

These two aims—personal and social flourishing—are distinguishable, even separable. Some people prosper though their society does not. A slave state may prosper for a time, though members pay for its success in their private lives. But flourishing is qualified when these two vary independently. Plato observed that personal and social well-being are mutually conditioning: a society flourishes, if and only if its social organization promotes individual well-being.[5] Small systems—families or villages—sometimes realize this ideal. It often evades larger ones: nation-states or cities, for example.

This strategy—distinguish determinables from their determinate expressions, then appraise the expressions for their contribution to well-being—reframes debate. It isn't enough to aver that we prefer our poison to theirs. Particular cultural styles are appraised—consequentially—from a standpoint that abstracts from them to ascertain their contribution to well-being. Are we nourished, whatever we eat; are we fit, however we play; do we have amiable relations to other, whatever the modes of cooperation? Distinguishing determinables from their satisfiers in order to determine the degree or quality of satisfaction is, nevertheless, contentious. It will delight antiabortionists who say that killing fetuses is bad for well-being, because it impairs a culture's ability to reproduce itself. But their objection oversimplifies. The prerogatives of women is a cross-cultural determinable, one whose determinate values are weighed in the balance with others. Autonomy for women is one such value. A stable, sufficient population is the value for a different determinable. Depopulating states may encourage pregnancy—using tax breaks or other advantages—without compelling it. What if these inducements make no difference to the birth rate? Then, corporate well-being or the well-being of many women will be diminished: the society will be enfeebled, or pregnancies will be coerced. This confirms something we already know: the conditions for personal and social well-being are complex and difficult to coordinate.

2. Aristotelian and Nietzschean Problems

Each of us is constrained by physical and social determinables that frame our places in nested systems, from the molecular through the cellular and bodily to the social and cultural. How can we tell in advance that a person or social system will tolerate a variation, or dissolve because of it: altered diet or marriage laws, for example? We need to know several things: conditions for the material well-being of the person or system; its relations to other systems, and the effect of altered circumstances on these two. This implies problems and solutions that may be Aristotelian or Nietzschean.[6] Aristotle is prudence. Nietzsche is imagination and risk. Both derive *ought* or *should* from *is*, with this difference: one emphasizes the is of experience, the other the *is* of imagination.

Aristotelian problems assume the stability of our circumstances, and the effectiveness of our solutions. Aristotelian projects are conservative. Their principle is a generalization of medical practice: do no harm. Understanding a system's structure and dynamics, knowing its place within a culture or society's settled practices, anticipating the likely effects of altering the system's constitutive norms and relations, we make incremental changes only. Aristotle believed that a culture's principal functions—its determinables—are plain, and that Hellenic expressions for them were mostly viable. He would fix a problem by altering a practice that usually works, if only imperfectly.[7] We raise or lower the accepted age for marriage, and, collaterally, we adjust practices that are directly linked to marriage: work and the care of children, for example.

Nietzsche demurred: cultural determinables are not a stable context particularized by time-tested solutions. Problems are Nietzschean when circumstances lack the stability—the inertia—of their materiality. No continuity is established by amending successive determinations, because reality, in itself, is Protean or formless. Human will prescribes form to a receptive void: there is no other stabilizing force.[8] Nietzschean solutions are radical, but vulnerable: they promise dramatic benefits, but threaten a system's stability. Circumstances may be hostile, or the systems we create may founder because of inherent but unknown structural flaws. Apparently good ideas may have consequences we rue. Stubborn will—our determination to make a comprehensible and satisfactory world—is Nietzsche's only defense against the flux.

Aristotelian solutions are sensitive to the reciprocities that sustain current systems. They search for normativity in the constitutive relations of systems, then tinker to make them work better. Nietzsche was contemptuous of every such solution, because he believed that people who need this stability—the "herd"—conflate *ought* with *is*. Their formulaic solutions and ossified social systems are defended reactively, however unresponsive to threats or ideals. Nietzsche would have us imagine our aims, then will and create conditions for their realization. Aristotle was equally confident that some *oughts* derive from *is*: family and civic duties, for example. He would remind us that Nietzschean solutions risk chaos. We shall be wrong more often than right. A succession of bad ideas will exhaust our capital, patience, and civil order. Yet, some developments encourage Nietzschean thinking. Molecular biology will make it possible to dispense with sexuality as we know it. Should we alter human genes to avert sexual travail? Efficiency might justify it; but there are other considerations, including the families that exist to produce, nurture, and educate children. Dare we jettison the familiar limits of these cultural determinables in the hope of a visionary equality and efficiency? People sometimes favor radical solutions when incremental, Aristotelian solutions seem grudging. But established ways have the advantage of supplying a normative, stable context in which to experiment.

Should slavery have ended incrementally, always taking care that we not get ahead of ourselves? Caution was unnecessary, because the dramatic change required in slave states was foreshadowed by civil society in other places, including other states of the Union: emancipation was not a shot in the dark. This is the example for molecular biology. Evolution supplies immanent biological norms, including the cultural variables. They are cross-linked in many ways: pull one thread, and the garment may unravel. We need to be conservative, never pretending to isolate a variable, when we don't know the consequences for other determinables if we alter its range of expressions. This isn't death to progress, merely the prudence of taking care where the ice is thin. But there is this other side. Careful, infinitely measured responses are retrograde when cultures are rigid and stale, because they don't change with altered circumstances and opportunities. Any change seems radical to people who fear everything unfamiliar. Variation is responsive and successful when it mixes incremental changes with radical innovations that work. Ideals that were imagined (and resisted) become norms. Too bad that we can't always predict the beneficial changes.

3. Change

People bemused by the strangeness of other cultures are surprised to learn that each is constrained by the same universals. This information is annoying if we bristle at the idea of immanent norms, believing that exemption from every limit is the hallmark of the good life. But annoyance is pointless, if cultural determinables—founded in the mechanics of human physiology and social practice—constrain us as surely as the laws of motion. Yet, cultural variables are more tolerant than those laws: every society expresses them in ways peculiar to itself. These two—constraining determinables and determinations more or less freely chosen or adapted—are the antitheses through which cultures and societies flow.

Radical change is graded. Body piercing seems odd to middle-aged men, though it is familiar to women, make-up artists, sailors, and other cultures. Encouraging polygamy or polyandry is still only imaginable; tolerating cannibalism is not. Acceptable changes satisfy three criteria: Altered expressions for a culture's determinables shouldn't destabilize or destroy core systems or their members. Changes should be viable in themselves. None should diminish an individual or system's compatibility with expressions for some of the sixty-six other determinables without enhancing compatibility with others. Body piercing and tattooing satisfy these tests, principally because they are trivial, though neither would survive anywhere if blood poisoning and death were their typical effects. The effects of polygamy and cannibalism are, respectively, bad and worse. Polygamy is bad, if one favors the equality of men and women in family life and beyond. Cannibalism destabilizes relations within a society, or it precludes relations with others.

Which changes should we welcome? What could we be that is better than what we are? Every culture could better integrate its practices: work and health with education, intelligence with cooperation. Most every expression for any culture's determinables could be improved. Imagine an illiterate culture that promotes literacy: people who don't read or write are encouraged to invent and use a written language, because it facilitates deliberations that give them unimagined control of their practical lives. Memory flourishes. Moral teaching is promoted when students read constitutions, moral arguments, histories, and novels. Now consider that our moral development may be incomplete. We, too, may have exploitable talents that are currently unknown. Morality was a feature of human life for millennia before the invention of writing, because systems and the obligations they promote were an everyday fact of life. But those lives were not moral in the respects that our lives are or can be, because the deliberations that literacy facilitates were unattainable then. It would be premature to say that literacy is the last latent talent having moral consequences. How do we bootstrap ourselves to a moral sensibility that currently exceeds us? We don't know.

Change is mostly puzzling when applied to the determinables themselves. Which of them can or should we modify? Are there desirable additions or subtractions? Human behavior is often primitive, because of our animal nature, but it will be our misfortune if bioengineers alter the human genome to make us work more efficiently, without regard for more ample interests. Their tinkering guarantees that we and our environment shall be different. Only the changes and their effects are uncertain. Consider, for example, biology's relative independence from cultural evolution. Biology supplied a framework that we humans couldn't significantly alter. Cultures could be elaborated over centuries without having to consider the possibility of significant changes in the biology of human populations or the environment (natural disasters and environmental degradation, apart). Now, when biological evolution accelerates under the propulsion of human intervention, culture may be incapable of adapting to unpredictable alterations in the biology of humans and our environment. What shall we do or be when human cleverness enables us to manipulate or eliminate both cultural and biological norms, leaving us vulnerable to *musts*, *shoulds*, and *oughts* that have imagination as their only basis?

CHAPTER SEVEN

Freedom

1. Positive and Negative Freedom

Freedom is our sacred word. It awes, intoxicates, and defends us. We praise it as a sanctuary and timeless right. This teleology ignores the historical changes that created our sense of entitlement. Six are critical: i. We say that God created us with free will so we might voluntarily observe his commandments. Yet, belief in a creator God is no longer the spindle about which every life turns. Skeptics don't believe that God is a presence in our lives. They do believe in free will. ii. Authoritarian political systems are anathema. Popular elections are a given in democratic states. Their citizens demand that government leave them alone, as typically it does. Civic duties reduce to voting, paying taxes, and serving (rarely) on juries. Some people do military service; but this is a choice. The arbitrary scrutiny of aliens is, we hope, a temporary aberration. iii. Poverty and drudgery are no longer pervasive. A thriving capitalist economy encourages initiative, and rewards talent. Its technology supplies machines for work and pleasure, the first to relieve odious tasks, the second to divert us. Many people can't escape dead-end jobs, but public rhetoric affirms that we or our children can find and thrive in other work. iv. Social relations are freer than before. Marriage is an arrangement, not an obligatory rite. We make friends across chasms of religion, race, or class that were once unbridgeable. v. A Great Community would temper our freedom in the name of the greater good by creating obligations to one another and the state. But the hope of universal solidarity is no longer inspiring, because the conditions for achieving it in the Soviet

231

Union were despotic. vi. The foregoing considerations are generic or global. This last consideration is personal and idiosyncratic. A saying has it that "Other people are hell." One wants a space for psychic repose. This desire may seem odd given that selfhood emerges in the midst of core and other systems, but the emergent self, aware of its social origins, wants barriers that limit intrusions, boundaries in which to deliberate and choose.

The first five of these obstacles to freedom are mostly vanquished in the West, though several are remembered fondly by people who want them restored. Some changes feel tentative and insecure, because they are new. All five are, nevertheless, perceived as a universal standard, because we shrink from imagining these histories reversed: we say no to theocracy, autocracy, poverty and indentured servitude, social barriers, and the utopian ideal used to justify a totalitarian bureaucracy.

Freedom in all six respects is real and transforming. But notice the version of freedom achieved by these changes. Each is a negative freedom, freedom from a disfiguring condition. Social doors once closed are open; psychic windows are shaded: we are free to do or be as we choose. The crux is here: systems that restricted liberty also provided contexts for choice and rewards for approved choices. There were partners for our undertakings, or circumstances that authority decreed. Personal identity and position were assured, however diminished our status. Before, we had little choice, but a rich context. Now, one has little context, but the freedom to create a place and identity of one's own. Experiencing oneself as free has become a personal imperative. Reliance on others—dependence—is weakness, moral failure. Nietzsche is the philosopher of the day, because his emphasis on the will and its world-making powers is the persuasion required by every self-made man or woman: we decide what to be and how to become it. But uncertainties remain: What are we to do with positive freedom? Is it sufficient to create both a self and the context appropriate to expressing worthy aims and interests when traditional supports have lapsed? Relativists won't like the qualification, *worthy*. Libertarians will be startled by the implied irresolution: we have freedom; they would have us defend and use it. Do things that secure and satisfy you, knowing that your constructive deeds also benefit people you affect. They want your help, as you want theirs. They will read what you write and hear what you say. Bootstrap yourself to stability, judgment, and well-being.

These responses leave principal issues unresolved. What shall we value, do, and be? How shall we find partners we can trust? Having the freedom to decide these things doesn't, itself, provide them. Hence, these questions: What are the conditions for having and using positive freedom? How is it frustrated or diminished if its conditions don't obtain?

2. Alternative Ontologies

Having freedom, we are quick to exploit it, usually without knowing its conditions. We let ideologists fill the space where accurate representation and understanding should go, though their "truths" about our character and circumstances are usually affirmed rather than tested. Hypotheses are true or false, given evidence for or against them. The ideologies proposing that we express freedom in one or another way are recommendations: they express preferences. Telling what we should be, they describe us in terms—whether utopian or despairing—that are often more fantastical than real. This bias is costly when freedom and its context are the matters at issue; freedom is harder to achieve if self-understanding is distorted because we and our context are misdescribed. Hence these questions: Who are we; what are we capable of doing and being? What are we free to do and be in the circumstances that currently obtain? What would we be free to do or be if circumstances were altered in specified ways?

Atomism, holism, and communitarianism are three hypotheses about our context, whether physical, biological, or social. One imagines eclectic combinations: an atomist in physics, holist in biology, communitarian when describing human social systems. This is possible, though arguments for or against each of the hypotheses are equally feeble or effective at each of these levels. It simplifies the issue and loses nothing dialectically if we suppose that each hypothesis is proposed as the right account for phenomena of all three levels. Why require that we decide among the three? Because we can't think clearly about freedom without having a clear idea of its context. Freedom without ontology implies freedom in the void.

Which hypothesis is true? Atomism postulates that individuals are separate and self-sufficient. Each goes his or her way. People do this more effectively than atoms, because we have perception, foresight, and intentions. But we, like atoms, are self-propelling. Neighbors to either side welcome us when we rent a space and open a store between them. Sharing our view that God helps those who help themselves, they are helpful, but distant and discrete. Employees we hire are equally incidental to our concerns, apart from the work they do. They have other lives, and, even within our business, other tasks. Subtle mores avert collisions by defending each one's space. We are careful not to harm other people, and are or ought to be free from their intrusions. Traffic laws are the signal example of atomist lives: we go alone or with only a few others, even when going, for a time, in the same direction. Atomism says that such laws and occasional shared interests are the principal social binders.

Holism inverts every atomist assumption. No one is alone, no one lacks a context, because each has a role that connects him or her, directly or indirectly, to every other. What are negative and positive freedom in these circumstances? None fears the intrusions of others, because each is busy doing the work of his role. This is negative freedom—freedom from interference—in the service of positive freedom: the power (talent and skill) and opportunity (circumstances and resources) to do the tasks appropriate to one's position in the whole. Do them knowing that the rest of us support you. Indeed, we give more than support. Like the interlocking pieces of a jigsaw puzzle, we who surround you delimit the place you occupy. Our relationship is your context: every other person is implicated in your role and the identity you acquire by filling it.

Think of people waiting on a crowded subway platform. Trains come and go. People get on or off, but nothing passes among them. No context encourages talk or civility. Fear is suppressed but pervasive: someone falling might be trampled or hit by a train. Holism would have us believe that things are better than they look. Every next person is looking out for your welfare as well as his own. It couldn't be otherwise if each person needs every other. For the system of roles is a delicate mechanism: no single part works, unless all work together. Parts that fail are replaced immediately (or the parts reorganize), so the whole functions as before.

Systems theory, communitarianism, objects that holists such as Leibniz compress an array of systems—some mutually independent, others reciprocally related—into a single network.[1] He argued that every contingent particular is a partition or shard of God's infinite mind, and that all are integrated by pervasive internal relations: each affects and is (as though) affected by every other. (This qualification—as though—provides for the autonomy of monads.) Less comprehensive relations would bespeak God's inability to integrate the multiplicity of things he creates, hence an imperfection contrary to his nature. This hypothesis is confounded by time: things to come do not influence those preceding them. Leibniz answers that time is unreal to the God who perceives everything at once. But this complicates the story without saving it. For how does God relate to the whole he thinks: does the postulate of internal relations also apply to their relationship? If yes, God is affected by the contingent world created within himself. If not, God is limited by the world that stands apart from him. Either way, God is not God: he is finite, not infinite because affected or limited by the world he creates. A suggestive postulate becomes a dialectical embarrassment.

Atomism, too, has unacknowledged theological origins. Its notion of individuality derives from Augustine and Descartes: we think and have free will, because God has endowed us with powers like his own. Souls or minds are partitions, shards, of the infinite One. They are mutually independent, because self-sufficient in every respect but one: the contingency of their existence makes them dependent on God, their maker and cause. Few contemporary individualists formulate their views in these terms, but the gravitas, the near sanctity, of the autonomy claimed for thinkers and moral beings intimates its origin. How is belief in our autonomy undermined? Merely by adducing empirical evidence that humans are neither mutually independent nor self-sufficient. Bodies need food and warmth; education requires language and the community where we learn and use it. Here, too, a postulate partly inspired by theological assumptions is subverted empirically.

Communitarianism starts as an innocent observation: things are connected spatially, temporally, and causally. Every thing—any molecule or human body—is a system constituted by the reciprocal causal relations of its parts. Each system is a module: its internal reciprocities establish both its identity and its relative autonomy. Atomism fails, because each system is embedded in the network of reciprocities that bind it to one, several, or many others. Relations to them are mediated by the functional membrane that filters their effects, but independence is qualified because these relations establish the higher-order systems in which constituent systems participate: atoms in molecules, individual persons in families or teams. Holism fails, because hierarchies of nested systems are often mutually independent. Kinship relations on Mars have no effect on those in Philadelphia. My neighbors' religious beliefs have no effect on mine.

Atomism and holism misrepresent reality at every order of complexity. There are no internal relations that make the existence and character of each thing a function of every other. Nothing is self-sufficient: even protons require an environment that tolerates (fails to disrupt) their internal bonds. There is relative autonomy—modularity—and there is an array of systems, some that are nested or overlapping, others that are mutually independent. Systems theory accurately describes this mix of autonomy and context. Its hypothesis is the baseline for a discussion of freedom.

We have a better answer now for the questions that motivate this section: Why is ontology pertinent to freedom? Because freedom of choice and action implicates the network of systems in which we participate: no one acts or chooses in a plenum or void. Filling, creating, or rejecting a role, we discover two things: systems that form, stabilize, or dissolve, and the character—the habits, beliefs, and attitudes—that forms in us as we participate in them. This tension is freedom's context: people of established but alterable character live and work in circumstances that are rigid in some respects, pliable in others. These two—character and context—are the inviolable limits to negative freedom: no one is free of either. But neither is formless or fixed, and neither fits the other like lock and key. There is negative freedom—slippage—in systems too complex or clumsy to coerce every participant. There is positive freedom—leverage—in contexts that supply the people or things appropriate to one's talents or dreams.

3. Free Will

Positive freedom implies free will, but what could that be if we assume the principle of sufficient reason, hence pervasive determinism? Why call choices mine if all I am and do is a moment in one strand in the cosmic world line? The distinction of positive and negative freedom also needs rethinking if nothing is exempt from determination by its antecedents and context.

We justify this distinction by considering the modularity of systems. They form in circumstances that supply vital information, energy, and materiel, yet every system has a degree of autonomy—living systems, especially, are self-sustaining—because each is cocooned by the reciprocal causal relations that create it. Modularity implies an internal economy, one that requires specific resources. Systems respond selectively by filtering inputs in ways appropriate to their safety and needs. Turn away or close your eyes and annoyances may disappear. Reciprocities that filter inputs don't eliminate determining conditions: gravity, work, and noisy neighbors may be constants. Negative freedom originates here, where some things are ignored because they are inimical or useless to a system's welfare. Reduce political and social intrusions—in the six ways cited above—and we fortify modularity by exempting systems from constraints that diminish their freedom of action.

Positive freedom—implying free will and choice—comes with the elaboration of human systems. Infants have a degree of choice when autonomic behavior is subject to the over-ride of controls called *voluntary*. But voluntary actions are not undetermined. They mediate between stimuli and automatic responses in the matter described by Dewey's paper on the reflex arc:[2] actions are inhibited or initiated because of information or interests additional to factors that would incite automatic responses. These additional causes—and the newly formed hierarchy of neural or neuro-muscular formations they provoke—enhance the options for choice. For what is education or nutrition if not the external cause of internal formations that have liberating effects? Speech requires new connections and pathways in an infant's evolving brain, but there is more freedom and more control when a child exchanges information or makes plans with others by speaking. This new ability is a condition for choice, but an effect of determination.

Volition—will—is the activation or inhibition of neural circuits. The stimulus may originate externally (something heard) or internally (a mood, thought, or memory). Free will is the activation or inhibition of higher-order neural subsystems that control other neural or muscular functions. The action may be internal—private—or overt. Walking—at a pace and in a direction of one's choice—is an expression of free will. Writing is also a choice, though the flow of words and ideas is not subject to voluntary control. Editing is freer: there is more choice and control, but less invention. Both are expressions of positive freedom: each is the activity of an acquired internal formation. Either may be activated by a stimulus generated internally. We often suppose that free choice is conscious and self-conscious, and this may usually or always be true, but self-consciousness, too, is hierarchical: one subsystem reads and controls others. Yet all subsystems are neural, and each is connected to some or many others, so higher-order systems responsible for self-consciousness or free will are affected by others including those they control. Making a choice, one reads its effect in order to calculate the next choice.

This formulation construes free will in the spirit of soft-determinism. It gives no credit to the conscious evidence for free will—acting when and as one wants—because these obscure feelings provide no access to the whole complement of their neural conditions. The evidence of consciousness raises a question—what is free will—but making it one's sole point of reference all but guarantees question-begging answers: wanting to be free, we contrive reasons for believing we are. We extrapolate, for example, from chaos or quantum theories, though chaos theory is deterministic (small differences in initial conditions make a considerable difference to latter effects, but their evolution is determined) while quantum theorists say that quantum indeterminacies wash out at larger scales. Why are these indeterminacies nevertheless chronic in brains? Is there evidence for them in the transmission of signals across neurons responsible for choice, or is this—for want of evidence—an ad hoc rationale for free will? Other arguments for free will are only conceptual. Rethinking Aristotle's claim that there is no truth or falsity to claims about tomorrow's sea battle—nothing is decided—we choose among possible predictions about the future. Strict determinism is defeated, it is alleged, because our expectation cannot have been determined by a state of affairs which hasn't yet come to pass. Yet, the future is incidental (determined or not), because the choice of predictions is determined by causes or by reasons (acting as causes) in a present that is fully conditioned. Why say categorically that choice is wholly determined? Because empirical and conceptual evidence strongly confirms it. Indeterminacy is a serious challenge to classical ideas about sufficient reason. But all the alleged indeterminacies currently proposed, those of quantum theory included, are responsibly doubted.

Those mooted by the sciences are misappropriated when used to vindicate moral or political commitments to freedom. Robert Kane makes his objective explicit:

> Libertarians and incompatibilists do not want indeterminism for its own sake. If the truth be told, indeterminism is something of a nuisance for them. It gets in the way and creates all sorts of trouble. What they want is ultimate responsibility, and *ultimate responsibility requires indeterminism.*[3]

This partisan candor is alarming, if one believes that philosophy is disinterested inquiry: it recalls theists who use philosophy to confirm that there must be a God of the sort they favor. Such arguments rarely or never do the work for which they are designed. Solutions invented to save free will—processes that are "macro-indeterminate as a result of amplification of micro-indeterminacies in the brain"[4]—compound a simple error: we want to believe that the euphoric sense of choosing freely is veridical and unconditioned. But neural circuits have only two settings: on or off. A signal is or is not strong enough to provoke the activation or inhibition of associated ganglia. The idea of neural indeterminacy seems to have no basis but its role in Kane's argument.

Soft determinism—especially the emphasis on modularity—allays fear that each person has no resources with which to resist the tide of determinations running through him or her to a distant end. Each of us selects among his or her inputs, and each engages other things under personal control. But there is no disguising the implication that every state and process within us has a history of sufficient conditions. What is moral responsibility if every choice is fully conditioned? The determinist answer has two parts: Seeing the autonomy of human systems, we hold one another responsible for duties assumed and affirmed. Yet, we acknowledge universal determination, so moral appraisals are as much aesthetic as judgmental. Sensitive to duty and law, we favor people and actions that observe them. But core attitudes are mostly formed by the age of ten. They are not easily changed short of vigorous intrapsychic struggle, punishments or inducements that inhibit pernicious inclinations. We see conduct as it is—the aesthetic attitude—without being able to do more than deter, rather than alter, those who do it.

Is this response—approving or reproving the attitudes or conduct of other people or oneself—an expression of taste? No, like the desire that beliefs be true, it expresses a point of view determined by persistent reality testing: we prefer that human behavior satisfy duties and rules that make life viable. We are morally educable—training in the obligations of social life is similar to instruction for any skill—but we learn morality early. Failure is costly: one is excused for never learning to drive, not for chronic thieving. Could failure have been averted? It might have been had the thief or his circumstances been different: there are myriad counterfactuals. But all are incidental, because history is a record of sufficient conditions, hence evidence that there was little he could have done to alter his core attitudes and orientation. One gets credit or blame (aesthetic or judicial) for one's acts and their effects, not for having chosen one's character.

4. Positive Freedom: Character and Opportunity

Positive freedom has two conditions: a character empowered by talent, habit, or desire and the opportunity supplied by one's context. One isn't free to play the piano unless one has skill and a piano. Negative freedoms are assumed, because positive freedom is impaired (as it always is to some degree) without them.

Character is cognitive-affective posture.[5] It develops as one participates in the families, friendships, and schools where information, attitudes, and habits are acquired. What do I believe? What can I do; how ably and reliably do I do it? What do I favor, or resist? Answers come as we participate in systems that teach and test us. People growing up in desert tribes don't learn to swim. There are no shortstops where baseball isn't played. Context explains both sorts of incompetence. It also explains one's skills: a boatman's children learn to row or sail. Finesse of one sort facilitates others: musicians are better able to play the music of composers inspired by folk rhythms if they grow up knowing the dances. Character evolves as I distinguish myself from my roles, reflecting on them and my aims. It matures as I join or help to create the systems that engage my talents and time. I don't choose my place in the birth order of siblings; I can resist an arranged marriage.

An evolving character is part of the context for subsequent growth: we bootstrap ourselves to more character on the basis of the character we have. For the dialectic of participation and appraisal is constant: What are we doing and why? Is it good for others? Is it good for me? Conflicts between early roles—family and friendship—force us to distinguish roles from one another, and oneself from the roles. Autonomy emerges with development, because one is more and more aware that he or she controls the terms of participation to some degree. Awareness is intensified when reciprocities that create a system break down, perhaps because the members' aims diverge. Every such experience heightens the sense that I participate in systems because of affirming or accepting their terms, not because they could not be resisted. Or I do what a system requires because I lack the power to do otherwise, though I quietly repudiate its aims. I am its captive, not its creature.

Each of us is a center of reflection and choice. Both pilot and navigator of our private lives, we compare our aims to those of systems that engage us. Where the match is good, we are loyal members. Find a discrepancy, and we rethink the terms of engagement, weighing the costs of withdrawal to oneself and valued others. This posture—engaged but separate—is the all but certain outcome of participating in several systems at once. But autonomy is a crippling fantasy, if we insist, impossibly, that every affiliation must have irreproachable, justifying reasons. For opportunity does not require the void of the atomists or the closed system of the holists. Its three conditions—*context, resources, and a reconciling interpretation*—are individually necessary and jointly sufficient.

Context has eleven variables: i. systems in which one participates; ii. personal health or illness, and the health of one's core or other systems; iii. economic organization and productivity; iv. civil peace and stability; v. physical topography and climate; vi. culture; vii. technology; viii. conventional laws; ix. logical and natural laws; x. personal and social history; and xi. conflict. Some, though not all, may be incidental to any particular expression of freedom.

i. The *systems in which one participates* include one's family and state, and every system established (friendships or marriage), joined (schools or work), or acknowledged (a religious sect). Systems are the incubator of personal identity, hence character, intellectual style, skills, sensibility, and choice. They supply differentiated roles, then allow or encourage us to choose roles appropriate to our talents. Inheriting or acquiring responsibilities to them and their other members, they require us to balance choice with obligation. Duties qualify freedoms of both sorts, but they needn't be onerous. We are not free to do as we like while ignoring duties to core or other systems, but these systems may be sanctuaries if they free us of other demands and intrusions. Families do this (ideally) for all their members, children especially; states do it (ideally) for their citizens. Members sometimes rebel at this constriction, though a taste of experience without this buffer is often enough to convince them that life is better in partnerships that supply it.

ii. *Personal health or illness* facilitates or limits initiative and one's ability to learn or fill a role. Or it determines the manner of one's responses to a role's demands. Not seeing well, a child doesn't learn to read. That restricts the roles he fills and degrades his self-esteem: he isn't free to read or free from the embarrassment he feels. The health of core and other systems—their sustainable equilibrium—is critical to the well-being of their members: parents rightly worry that divorce or bad schools will injure their children.

iii. *Economic organization and productivity* affect systems of all sorts, because they supply the goods and services that enable systems to function. They are decisive, too, because a society's modes of production enable it to support and secure its members, while restricting the work available to them: sheepherding and shearing are not realistic options in Manhattan. It does have bars and dance halls, lawyers, and construction companies. They promise freedom from want, and an inventory of choices appropriate to specialized talents. Access to the system is critical. The rich are different, because they have money, but the poor are different too. They can't plan or otherwise stabilize their lives. Vulnerability to illness and depression, lethargy or resentment is keener in them.

iv. Everyone approves of *civil peace and stability*, at least for himself and his friends. Hobbes wrote his *Leviathan* to argue that there is no freedom or efficient social organization without civic harmony.[6] People having it are oblivious to the difference it makes. Those who do not are tortured or numb for want of it. Both effects are decisive for the formation of character and systems.

v. The *physical topography and climate* of our circumstances affect both character and the systems people establish. They shape our opportunities—fishing or farming, for example—and limit our projects. First-time sailors are seasick. Country people are disoriented in cities. We embody the places where character evolves. Systems, too, are appropriate to their circumstances: Botswana doesn't have a navy.

vi. *Culture* is the subtle context that invades and shapes everything we think, feel, or do. Language, sport, or politics, city, family, or farm: there is no evading it. Violate a culture's regulative principles—its mores, rules, or laws—and you make yourself conspicuous. No matter that the norms are loose and variable. Think of slang or fashion: people who know the rules are acutely sensitive to those who do not. It happens occasionally that someone in authority decrees a standard that becomes a norm (the Spanish lisp). More often, cultural norms emerge from the give and take of people and systems. Baseball was played for a time to the design of its maker; but the game has evolved. Children who play it use the new rules: the adult game is their paradigm and context. Clever innovations in the Japanese or Cuban game would prompt us to modify ours. Context isn't less inclusive for being international.

vii. Technology may be perceived as an aspect of culture, but technologies quickly spread from cultures that generate them to others that apply them: airplanes are commonplace in many cultures and societies where they could not have been invented.

viii. Conventional laws—including tax, marriage, or traffic laws—determine the limits and modalities of action. Their message is implicit: one who falls within the domain of the law will act as it prescribes.

ix. Logical and natural laws (more, fundamentally, the dispositions of things) are the developmental context for character and every other state or process. We ride the waves, accommodating to circumstances assembled as laws determine. Or we are alchemists who learn what laws permit, then organize to exploit them.

x. Personal and social history are implicit in one's current posture and circumstances. Choice is constrained by formations having unknown origins, and by the memory of past successes and failures.

xi. Conflict is endemic, because individuals must choose among the competing requirements of systems that engage them and because systems compete for scarce resources and opportunities. Like climate and topography, it is stubborn and enduring: we mitigate, but never cure it. But conflict, like other aspects of context, is equivocal. It may be a condition for positive freedom (employing the skills of a mediator, for example), though, more often, it is one of the factors from which the negative freedom of an ideal world would exempt us.

The *resources* required for using a talent or skill may be construed as contextual goods—they may be counted under any of the eleven aspects of context—but they deserve separate mention: no reading without light, books, or papers.

A *reconciling interpretation* integrates character and resources with context. There are obstacles and priorities—red and green traffic lights—everywhere. Each of us integrates and construes them, telling a story about reality and its valences: where am I safe, where endangered, what is or is not appropriate in my circumstances? The story we tell neutralizes some of our vulnerabilities, though conjuring it intensifies them if there is a spreading gap between reality and interpretation. This is dangerous but not always fatal: someone bold in adverse circumstances may succeed despite his inaccurate maps, because things change, unforeseeably, to his advantage. Every interpretation is suffused with hopes and fears, many of

them unacknowledged. They explain both the disparity between interpretations and reality, and their resistance to decisive empirical tests.
Expressing one's history, attitudes, and expectations—persistent though
mistaken—interpretations are slow to change.

Opportunity is a function of context, resources, and interpretation.
Or we construe it more amply as the complex of these three plus character: what might be done given what I understand of myself and my
situation? Circumstances mix rigid structures that won't change with
opportunities for altering old systems or forming new ones. One implies
stasis, the other encourages innovation. There are stable cultures where
change is imperceptible or slow. Limited imagination, ample resources,
and a reconciling interpretation of their place in the world explain this
people's reluctance to change. Other cultures are self-transforming. Innovation can't be programmed, but it is facilitated by the cross talk of
people who leapfrog one another on the way to something new. Science
and technology have this effect among us. Our systems are pliable; we are
restless and adaptable.

Each of the foregoing variables is suffused with norms. This is
explicit with cultural norms and laws; but it is also true of the others,
with this difference remarked in chapter 2. Some norms—the laws of
logic—apply universally: they establish the domain of possibilities.
Others are parochial necessities: they apply within this world, but not in
others that are possible. Customs and conventional laws are all the more
specific: customs distinguish a culture whatever its national borders; conventional laws apply within a jurisdiction (Illinois, but not Iowa; Peoria,
but not Chicago). These are successively restricted, large-scale dimensions of context. Others are more circumscribed. My situation is shared
with the people of my city, but it narrows to the scale of my small house,
my family, and friends. Health and character are only mine. Norms as
local as these are particular and contingent, but they constrain me as
fully as the laws of logic. The design of my rooms dictates their possible
uses; character limits my choices. *Musts* are everywhere overlaid with
shoulds and *oughts*.

This cascade of limits is a nested set of contexts. Positive freedom is
qualified accordingly. I am free to do such things as skill and opportunity
permit, or somewhat more if I am willful and lucky. I can do nothing at
all in a void where there are no limits, but also no possibilities. Context—resistance and leverage—is freedom's necessary condition. My freedom is shaped by this complex of factors: I cannot do or be any- and

everything, or merely what you can do and be. We neglect these nested conditions, because the stability of many situations justifies ignoring it. But then circumstances betray us. Everything favors lunch in the garden, until the weather changes. Hopes prosper, until health fails. It then seems miraculous that context was, for a while, both propitious and invisible.

Before, our preoccupation with liberty was focused by considerations cited at the top of this chapter: theology, autocracy, poverty, and social biases quashed the freedom to act in one's interest. Now, with these conditions altered, we emphasize freedom without realizing that its reference is uncertain. Do we celebrate freedom from repression, or the fantasy that choice and action have no context?

5. Pathologies of Freedom

The dissolution of traditional constraints is wrongly construed as the new and desirable exemption from every norm. License—do what you like—is a crude response. Others are more subtle, and they, too, are evidence that we are deceived. Philosophy is complicit. Its idealists say that context is a deception: reality is a blank slate, one that takes whatever form is projected onto it by the theory or interpretation used to think it. Previous generations believed that context and constraint were appropriate or inevitable, because they were propagandized by stories congenial to priests or kings. We prosper, because a skeptical wind has blown away their myths. Reality has no differentiations and relations but those introduced by the conceptual systems used to create a thinkable experience. Does your situation seem unyielding? Liberate yourself by rethinking it.

This program, so evocative of Rousseau—"Man is born free but is everywhere in chains"—is the responsibility in our time of philosophers who describe themselves as *pragmatists*. The name signifies that thought is hardheaded—realistic—and practical, though the conceptualizations used to create thinkable worlds are neither. They schematize reality in ways congenial to a thinker's interests. They promise fresh air, but the choice they offer is suffocating: we can address the void—reality as it is without the intervention of a theory that gives it differentiations and relations (character)—or we can replace a current world-making interpretation with one or a sequence of others, each formed to gratify an interest or desire. This power comes in three steps Kant cited in the *Critique of Judgment*: specify, perhaps justify your desires; choose appropriate empirical schemas; then create thinkable objects by using the schemas to differentiate and organize sensory data. Create any world that suits you, up to the point of contradiction.[7]

Pragmatists who endorse this project concede no reality but the one (or many) of our interpretations. But interpretation is selective. Never wanting to sabotage ourselves, we construe reality in ways that make it amenable to our interests. Not everyone is as sanguine. William James wrote "The Will to Believe," but he was careful to distinguish the effects of will from the hard facts of mathematics and science.[8] Peirce and Dewey were also pragmatic, but they emphasized initiatives that couple us to a world we do not make.[9] These earlier thinkers expressed and justified the muscular experimentalism of nineteenth-century American experience. Neither doubted that frustration, error, and death are the evidence of contexts that resist us. Pragmatists of the late twentieth century express the triumphalism of a people whose recent experience confirms that, sometimes, reality is made, not encountered. But how is it made? This is a place where philosophy and life diverge. The new pragmatists suppose that reality derives from texts and talk:

> Truth isn't outside power. . . . Truth is a thing of this world: it is produced only by virtue of multiple forms of constraint. And it induces regular effects of power. Each society has its regime of truth, its "general politics" of truth: that is, the types of discourse which it accepts and makes function as true: the mechanisms and instances which enable one to distinguish true and false statements, the means by which each is sanctioned; the techniques and procedures accorded value in the acquisition of truth; the status of those who are charged with saying what counts as true.[10]

> This hard saying [Sartre's "In reality, things will be as much as man has decided they are"] brings out what ties Dewey and Foucault, James and Nietzsche, together—the sense that there is nothing deep down inside us except what we have put there ourselves, no criterion that we have not created in the course of creating a practice, no standard of rationality that is not an appeal to such a criterion, no rigorous argumentation that is not obedience to our conventions. A post-Philosophical culture,

then, would be one in which men and women felt themselves alone, merely finite, with no links to something Beyond.[11]

Truth itself gets its life from our criteria of rational acceptability, and these are what we must look at if we wish to discover the values which are really implicit in science.[12]

'Every fact is value loaded and every one of our values loads some fact.'[13]

You don't like your neighbors or the laws of physics? No problem. They are posits of your interpretation. Tell a different story, and they disappear.

A second gesture is more effective. It, too, has the effect of shaking our reasonable belief that each of us is located in nested hierarchies of constraint, from logic and natural laws at one extreme, to the idiosyncrasies of character, work, and local weather at the other. This program construes every vital service or product as a commodity and every place of exchange as a market. It would have us purge every system that interferes with "market mechanisms," including monopolies and traditional village economies. The deleterious effects on liberty are obscured, because we often elide the freedoms required for participation in market economies with those of political freedom. We believe with Hayek[14] that markets promote the competition, tolerance, and flexibility that nourish democratic regimes, though China is evidence that market economies do not require or create the civic freedoms of an open society. Labor, resources, investment capital, banking and legal systems, management, deregulation, competition, initiative, and buyers are jointly sufficient for one, but not the other. Only free markets—not the political freedoms of an open society—concern us now.

Market economies promote health, literacy, the welfare of women, and (sometimes) democratic practices. They reduce poverty and dissolve traditional biases because merit—not race or gender—generates profit. They reward initiative and encourage the devolution of moral authority from religious teachers to individual scruples. Markets are admirable for all these reasons, yet freedom is reduced when markets diminish character and opportunity by homogenizing and regimenting contexts where taste and intelligence are acquired and expressed. Thought requires the stimulus of ideas that are freely heard, considered, and exchanged, but ideas languish, and thought is impaired when publishers, even university presses, insist that unprofitable books cannot be published, because publishers, too, are businesses obliged to earn their way. The Internet may save ideas from oblivion by replacing traditional publishers, but this is a fortuitous effect of computer technology and marketing. How long before it, too, is subordinated to market imperatives?

Market effects are framed by six considerations: i. the utility of markets for some economic purposes versus the belief that markets are the appropriate organizational mode for every vital social function; ii. conflicts that result when interests at one scale of systemic organization (individual persons) oppose interests of another scale (businesses, for example); iii. the myth that markets are the guarantor of social fluidity and freedom; iv. the difficulty of acknowledging market costs when benefits are conspicuous; v. the impotence of political regulation in local communities when transnational companies control their economic well-being, and vi. my claim that positive freedom is a function of character and the opportunities afforded by one's context. The sixth point is assumed. Its bearing on the five prior considerations is the issue to be clarified.

i. *The value of markets for some economic activities versus the belief that markets are the appropriate organizational mode for all vital social functions.* Thinkers impressed by our ability to plan—Plato and Hegel, for example—believed that individual and corporate well-being is enhanced when states enact projects that are bold and well-conceived. Centrally organized governments and command economies are their heirs. But this claim depends too much on analogy: controls appropriate to a family on a tight budget aren't efficient in large societies. Interests are too divers, the allocation of resources is too slow for efficient production or distribution. Command economies are less flexible, less responsive, and more wasteful than market economies, because the powers centralized in one are dispersed in the other. Let buyers and sellers find one another. Having initiative, goods, or cash, eager to deal, each perceives and responds to opportunities that would be invisible in a centralized economy. But market economies, too, are inefficient, because wasteful. Wanting things to sell, creating demand, then producing to fill it, business makes and sells more than buyers need. Like a firestorm feeding on itself, we use and degrade vital capital resources—the environment, for example.

We don't notice the cost, because we are distracted by the near term advantage: market economies are vastly profitable to entrepreneurs and workers, alike. Both can have things and services that make them healthier, better educated, and more secure. Yet, profit is subverting when it becomes our only motive. This is less apparent if wealth is widely distributed: your well-being comes at no cost to mine. Still, the elision of wealth and well-being is insidious. Recall Aristotle's three kinds of friendship: those based on utility, affection, and mutual respect. Aristotle ignored friendships that emerge between or among people engaged in systems they value. This is the fellowship of citizens signified in French by *fraternité*. Its sense is generalized without distortion: civic friendship is expressed as the generosity and mutual respect of people engaged reciprocally in activities impelled by shared interests. They know one another's skills, temperament, and idiosyncrasies, because they depend on one another to do the work of their respective roles. This bond is familiar to spouses, team-, and workmates. Extrapolate, and it includes the relations of parents and children. Fellowship is practical, not only sentimental. Its aim is effective solidarity, for it creates the core systems where life's principal work is done. Friendships of this sort are not inimical or hostile to profit, but that is not their primary aim. Aristotle may have supposed that such friendships are merely utilitarian, though he prized effects they enhance or create, including moral virtue and solidarity.

Markets eviscerate fellowship. Subordinating it to profit, efficiency, and the idea of freedom, we turn cynical about duties that once seemed inviolable. Responsibility to others comes to be perceived as a burden: one wants exemption from duties to them and shared systems. Society seems vigorous—initiative is everywhere—but personal relations wither, because no one aware of his own opportunism trusts the friendship or respect evinced by others. Character is altered and reduced. We get social atoms—isolated persons—where previously there was fellowship in core systems. This first seems a boon to freedom. Constraints are few; there are innumerable opportunities. The unbounded, nearly empty space of Newtonian cosmology is reinterpreted as the space of economic activity: do as you like while doing no harm, and you are or ought to be free to go your way without interference.

Yet, free markets are a different context for social purpose and activity, not the bare cupboard where every context is eliminated. Business is conducted within an ecosystem of deeply nested, overlapping hierarchies of evolving systems, including factories and banks, companies that transport goods, and networks that communicate information. Businesses are free to buy or sell, invent, produce, or invest, but they are everywhere constrained by opportunities determined by their relations to clients, suppliers, or competitors. Each defends its more or less stable niche. Atomist rhetoric would have us believe that any interest or motive detracting from or interfering with honest exchange—buying and selling—is incidental to the market's purpose. Let nothing impede the enterprise of those who are careful not to damage others while pursuing their commercial interests. Deregulate: clear the petty rules that reduce freedom by petrifying initiative. This slogan is more posturing than persuasion. Markets are laced with norms: banking laws, rules that govern interstate or foreign commerce, laws that protect contracts and the safety of workers, laws against anticompetitive practices, and laws that make businesses responsible for renewing or protecting resources. These, too, are constraints. They limit choice when alliances for mutual advantage have displaced fellowship.

Profit and freedom are two of the three principal benefits markets are said to promote. Globalization is often a shorthand justification for the third, market efficiency: the larger the client base, the greater the economies (and profit) of production and distribution. We are encouraged not to resist when businesses of various sorts establish the global market in which all may flourish. Adam Smith's marketplace of relatively small competitors[15] seems quaint to business leaders who organize companies that reach across borders. Imagine them having political power sufficient to organize economic space any way that suits them. Would they prize and maintain a free market, an open playing field that guarantees access to any agent with the daring and means to pursue an idea? It isn't unlikely that business conditions would be transformed because rationalized: meaning, organized and supplied by a small number of dominant producers. It would resemble an open market much as zoos resemble the wild.

This would be a mixed blessing, still only fractionally realized, because a market dominated by companies having mutual interests and polite understandings would be a bureaucratized and sclerotic command economy. Producing to fill created demands, it would tell consumers what to buy. Companies that would dominate such an economy might be efficient and profitable. The benefits to individual workers would be considerable, but equivocal. Poverty would likely be reduced, and equality promoted: many of its women would be educated and employed. But few would be exempt from the constraining effects of labor markets or repetitious work. Fewer, still, would be free to shape their private lives in ways unaffected by the homogenized social contexts that markets create.

We don't have to imagine this result because the market economies established in America and other industrialized states already dominate cultural and social life. Hence, this question: Is a market appropriate to every context of activity and exchange: thought or friendship, for example? Mill proposed a market of ideas, but he meant that ideas ought to be widely available and openly discussed. They are not exchanged freely—at cost to thought, research, and eventually business—if patented and sold. Free marketeers respond that ideas have value. Don't be naïve, selling yours cheaply, for nothing. Take care, as well, that self-perception doesn't outrun your market value. For the worth of every human and every hour of labor is decided by the market's assessment of its cost and utility. Some older interpretations of our nature and context—"Made in the image of God"—were grandiose and unverifiable. But they had the virtue of dignity. Markets correct this impression by making us sober. Where money measures value, we convert every context for human exchange into a market where values are determined by prices freely paid. Do coagulated practices protect inefficiency? Withdraw subventions so every activity or system may be tested by competition. Let inefficient producers fail. The market will set fair values.

Yet, *market* is a misnomer in domains that are critical to personal and social well-being, but rarely or never profitable. Should farmers compete? Perhaps. Should schools, hospitals, and police departments be privately held? These are doubtful candidates for market economies, given that education, health, and safety are conditions for creating the services and products that markets exchange. Perceiving these services as commodities risks the harm of a bee stinging itself: don't use public money to pay for education unless it's profitable, fail to educate large numbers of people (your potential workers and customers), then try to sustain an industrial economy. The effect is comparable if we ignore people who have no health insurance. Many of them don't work, but that has an unforeseen benefit: demoralization makes them unlikely to skew election results by voting their preoccupations. That's just as well, given that they are incidental to economic life. But the uninsured do receive public money, they could work in other circumstances, their illnesses might spread like plague, and they do suffer. The market doesn't help them. Is there no other way to organize for individual benefit and mutual support? There is: we aren't obliged to assume that every significant human need or activity is usefully construed or reconstructed in market terms.

ii. Conflicts that result when interests at one scale of systemic organization oppose interests of another scale. These conflicts are explicable, even predictable, in the terms of systems theory. Orders in a hierarchy of systems—New York City and New York State, for example—may be significantly decoupled in the respect that the operation or well-being of one may be somewhat independent of the operation or well-being of the other. This is counterintuitive when one rightly supposes that the working parts of the higher-order system are the individuals of the lower one. The higher-order system may nevertheless achieve considerable autonomy, either because of power over its parts or because it has access to surrogates, as companies replace workers in a fluid labor market. Accordingly, conditions or effects favorable to one level in a hierarchy of systems may be good or bad for people or systems at other levels. This is a limit to the utility of markets: they are inimical to the richly textured contexts where personal freedom is taught and expressed, and, conversely, the inertia and idiosyncrasy of such contexts makes them adverse to the efficiency of the higher-order systems—the businesses—on which economic well-being depends. Business cycles or conditions are relatively independent of the private lives of workers, though workers can hardly withstand the conditions imposed by markets and employers.

One expects to see evidence of this difference in Karl Marx's understanding of business–worker relations. It may be there, but one suspects that Marx didn't perceive the relative autonomy of higher-order systems, hence these two sometimes adversarial domains of freedom: one pertinent to markets where businesses compete, the other to the choices of private individuals. Dialectical materialism foresees the dissolution of both the state and the class structure it serves; workers will assume ownership and control of the means of production, including all businesses.[16] But then, machines are to assume the burden of production, while liberated workers learn the bliss of poetry and music. The class struggle is vindicated and resolved as individuals emerge from proletarian anonymity. But what happens to higher-order systems, the profitable businesses that were the fulcrum for labor's struggle with capital? Do they lose their corporate identity as higher-order systems, for the reason that their functional autonomy had no purpose but the one of subordinating labor? There is an instructive parallel: Marx supposed that nuclear families will disappear when women—a different sort of property—are no longer subordinated by their worker husbands.[17] Marx, the Hegelian holist, becomes Marx, the liberal individualist.

This may or may not have been Marx's prediction for the corporate autonomy of businesses, but the error implied is germane. Higher-order systems persist for many reasons; businesses of some form will endure as long as they supply goods, services, and employment to needy people. There is no obvious way to mitigate this conflict: the freedom afforded these businesses by markets opposes the character and contexts vital to individual freedom.

iii. The myth that markets are the guarantor of social fluidity and freedom. *Free markets* suggests the unfettered exchanges—street fairs, for example—where buyers and sellers meet and bargain, though there is little similarity between their exchanges and the competition that opposes Daimler-Chrysler to Honda, Ford, and General Motors. Many small vendors sell goat cheese or tomatoes they produce. The few gargantuan carmakers employ thousands of workers whose lives are ever more regimented by the conditions of work and ever more vulnerable to the risk that they shall lose jobs if they reject its terms. Labor costs—in salaries and benefits—are the principal cost of producing cars. Efficient management of the workforce is a principal way of reducing costs.

Workers are trapped by the requirements of work—narrowly focused tasks and extended hours, for example—the risks of unemployment, and the learned social persuasion that one's life is flawed in the absence of the advertised fantasies of contemporary life: cars, houses, status, and excitement. One is too busy, tired, or anxious to cultivate simple skills or too elated by purchases and possessions to care. The effect is constriction: constricted concerns, skills, opportunities, and affect. We care too little about what we are or could have been. Positive freedom is crippled though it seems pervasive, because we construe it narrowly as the power to choose and buy. It can't be recovered without negative freedoms: freedom from regimentation and vulnerability and freedom from fantasies about the least tolerable conditions for well-being. We are vulnerable if the employment that pays for our needs and wants is precarious. We are deluded if we believe the advertisers who tell us that our lives are flawed without their products.

We are regimented, say Weber and Marcuse, because the conduct and context of work are ever more rationalized in the name of efficiency:

> [T]he American system of "scientific management" triumphantly proceeds with its rational conditioning and training of work performances, thus drawing the ultimate conclusions

from the mechanization and discipline of the plant. The psycho-physical apparatus of man is completely adjusted to the demands of the outer world, the tools, the machines—in short, it is functionalized, and the individual is shorn of his natural rhythm as determined by his organism; in line with the demands of the work procedure, he is attuned to a new rhythm through the functional specialization of muscles and through the creation of an optimal economy of physical effort. This whole process of rationalization, in the factory as elsewhere, and especially in the bureaucratic state machine, parallels the centralization of the material implements of organization in the hands of the master. Thus, discipline inexorably takes over ever larger areas as the satisfaction of political and economic needs is increasingly rationalized. The universal phenomenon more and more restricts the importance of charisma and of individually differentiated conduct.[18]

Marx believed that technology—machines and efficient social organization—would liberate men and women to discover and realize their particular talents: "we shall have an association, in which the free development of each is the condition for the free development of all."[19] But we are not liberated, because the demand for the efficiency that conditions profitability in a competitive market has turned the very context of work into a machine that mixes technology with organization. Veblen described the effect:

> The share of the operative workman in the machine industry is (typically) that of an attendant, an assistant, whose duty it is to keep pace with the machine process and to help out with workmanlike manipulation at points where the machine process engaged is incomplete. His work supplements the machine process rather than makes use of it. On the contrary the machine process makes use of the workman.[20]

These passages are not discredited by their age: substitute computer screens, Blackberries, and cell phones for stamping and sewing machines. Then add that workers using these devices are frequently on-call all day, every day.

Every mode of production transforms the people who work within it: fishermen and farmers, for example. Their lives, too, were and are regimented. But we who live with the rhetoric and conceit of a perfected freedom are slow to perceive that regimentation abetted by technology makes many workers less free. They are obsessed by work and fear of losing it. The demands of profitability consume their time. Addiction to market goods makes other goods invisible. Weber, Marcuse, and Veblen knew us better than we know ourselves. This is our dilemma: the benefits of the economy we have versus the goods and freedoms of a simpler life, one we can imagine but not easily create.

Evidence is as close as the automobile one carefully chooses and maintains. Advertisers tell us that one's car is a close match to whatever is distinctive in one's personality. Dashing or romantic, prudent and safe: we express ourselves by the cars we buy. Television advertisements show cars on the open road. Actual driving time is more often passed on crowded roads in traffic jams, where Bentleys go no faster than Fords. How shall we distinguish ourselves as we sit in traffic, or drive, bumper to bumper, in and out of clogged cities? By closing the windows, turning up the air conditioner, and listening to a favorite song, basking in the pleasure of this distinctive motorized nest. Are we free? Yes and no. Yes, because this is my car and my music. No, because the rationalization of mass society radically constricts my choices. The market that promotes automobile manufacture and sales cripples the lives it transforms. Marcuse described this trajectory:

> The spreading hierarchy of large-scale enterprise and the precipitation of individuals into masses determines the trends of technological rationality today. What results is the mature form of that individualistic rationality which characterized the free economic subject of the industrial revolution. Individualistic rationality was born as a critical and oppositional attitude that derived freedom of action from the unrestricted liberty of thought and conscience and measured all social standards and relations by the individual's rational self-interest. It grew into the rationality of competition in which the rational interest was superseded by the interest of the market, and individual achievement absorbed by efficiency. It ended with standardized submission to the all-embracing apparatus which it had itself

created. This apparatus is the embodiment and resting place of individualistic rationality, but the latter now requires that individuality must go. He is rational who most efficiently accepts and executes what is allocated to him, who entrusts his fate to the large-scale enterprises and organizations which administer the apparatus.[21]

iv. The difficulty of acknowledging market costs when the benefits are conspicuous. The alleged impediments to freedom seem stagy or false when one thinks of the many businesses started and sustained by individuals. People of initiative never doubt the market's empowering effect. The risks they take and the successes they achieve are sufficient evidence of that. But not everyone is or can be an entrepreneur: there are also the many workers whose lives are subject to the norms of employment. The freedom of self-employment in a vocation of one's choosing is not for them. But they too want freedom, freedom to make choices that will enrich their private and social lives. They can't have it when markets leach contexts of features, relations, and values that are critical if character is to develop the skills and context is to provide the opportunities required by positive freedom. The losses are obscure, because sloganeering about freedom deters our seeing them, or because we prefer to emphasize the benefits markets promote. Wages (usually) rise for those employed in firms that survive. They and their families are better housed and clothed. More of their children go to school; most are healthier. Birth rates drop, and women achieve the autonomy once reserved to men. Products that were made locally are now produced in fewer styles (by remote factories that are more profitable because unit costs are lower), but their uniformity is reassuring. There is comfort in the familiar goods available wherever one goes, especially to those who relocate in strange places in hope of work. But there is a cost: contexts that were local and distinctive are homogenized. Stand in a cafe, store, or hotel lobby. Notice how much it resembles all the cafes, stores, or hotels of this chain, then look to see if you can tell, without asking, which city this is.

We underestimate the implications for positive freedom, because we have not understood that conditions for many of its expressions are independent of and opposed to the conditions for market efficiency. This failure has seemed incidental, because our conception of markets is distorted by the rhapsodic notion that individual liberty implies an open playing field where every participant enjoys his private game or lolls on the grass

without impeding others. But this is the elision to resist: freedom of initiative—liberty to compete in the market—is not identical with the liberty to make the textured choices that are defeated because no business
finds it profitable to support them.[22] Should we eliminate violins or
mathematicians because the money spent making them could be used
more efficiently—more profitably—elsewhere?

No one minds that logic and physical laws apply throughout the natural world. But the effects of social homogenization are more unsettling.
Markets that improve health, education, and welfare reduce the variety
of cultures, discourage idiosyncrasy, and dissolve moral bonds. A culture's
ways are points of pride; its curmudgeons are tolerable annoyances; duty
is moral glue. We notice, but don't care that no one shaves the barber
who shaves the rest of us. We do care that a job interview goes well, as it
does not if we are conspicuously different. The market saves us this
embarrassment by dressing us in standard ways. It supplies products, style,
and jargon to guarantee that we shall be recognizable, efficient, and safe.

Those who labor—most people—have interests that are opposed
and all but mutually annihilating. We want productive economies and
our freedom. Market economies seem to promise both: they repay initiative. But this benefit—freedom rewarded because effectively used—is
reserved to a few. Many more live with the consequences of an economy
that calculates its efficiencies and profits, not the consequences for lives
diminished by homogenized contexts. Markets create generic people as
surely as their factories produce serviceable but generic goods. This must
have consequences for freedom, because freedom stripped of context and
character is more slogan than power. We resist homogenization because
variations of family dynamics, birth order, wealth, religion, locale, or education guarantee differences among us. But variability is a cost: business
prefers compliant consumers and fungible labor. Education is one victim:
literacy is pervasive, but cultivation is ever more shallow as context loses
its complexity. We learn fewer ideas, and imagine fewer ideals. Freedom
withers, because the people taught to revere it are trained to make the
same choices. Rafts of statistics demonstrate the contrary by citing initiatives taken or innovations that improve the quality of life. But one is
skeptical, because freedom's constriction is obscured in two ways and
clarified in a third.

Public esteem for liberty is beyond dispute. The last sixty years of
American history are testimony to our good intentions. Successive differences—race, religion, ethnic difference, gender, sexual orientation, and

physical disability—have fallen to the principle that equal opportunity is a paramount value. We believe in negative freedom and legislate to enforce it. Yet, our zeal for freedom obscures its conditions: we consolidate negative freedom but ignore the requirements for positive freedom. Character and context—core systems, especially—are its principal, material conditions. The intelligent child is free to profit at school, because he or she has learned to read. Context—teachers and a literate family—completes the circle by supplying books.

Context confuses us—a first obscurity—because of its ambiguity. It signifies both the array of malign circumstances from which we seek freedom—autocracy, oligarchy, and exploitation of every sort—and conditions that promote choice. We usually think of context in terms of negative freedom—exempt us from interfering contexts—before projecting this ideal as the condition and content of positive freedom: let there be nothing in our circumstances to shape or direct us. But nothing is learned or done in the absence of contexts that promote learning and doing.

How rich must contexts be to support robust expressions of freedom? What strength should they cultivate? Just the power Nietzsche described, the power to remake given materials in a way that stamps them with the distinctive craft or perspective of this or that personality.[23] The artist (a painter or poet, gardener or cook, spouse, parent, or friend[24]) transforms malleable materials in ways prescribed by an idea or value. The result is calculated or inspired, graceful and clever or seismic. Its authenticity speaks for itself. Artists have a taste for freedom's transforming power, but nothing they accomplish is achieved without contexts that supply teachers, ideas, examples, and materials. Compare homogenized products: they are made most efficiently in standardized facilities by employees who consume the products and information they produce. We are seduced by an advantage that subverts us: homogenizing the textured contexts where skills are learned and exploited reduces our freedom to make significantly different choices. I do what you do and can't imagine doing it otherwise. We are diminished by the result, whether or not we perceive it.

This point of view seems redolent of the elitism markets quash: many now enjoy opportunities and pleasures once reserved to a few. But—a second obscurity—the issues are diversity and standards, not status. Bakeries were once a fixture in every city neighborhood. Many bakers had a special recipe or knack that customers savored and remembered into old age. But commercial bakeries and supermarkets undersold them; their stores didn't survive. Now, virtuoso bakers open shops in big cities, selling bread and cake at prices no neighborhood baker imagined. Wealthy customers pay to recover tastes they had forgotten or despaired to satisfy. Bookstores were also common. They, too, had proprietors with special interests. Rents were cheap, shelves groaned with books that could wait for buyers. Publishers warehoused their backlists for times when customers asked for books unavailable on the shelves. But warehouses and stores have closed, because rents are higher. There are supermarket bookstores, and they do have cafes; they don't have backlists. There were also hat stores, stores selling buttons and ribbons, and the tailors who made clothes to measure for people who couldn't pay today's prices for bespoke tailoring. Much that we call elite is basic and functional, but expensive. The market that lowers unit costs and standards—spreading wealth to entrepreneurs and workers, too—has a price structure (in rents, raw materials, and salaries) that penalizes everyone who supplies or buys a better product.[25]

Responses to this charge go either of four ways: they reject nostalgia, reminding us of the many people who couldn't afford books or bread; they tell us not to complain amidst our unparalleled wealth and opportunities; they exaggerate the opportunities for choice; or they suggest diversions for people disoriented or bored by uniformity. Each of these responses misses the point. We (or our grandparents) derive from communities differentiated by networks of nested and overlapping systems: families, neighborhoods, schools, churches, and jobs. Many of us now live and work in circumstances stripped of the chance to learn the subtle talents once acquired in those settings. The reciprocities and intimacies of life in an extended family and neighborhood are a principal victim. There are fewer duties to others in nuclear families, but also fewer opportunities to learn and bond.[26] We don't know the athletic uncle or aunt, the musical grandparent, or bookish neighbor. We are less at ease socially, because self-definition comes later with school or work. Nuclear families are a fragile base for the psychic well-being of their members, but even this support dissolves when children disperse to jobs in remote places. We live longer, but loneliness is chronic. Yet, life is congenial, because substitutes provide a surrogate identity, one founded in the advertised marks of work, status, and wealth. Chummy and alluring, movies, magazines, and television tell us that all is well, if brittle. Liking music, we listen on radios or headphones, hardly remembering the music of our grandparents. Many of them sang and played local tunes. A few stood about the family piano singing Schubert. But all played together, at home or nearby with children and friends. They heard less music, but knew it better. We are prosperous in many ways, but there is less of the freedom nourished by the articulated, local contexts where idiosyncrasy, skill, and reflection were encouraged.

A third consideration is clarifying. Mill distinguished three regions of liberty (freedom to chose and act): consciousness (thought) and conscience, tastes and pursuits, and the freedom to join with others to satisfy common or complementary interests. Thought is first, because one cannot have worthwhile tastes or pursuits without understanding pertinent opportunities and their differences. Homogenization and market values reverse the order Mill prescribed: advertisers tell us what is good, thereby reducing the differences of taste that diminish profits by creating small markets. Mill knew this possibility and considered it when defending utilitarianism against the charge that it makes pigs of people. His utilitarianism distinguishes three kinds of pleasure: animal, moral, and intellectual. Moral pleasure—taking responsibility for the well-being of another—is said to be finest, but intellectual pleasure, too, is said to be better than animal pleasure. Homogenization aims lower. It promises diversion for people who buy the means to please themselves. What shall we do if subtle pleasures—thought, for example—are costly to produce though they often fail to return a monetary profit? Should we lower the cost of producing them, or marginalize and disable people who aspire to them: by ridicule, perhaps. This is costly in a different way: homogenize and debase vital contexts, anesthetize us with pleasure, and we are less free.

The freedom to choose and act comes in degrees. There is more or less of it depending on contexts where character develops: are they impoverished or enriched? I have no duties to family, friends, neighbors, or workmates if the insecurity of my every job precludes marriage, friendships, or a stable address. I can't learn or do such things as can't be done, either because I can't imagine doing them, or because there is no longer a motive or means. Writing letters was once a respected practice: people enjoyed writing, others expected their letters, there were no alternative, inexpensive ways to communicate. E-mail is more efficient. Will it promote the literary style or reflection letters did? One isn't sure. Depleting a context, we lose its norms and guarantee that we shall lose the freedoms expressed in things it enabled us to do. This isn't new: technology and contingencies such as flood or drought have always altered circumstances and the talents they supported. Carving seals' teeth was also a skill once prized. Yes, but losing it is not so consequential as splintered families, lapsed duties, or formulaic thought.

What sort of freedom do we prefer? People recently liberated from oppression—be it poverty, priestly authority, or discrimination of any sort—don't ask. Their exhilaration speaks for itself. But there is a question to answer: is it sufficient that we have freedom from interference and want, freedom to choose our partners, freedom to start a business, and freedom to please ourselves in ways prescribed by our flourishing consumer economy? Or should we learn and use the power to do subtle things? Both aims are worthy, though a principal condition for the first— a market economy—diminishes the second. Free markets are welcomed for their singular benefits, but they can be resisted in circumstances where they compromise freedom by draining complexity from contexts where character forms and decisions are made. Ignoring this dilemma, we choose what we have: better health, liberated women, less poverty, and more goods, but meaner choices, meaner skills, and the diminished selves that make us blind to our loss.

Marketeers have a simple rejoinder: all the abuses alleged are distortions. Regulate markets to purge these abuses, and we eliminate regimentation while assuring the maximally practical condition for both free choice and the production of goods that vary with the cultivation of their buyers. This would be ideal—liberty would flourish—but the project founders. Profit is the crux. Producers don't like regulation and lobby effectively against it, because market dominance enhances profitability and because financial power buys the political influence that deters regulators. Shareholders demand profit on their investments, thereby obliging producers to minimize costs by regimenting the labor that produces the homogenized goods that coarsen the tastes of these shareholding consumers. There are no simple solutions for these tight circles.

v. The impotence of political regulation in local communities when national or transnational companies control their economic well-being. Negative freedom is imperiled, positive freedom is crippled if people—citizens—cannot regulate their relations. This is true of families, neighborhoods, cities, and nation-states. Every system's members must be able to negotiate and legislate the terms of their sociality and well-being. This is prudent, because others know less of one's circumstances and care less for one's interests. It is potent, because the regulation of one's community—its economy included[27]—is an extension of self-control, a power that is incontestably essential to positive freedom. The risks are considerable when a community is careless about self-regulation (many of its able citizens don't vote, for example). Risks are grave when the power of communal control is decoupled from the economic conditions for its well-being, as happens when local economic activity is subordinated by large market economies. Dominant factories and stores are units in companies whose decisions are made elsewhere. Communications of all sorts—electronic media, airplanes and airports—are links in networks that exceed local control. This hazard—the effect of technological and economic integration everywhere—is all but unavoidable; but its consequences for freedom are devastating: local people lose the power to regulate critical aspects of their lives. The chances for employment and unemployment become adventitious: will anyone locate a factory among them? The airport or hospital closes for reasons beyond their control. Money for public services evaporates. Demoralization and passivity—with all their effects—are pervasive.

This decoupling of scales—political and economic—is invisible in large business centers where commercial taxes pay the ample costs of local government. It is wrenching and perilous in towns and nations where citizens are torn between the desire for jobs and the demand for political autonomy. Some states willingly sacrifice their independence for foreign investment. Others writhe: proud of their political traditions, zealous in defending their autonomy, they struggle to maintain self-respect as their economies founder. Their choices seem poisoned: cede freedom to powers one can't control, or save freedom but suffer the indignity of unemployment and disintegration while neighbors enjoy their wealth.

❋

Living in contexts, needing the leverage they supply, doesn't entail that we can't remake them to serve us better. Some are resisted, others reformed. The history of negative freedoms, each requiring a specific struggle and ideal, reminds us that barriers sometimes yield to intelligence and strength. Markets are puzzling, because they work. Allied to technology, they remake our lives in ways that are all but irresistible. Thoreau's life at Walden Pond—close enough to town and friends—balanced negative with positive freedoms, but who today prefers 1820s dentistry or transport? How to profit from markets without being consumed by them? Scandanavia, France, Germany, Singapore, and Japan temper market economies with local control and social protection: in health and education, for example. But the task is deceptive because the target seems defuse—less visible than a domineering church or tyrant—and because we like so many of its effects. Half seduced, half comatose, we are slow to struggle. Our alternatives, accommodation or reform, are nevertheless incidental here. My concern is freedom, and the contexts that facilitate or impede it. Markets are an illustration: they have both effects.

6. Is Freedom Good-in-Itself?

Should we endorse the magical belief that freedom is a good in itself, perhaps the only intrinsic good? How shall we answer someone who argues that choices are secondary to the power they express? Thinking of revolutionaries in art, politics, or science, he avers that liberty is our distinctively human capacity and virtue, our hallowed ground. Or he remembers Descartes' question—"What am I"—and the answer that still dominates our thinking about freedom: "A being which doubts, . . . denies, . . . refuses."[28] We reveal ourselves by resisting contexts we disapprove. Other animals are captive to their context and hard wiring. We are not.

Descartes' first *Meditation* exposes our freedom by denying us context. This is the atomist myth, one that would reduce freedom—were it true—to gestures in the void. What follows when we concede that freedom is situated? One side argues that freedom is a utility, a condition or cause of effects; the other regards it as an effulgent ground—a node—recognized by its consequences. This is a dispute about perspective. For the same empirical data support both claims: we give priority to the ground or value it instrumentally as cause of its effects. Either way, freedom's value is practical: it is good (or bad) as an instrument, and good (or bad) for its effects. We who celebrate freedom should also want to know the uses made of it.

Conclusion

The tools and methods of contemporary conceptual analysis come from Descartes: separate whatever is distinguishable; discern the essential form of an idea. Examining a notion used casually, conceptual analysts strip the dross to expose the unembellished core. Hume was Descartes' best student. Ideas of cause and effect are not clear and distinct, until we eliminate gratuitous inferences from the bare observation that phenomena are constantly joined in space and time. Psychology explains the rest: we expect one conjunct when the other is perceived.[1] Ideas of fact and value are equally encumbered. Wanting something seen, I wrongly infer that its value is inherent. Analysis clears the air by distinguishing the item wanted from my desire. This exercise has a complementary motive. Descartes and Hume supposed with Plato that clear and distinct—analyzed—ideas are reality's template.[2] If cause and effect, fact and value are separate in thought, they are and must be separate in the extra-mental world. It is sloppy, undisciplined thinking that encourages us to see essential, necessary relations in couplings that are never more than contingent.

This conclusion would be plausible if the products of conceptual analysis were the lens through which reality is and must be perceived. It is implausible, distorting, and false when mind has lost its a priori, prescriptivist authority. Thought is a complex bodily activity that supplies fragmentary information, tentative ideas, and fallible hypotheses about the material world, itself included.[3] Knowing other things requires that we engage them in relations that are physical and causal. One well-confirmed hypothesis affirms that causation is energy exchange: no effects result without the interacting causes—and motion—that induces them. Another hypothesis proposes that there are no values—no norms—without the material relationships that generate *musts*, *shoulds*, and *oughts*.

Must sometimes emerges without human intervention, as when $e = mc^2$ is nature's signature law of motion. *Shoulds* and *oughts* emerge as we engage one another. But this is not, as Descartes, Hume, and Kant supposed, the difference between empirical content (however received or created) and the interventions of reflection or transcendental desire. The repertoire of human capacities is broader, but not less material, than those of squirrels or steel. Loyalty solders us to other people and systems, but this is a material bond, not an effusion in a luminous, immaterial mental space. An elderly woman is sick and alone; her neighbor takes an interest. He intensifies relations that were previously remote and formal. One promises to help; the other waits and hopes he will. The promise should be kept. But why? Her need is distinguishable and separable from his response: it is no contradiction that he not respond. But he does, because he wants to. For it is no secret that interdependence is a sustaining constant of human life and a condition for the worth and well-being of individual lives. Do many people fail their responsibilities? Certainly. Why do we condemn them? Because they sabotage relations that support and defend us. *Should* and *ought* are practical values. Betraying them has inimical effects on everyone, a circle that includes oneself.

Descartes' *Meditations* elevated mind to the vantage point where it doubts everything—including material *musts*, *shoulds*, and *oughts*. His successors, Kant especially, loaded norms and every thinkable difference and relation into the minds that use them to create the intelligibilities of practical life or theoretical science. Their program expressed a principal Enlightenment motive: liberate people from their oppressors, whether church, state, personal ignorance, or the alien and punishing material world. The program succeeds by restricting mores, laws, and rules to minds that think or will them; other thinkers may scrutinize and reject the norms proposed as they would any other suggested idea. It falters, because freedom from the vulnerable material body requires mind's separation from body. Descartes' introduction to the *Meditations* promises this benefit: he will prove mind's immortality—and freedom—by confirming its exemption from body's corruption.[4] The mind he described tends to itself and its ideas, ignoring its coupled body as best it can.

This is the tradition that yields when mind is understood as the activity of thinking bodies, bodies that do and must adapt to their material circumstances.[5] We live in a network of layered systems: the natural world known to physics, chemistry, and biology, plus the domains of practical, moral, political, and aesthetic life. Each is a context where behaviors are shaped by relevant *musts*, *shoulds*, or *oughts*. Tripping, we fall; having roles that were inherited or sought, we satisfy them; seeing shapes emerge through fog on a Venetian canal, we see beauty. These are material constraints. They don't need an additional—transcendental, theological, or a priori—justification.

Is freedom compromised if we can't override material norms in the name of values we choose? It is, if Descartes' cogito or Kant's transcendental ego is the baseline for freedom, for then thought is the only action and every consistent thought is permitted. But this is a disabling fantasy. Denying the existence of natural norms isn't effective, if skepticism doesn't make them go away. Doubting—annulling—traffic laws guarantees chaos: think of cars driven in all directions, like molecules in a hot gas. Why would it be less disruptive if every material norm were to fail? We live within the boundaries—of character, social relations, biology, physics, and logic—fixed by a cascade of norms that are immanent and material. But we are not defenseless. Imagine surfing a wave. Lose it, and you fall. Character, systems, and their norms are also leverage. There is no freedom without them.

Notes

Introduction

1. René Descartes, *Rules for the Direction of the Mind*, in *The Philosophical Writings of Descartes*, vol. 1, trans. John Cottingham, Robert Stoothoff, and Dugald Murdoch (Cambridge: Cambridge University Press, 1985), p. 20.

2. René Descartes, *Meditations*, in *Discourse on Method and Meditations on First Philosophy*, ed. David Weissman (New Haven: Yale University Press, 1996), pp. 70–83.

3. Nicholas Malebranche, *Dialogues on Metaphysics and on Religion*, trans. David Scott (Cambridge: Cambridge University Press, 1999), pp. 76–77, 95–96.

4. George Berkeley, *Three Dialogues* (Indianapolis, Ind.: Bobbs-Merrill, 1954), pp. 81–82.

5. David Hume, *A Treatise of Human Nature*, second edition, ed. L. A. Selby-Bigge and P. H. Nidditch (Oxford: Clarendon Press, 1978), p. 165.

6. Immanuel Kant, *Critique of Pure Reason*, trans. Norman Kemp Smith (New York: St. Martin's, 1965), pp. 102–208.

7. Immanuel Kant, *Critique of Practical Reason*, trans. Thomas Abbott (London: Longmans, 1963), pp. 131–140.

8. Hume, *A Treatise of Human Nature*, p. 469.

9. Immanuel Kant, *Critique of Judgment*, no. 18, trans. Werner Pluhar (Indianapolis, Ind.: Hackett, 1987), pp. 16–17.

10. Heraclitus, *The Presocratic Philosophers*, eds. G. S. Kirk, J. E. Raven, and M. Schofield (Cambridge: Cambridge University Press, 1993), p. 187.

11. Hilary Putnam, *Ethics without Ontology* (Cambridge: Harvard University Press, 2004), p. 10.

12. Ibid., pp. 77–78.

13. Ibid., p. 61.

14. Ibid.

15. Ibid., p. 85.

16. Ibid., p. 117

Chapter One. Categorial Form

1. Rudolf Carnap emphasized syntax, semantics, and pragmatics, the latter implying that theories are used to satisfy the interests of the theorizers. There is, apparently, nothing beyond language to constrain them:

> If someone decides to accept the thing language, there is no objection against saying that he has accepted the world of things. But this must not be interpreted as if it meant his acceptance of a *belief* in the reality of the thing world; there is no such belief or assertion or assumption, because it is not a theoretical question. To accept the thing world means nothing more than to accept a certain form of language, in other words, to accept rules for forming statements and for testing, accepting, or rejecting them. Thus the acceptance of the thing language leads, on the basis of observations made, also to the acceptance, belief, and assertion of certain statements. But the thesis of the reality of the thing world cannot be among these statements, because it cannot be formulated in the thing language or, it seems, in any other theoretical language.

Rudolf Carnap, "Empiricism, Semantics, and Ontology," in *Semantics and the Philosophy of Language*, ed. Leonard Linsky (Urbana, Ill.: University of Illinois Press, 1952), p. 211.

Also, see Richard Rorty:

> [Dewey's] chief enemy was the notion of truth as accuracy of representation, the notion later to be attacked by Heidegger, Sartre, and Foucault. Dewey thought that if he could break down this notion, if

scientific inquiry could be seen as adapting and coping rather than copying, the continuity between science, morals and art would become apparent. We would no longer ask ourselves questions about the "purity" of works of art or of our experience of them. We would be receptive to notions like Derrida's—that language is not a device for representing reality, but a reality in which we live and move. We would be receptive to the diagnosis of traditional philosophy which Sartre and Heidegger offer us—as the attempt to escape from time into the eternal, from freedom into necessity, from action into contemplation. We would see the social sciences not as awkward and unsuccessful attempts to imitate the physicists' elegance, certainty, and freedom from concern with "value," but as suggestions for ways of making human lives into works of art.

Richard Rorty, *Consequences of Pragmatism* (Minneapolis: University of Minnesota Press, 1982), pp. 86–87.

2. David Weissman, *Hypothesis and the Spiral of Reflection* (Albany, N.Y.: State University of New York Press, 1989), pp. 17–61.

3. Benjamin Whorf, *Language, Thought, and Reality* (Cambridge: MIT Press, 1956).

4. Kant, *Critique of Pure Reason*, pp. 645–652.

5. Democritus, *The Presocratic Philosophers*, p. 405; Aristotle, *Metaphysics*, in *The Basic Works of Aristotle*, ed. Richard McKeon (New York: Random House, 1941), p. 784.

6. The thirty-seventh of Luther's ninety-five theses reads: "Every true Christian, whether living or dead, has part in all the blessing of Christ and the Church, and this is granted him by God, even without letters of pardon." This is *grace*, God's inexplicable generosity to fallen humans. It is his gift to individual souls. Luther supposed at the time of writing his theses that ecclesiastical intervention is helpful, but secondary. He would argue later that it is an obstacle to salvation. See Descartes, *Meditations*, pp. 63–70 for the idea of autonomous minds, and John Stuart Mill, *On Liberty* (New York: Macmillan, 1956), p. 13, for his regions of liberty and no-harm principle.

7. G. W. F. Hegel, *The Phenomenology of Mind* (New York: Harper, 1967); and F. H. Bradley, *Appearance and Reality: A Metaphysical Essay* (Oxford: Oxford University Press, 1969).

8. Ludwig von Bertalanffy, *General System Theory*, revised edition (New York: George Braziller, 1968); Justice Buchler, *Metaphysics of Natural Complexes* (New York: Columbia University Press, 1966); Mario Bunge, *Treatise on Basic*

Philosophy, vol. 4, A World of Systems (Dordrecht: D. Reidel, 1979); David Weissman, *A Social Ontology* (New Haven: Yale University Press, 2000).

9. Weissman, *A Social Ontology*, pp. 59–61.

10. Stephen Pepper, World Hypotheses (Berkeley: University of California Press, 1942).

11. Richard McKeon's views are presented systematically (with neologisms by the author) in Walter Watson's *The Architectonics of Meaning: Foundations of the New Pluralism* (Chicago: University of Chicago Press, 1993).

12. Kant, *Critique of Pure Reason*, pp. 384–484.

13. John Locke, *Two Treatises of Government* (Cambridge: Cambridge University Press, 1988), pp. 99, 301.

14. Thomas Hobbes, *Leviathan* (Amherst, N.Y.: Prometheus, 1988), pp. 87–89.

15. Mill, *On Liberty*, p. 13.

16. Jean Jacques Rousseau, *The Social Contract*, trans. Maurice Cranston (London: Penguin, 1968), pp. 60–61.

Chapter Two. Nature

1. See Rorty, *Consequences of Pragmatism*, p. 153; and John Dupre, *Human Nature and the Limits of Science* (Oxford: Oxford University Press, 2001). Their views conflate interpretation (construing phenomena in ways that introduce significance while satisfying attitudes) with inquiry (a procedure for determining the character and conditions of things). See David Weissman, *Styles of Thought: Interpretation, Inquiry, and Imagination*, forthcoming.

2. See Nancy Cartwright, *The Dappled World* (Cambridge: Cambridge University Press, 1999).

3. See John Earman, *A Primer on Determinism* (Dordrecht: Reidel, 1986)

4. Morris Cohen, *Studies in Philosophy and Science* (New York: Henry Holt, 1949), p. 150.

5. Joseph Butler, *Sermons*, in *British Moralists: 1650–1800*, ed. D. D. Raphael (Oxford: Clarendon, 1969), para. 384.

6. Zeno, *Presocratic Philosophers*, pp. 264–265, 269–276.

7. David Weissman, *Eternal Possibilities* (Carbondale, Ill.: Southern Illinois University Press, 1977), pp. 86–89.

8. Gilbert Ryle, *The Concept of Mind* (New York: Barnes & Noble, 1949), pp. 16–18.

9. Putnam, *Ethics without Ontology*, p. 60.

10. Weissman, *Eternal Possibilities*, pp. 68–72.

11. Ibid., pp. 93–95.

12. Hume, *A Treatise of Human Nature*, p. 172.

13. Ibid., pp. 531–532.

14. Ibid., p. 172.

15. Ibid., p. 173.

16. Ibid., p. 5.

17. Ibid., p. 172.

18. Ibid., pp. 66–67.

19. Berkeley, *Three Dialogues*, p. 81.

20. Descartes, *Discourse on Method*, in *Discourse on Method and Meditations on First Philosophy*, p. 13.

21. David Weissman, Lost Souls (Albany, N.Y.: State University of New York Press, 2003), pp. 81–96.

22. Richard Feynman described the conflict:

> When the new quantum mechanics was discovered, the classical people—Which included everybody except Heisenberg, Schrodinger, and Born—said: "Look, your theory is not any good because you cannot answer certain questions like: what is the exact position of a particle?, which hole does it go through?, and some others." Heisenberg's answer was: "I do not need to answer such questions because you cannot ask such a question experimentally." It is that we do not have to [ask such questions].

Yet, Feynman continued:

> It is always good to know which ideas cannot be checked directly, but it is not necessary to remove them all. It is not true that we can pursue science completely by using only those concepts which are directly subject to experiment.

Richard Feynman, Robert Leighton, and Matthew Sands, *The Feynman Lectures on Physics*, vol. III (Reading, Mass.: Addison Wesley, 1965), p. 2–9.

This qualification is properly cautious, because the application of some leading principles of inquiry—the principle of sufficient reason, for example—is not always subject to direct experimental confirmation. Sufficient reason is itself a hypothesis repeatedly tested and confirmed: smoke then fire, for example. We extend its application by applying it in cases for which we currently have and may never have confirming empirical data. So, we extrapolate from the many cases for which there is direct evidence to particles too small to see, particles covered by laws that cannot differentiate among them. The extrapolation may prove mistaken. But why suppose—as Feynman did—that philosophic doubts about the "identity" of particles that behave differently under "identical" conditions are trivial or spurious, when physical theory and experiment are limited by the size and sensibility of the things described? The considerable experimental evidence justifying applications of sufficient reason in cases where direct evidence is available make us skeptical that our current, statistical understanding of elementary particles is comprehensive.

23. This assumption is implicit in Descartes' distinction between temporalized mental phenomena and spatialized matter. It is duplicated when Kant alleges that time, the form of internal intuition, is the universal medium and unifier of experience.

24. C. S. Peirce, "Pragmatism and Abduction," in *Collected Papers of C. S. Peirce*, volume. V and VI, eds. Charles Hartshorne and Paul Weiss (Cambridge: Harvard University Press, 1960), paras. 5.195–205.

25. It may seem that this mechanical interpretation of causation is appropriate only to middle- and large-sized things that behave classically, meaning deterministically. Quantum theory is statistical and probabilistic, but also deterministic: it predicts an array of alternative possible effects, assigning specific probabilities to each. It doesn't predict randomness, and randomness is not observed.

26. Ludwig Wittgenstein, *Philosophical Investigations*, trans. G.E.M. Anscombe (New York: Macmillan, 1953), para. 217, p. 85.

27. Ernest Nagel, *The Structure of Science* (New York: Harcourt, Brace & World, 1961), pp. 345–358.

28. David Weissman, *Dispositional Properties* (Carbondale, Ill.: Southern Illinois University Press, 1965), pp. 53–56, 61–62, 116–117; *Eternal Possibilities*, pp. 62–64, 75; "Dispositions as Geometrical-Structural Properties," *Review of Metaphysics*, vol. XXXII, no. 2, December 1978, pp. 285–286; Nancy Cartwright, *Nature's Capacities and Their Measurement* (Oxford: Oxford University Press, 1994) and *The Dappled World* (Cambridge: Cambridge University Press, 1999), pp. 66–67.

29. Aristotle, *Metaphysics*, 1033b20–1034a8, pp. 794–795. Stephen Wolfram describes the evolution of cellular automata when simple instructions are repeatedly applied to each previous state of a machine. So, cells of a lower rank are colored or not given an algorithm and the color of cells in the rank above. Wolfram's account is incomplete, because he fails to ask and answer an elementary question. Machine instructions for cellular automata require an agent—a human or a machine—to complete every next line of the graphs that fill his book, rather as every next move in a game requires the players who move the pieces. Where is the surrogate for agents such as these in nature? None is required, because the dispositions of structures limit the effects of the motions that run through or join them. Wolfram's account is also incomplete in this other respect: it doesn't provide for the motion and transformation of its elements—colored squares. Changes are serial and discrete, not continuous: a square may be repeated or replaced, but not transformed. Wolfram assumes, with only the discreteness of his representations for evidence, that space, time, and motion are discrete, not continuous. We need more than his graphs—one line filled at a time—to justify this inference. Stephen Wolfram, *A New Kind of Science* (Champaign, Ill.: Wolfram Media, 2002).

30. W.V.O. Quine, *The Roots of Reference* (La Salle, Ill.: Open Court, 1974), pp. 8–15.

31. Ludwig Wittgenstein, *Tractatus Logico-Philosophicus*, trans. D. F. Pears and B. F. McGuinness (London: Routledge & Kegan Paul, 1963), p. 25, para. 3.3.

32. Aristotle, *Organon*, 2a11–4b20, pp. 9–14.

33. Percy Bridgman, *The Logic of Modern Physics* (New York: MacMillan, 1927).

34. See, for example, Cohen, *Studies in Philosophy and Science*, pp. 216–217.

35. Einstein's views about quantum indeterminism are scorned nowadays. But his response is still cogent:

    Quantum physics formulates laws governing crowds and not individuals. Not properties but probabilities are described, not laws disclosing the future of systems are formulated, but laws governing the changes in time of the probabilities and relating to great congregations of individuals.

36. Weissman, "Dispositions as Geometrical-Structural Properties," p. 289: Albert Einstein and Leopold Infeld, *The Evolution of Physics* (New York: Simon & Schuster, 1938), p. 297.

37. See, for example, Plato, *Timaeus*, in *Collected Dialogues*, eds. Edith Hamilton and Huntington Cairns (New York: Pantheon, 1963, 53c–54b, pp. 1179–1180.

38. This point is mitigated by the conservation of matter or energy: anything that exists today comprises matter or energy that existed throughout the life of the cosmos. Whatever mass or energy constitutes contemporary entities (this cat and dog) is affected by things whose dissolution antedates their creation (stars that long ago imploded) if such things fall within their backward light cones. And equally, the matter and energy in these contemporaries may once have affected things that long ago ceased to be.

39. Hegel, *Phenomenology of Mind*, pp. 789–808.

40. Reality is more comprehensive: it includes all possible worlds, those instantiated and the many that may be uninstantiated. See Weissman, *Eternal Possibilities*, pp. 141–188.

41. John Bell, *Speakable and Unspeakable in Quantum Mechanics* (Cambridge: Cambridge University Press, 1987).

42. Aristotle, *Metaphysics*, 1025b28–1052a12, pp. 820–834.

43. G.W.V. Leibniz, "Reflections on Knowledge, Truth and Ideas," in *Monadology and Other Philosophical Essays*, trans. Paul Schrecker and Anne Martin Schrecker (Indianapolis, Ind.: Bobbs-Merrill Company, 1965), p. 7 and paras. 29–38; pp.152–154.

44. Weissman, *Lost Souls*, pp. 19–22.

45. Leibniz, *Monadology*, in *Monadology, Monadology and Other Philosophical Essays*, trans. Paul Schrecker and Anne Martin Schrecker (Indianapolis, Ind.: Bobbs-Merrill Company, 1965), para. 59–69, pp. 157–159.

46. Benedict Spinoza, *Ethics*, trans. R.H.M. Elwes (New York: Dover, 1883), p. 65.

Chapter Three. Practical Norms

1. Descartes, *The Passions of the Soul*, in *Philosophical Writings*, vol. 1, p. 349.

2. It is one or another set of alternative conditions that must be assembled and engaged, if the effect is to be achieved, not usually some particular set only. Every individual set of this class would be sufficient to produce the effect; only the class of alternative sets is necessary to produce it in our world. Other sets of causes would have this effect in other possible worlds.

3. Aristotle, *Metaphysics*, 1013a24–1013b3, pp. 752–753.

4. Plato, *Republic*, 349b–350c, pp. 598–590.

5. John Dewey, *Experience and Nature*, second edition (La Salle, Ill.: Open Court, 1929), pp. 67–72.

6. Ibid., pp. 133–134.

Chapter Four. Moral Norms

1. Kant, *Critique of Practical Reason*, p. 106.

2. Aristotle, *Nichomachean Ethics*, 1112b13–20, p. 970.

3. Kant, *Critique of Practical Reason*, p. 106.

4. Ibid., pp. 39, 47, 49.

5. Ibid., p. 17, no. 1.

6. Ibid., pp. 56–58.

7. Immanuel Kant, "Perpetual Peace," in *Political Writings*, second edition, ed. H. S. Reiss, trans. H. B. Nisbit (Cambridge: Cambridge University Press, 1991), pp. 107, 112.

8. Eleanor Roosevelt, speech to the United Nations, New York, March 27, 1958.

9. These views are similar to several of David Gautier's, though two of his conclusions are, it seems, inconsistent and materially false: "In effect, we assume that human beings are socialized into autonomy" (p. 350), but "Although social affective relationships are essential to the liberal individual, there are no essential social relationships" (p. 347). But consider: core systems—family or friendships, for example—are essential to the affect and autonomy required for the cooperation Gautier commends. The beliefs, attitudes, and feelings acquired in core systems are fundamental to one's psychic identity; autonomous reflection is not a power for superseding, then shedding them. These are factual claims for which there is, or is not, empirical evidence. Gautier might respond that his claims are conceptual, meaning that they occur within his rational reconstruction of morality; but then, one asks if his conceptualization accurately represents the moral attitudes and feelings of actual people. David Gautier, *Morals by Agreement* (Oxford: Oxford University Press, 1987).

10. G.W.F. Hegel, *Philosophy of Right*, trans. S. W. Dyde (Amherst, N.Y.: Prometheus Books, 1996), pp. 256–258.

11. Gautier discounts all that is local and particular when specifying the ideal, contractarian basis for morality:

What ideal of the person does the Archimedean point express? How does that ideal lead to a judgment of the structure of society, or of the basic principles that underlie social interaction? And what is the import of this judgment for reason and for morals? Briefly, we suppose that the ideal presents a rational actor freed, not from individuality but from the content of any particular individuality, an actor aware that she is an individual with capacities and preferences both particular in themselves and distinctive in relation to those of her fellows, but unaware of which capacities, which preferences. Such a person must exhibit concern about her interactions with others, and this concern leads her to a choice among possible social structures. But her concern is necessarily impartial, because it is based on the formal features of individual rational agency without the biasing content of a particular and determinant set of individual characteristics.

Gautier, *Morals by Agreement*, p. 233.
Compare this passage by Mario Bunge:

Impartiality can only be secured through active popular participation, so that everyone may defend his own interests without infringing on the rights of others. And justice can only be secured by combining popular participation (self-management) with knowledge (not ignorance) of the basic needs, legitimate aspirations, and abilities of the group members. Since such knowledge is only possible in comparatively small groups, integral democracy is necessarily of the grass roots or bottom-up kind.

Mario Bunge, *Treatise on Basic Philosophy*, volume 8, *Ethics: The Good and the Right* (Dordrecht, Holland: D. Reidel, 1989), p. 192.

12. This requires the qualification of note 25 in chapter 2: the matter and energy constituting any new thing are as old as the cosmos.

13. Mill, *On Liberty*, p. 16.

14. Ibid., p. 13.

15. Aristotle, *Metaphysics*, 1041a7–1041b33, pp. 810–811.

16. Descartes, *Meditations*, pp. 80–81.

17. Hume, *A Treatise of Human Nature*, pp. 173–174.

18. R. B. Braithwaite, *Scientific Explanation* (Cambridge: Cambridge University Press, 1959), pp. 301–303.

19. Hume, *A Treatise of Human Nature*, p. 1.

20. Plato, *Republic*, 369b, p. 615.

21. Leibniz, *Monadology*, paras. 84–87, p. 162; and Hegel, *Phenomenology of Mind*, pp. 507–610.

22. Mill, *On Liberty*, p. 13.

23. See, for example, Christine Korsgaard, *The Sources of Normativity* (Cambridge: Cambridge University Press, 1996), pp. 49–89.

24. John Dewey, *The Public and its Problems* (Athens, Ohio: Ohio University Press, 1991), pp. 3–36; Weissman, *A Social Ontology*, pp. 167–170.

25. Weissman, *A Social Ontology*, pp. 166–178.

26. A politically sensitive example illustrates the result when these three are poorly distinguished. Women are often vulnerable to confusion when feminist thinking moves among the three ontological hypotheses (atomism, holism, and communitarianism) and the three rubrics (idea, ideal, or ideology). Using the competing ontologies as ideas, we compare the lives of women soldered to other people in relations of duty and affection to those of women who are self-reliant. Construing the ideas as ideals, we emphasize their relative benefits and costs. Or we construe them as ideologies and propose that one or another be used as a formula for remaking women's lives: supersede communitarian ideas of family, for example, so women may have the autonomy of (idealized) men. These options yield nine possibilities: each of the three hypotheses construed under each of the three rubrics. Theorists are not always clear about these options, so that talk of gender and roles moves erratically among the nine options. Women hear the options as prescriptions, and they feel the nine contrary messages with tension and guilt: can one go either way without betraying oneself? Conflicts of this sort pervade the experiences of people whose lives are warped by contrary ontological theses. They live alternately or concurrently within the "worlds" theories articulate, trying to realize competing norms in their personal and social lives.

27. John Dewey, *Reconstruction in Philosophy* (Boston: Beacon Press, 1920), p. 187; Weissman, *A Social Ontology*, pp. 242–252.

28. Bernard Williams, *Ethics and the Limits of Philosophy* (Cambridge: Harvard University Press, 1985), pp. 66–69.

29. F. H. Bradley, *Ethical Studies*, second edition (Oxford: Oxford University Press, 1988).

30. Chapter 6 suggests a consequentialist basis for appraising such differences: we evaluate them by introducing a determinable but not empty notion of human

flourishing. Rather than measure the differences against one another—they may be incommensurable—we ask if each enhances or diminishes human flourishing in the context of a culture's other practices.

31. Martin Heidegger, *Being and Time*, trans. John Macquarrie and Edward Robinson (New York: Harper & Row, 1962), pp. 103–105.

32. Williams, *Ethics and the Limits of Philosophy*, pp. 129, 140.

33. Hilary Putnam, *The Collapse of the Fact/Value Dichotomy* (Cambridge: Harvard University Press, 2002), pp. 28–45.

34. Richard Rorty, *Consequences of Pragmatism*, pp. 150–154.

35. Nagel, *Structure of Science*, pp. 485–502.

36. Heidegger, *Being and Time*, p. 98.

37. William James, "The Will to Believe," in *The Writings of William James*, ed. John J. McDermott (New York: Modern Library, 1968), p. 723.

38. Hilary Putnam, *Reason, Truth, and History* (Cambridge: Cambridge University Press, 1981), p. 128.

39. Putnam, *Collapse of the Fact/Value Dichotomy*, p. 32.

40. Ibid., p. 33.

41. Ibid., p. 30.

42. Kant, *Critique of Judgment*, n. 18, pp. 16–17.

43. Putnam, *Collapse of the Fact/Value Dichotomy*, p. 33. For contrast, see John Searle, "How to Derive 'Ought' from 'Is'," *Philosophical Review*, vol. 73 no. 1, January 1964, pp. 43–58.

44. Plato, *Republic*, 502c–509c, pp. 737–744.

45. Kant, *Critique of Practical Reason*, p. 55.

46. Jean-Paul Sartre, *Being and Nothingness*, trans. Hazel E. Barnes (New York: Washington Square Press, 1966), pp. 147–155.

47. Descartes, *The Passions of the Soul*, in *Philosophical Writings*, volume 1, p. 349.

48. Descartes, *Meditations*, p. 64.

49. Kant, *Critique of Practical Reason*, p. 33.

50. Hobbes, *Leviathan*, pp. 140–154; Hegel, *Philosophy of Right*, p. 217.

51. John Rawls, *A Theory of Justice* (Cambridge: Harvard University Press, 1971), pp. 75–83; *The Law of Peoples* (Cambridge: Harvard University Press, 1999), pp. 65, 114.

52. See, for example, disagreements among the contributors to *Metaphilosophy*, vol. 36, nos. 1/2, January 2005, "Global Institutions and Responsibilities: Achieving Global Justice."

53. Descartes, *Meditations*, p. 63.

54. René Descartes, *The Philosophical Writings of Descartes*, volume 3, trans. John Cottingham, Robert Stoothoff, Dugald Murdoch, and Anthony Kenny (Cambridge: Cambridge University Press, 1991), p. 159.

55. Descartes, *The Passions of the Soul*, in *Philosophical Writings*, volume 1, p. 349.

56. Or one acknowledges the intergenerational duty to do for one's infant children what was done for oneself. It is also compelling that one participates, as a new parent, in a community where irresponsible treatment of one's children is perceived as an assault on the fabric of reasonable relations and expectations.

57. Plato, *Republic*, 368c–371e, pp. 614–618.

58. Weissman, *A Social Ontology*, pp. 161–162.

59. Plato, *Republic*, 619c, p. 843. See Carol Gilligan, *In a Different Voice* (Cambridge: Harvard University Press, 1982).

60. Descartes, *Meditations*, p. 66.

61. Søren Kierkegaard, *Fear and Trembling*, trans. Alastair Hannay (London: Penguin, 1985).

62. Plato, *Apology*, in *Collected Dialogues*, 17a–42a, pp. 4–26; Friedrich Nietzsche, *Genealogy of Morals and Ecce Homo*, trans. Walter Kaufmann (New York: Random House, 1969), p. 109.

63. Kant, *Critique of Practical Reason*, n. 2, p. 55.

64. See Max Weber, *Economy and Society*, vols. 1 and 2, eds. Guenther Toth and Claus Wittich (Berkeley: University of California Press, 1978), vol. 1, pp. 40–56.

65. Rousseau, *Social Contract*, p. 49.

66. Thomas Pogge, *World Poverty and Human Rights* (Cambridge, Mass.: Polity, 2002), pp. 64–67; David Rodin, "The Ownership Model of Business Ethics," *Metaphilosophy*, vol. 36, nos. 1 and 2, January 2005, pp. 167–168.

67. Niccolò Machiavelli, *The Prince*, trans. Robert M. Adams (New York: Norton, 1992).

68. Thomas Pogge, "Human Rights and Global Health," *Metaphilosophy*, vol. 36, nos. 1 and 2, January 2005, pp. 182–209.

69. Jürgen Habermas, *The Theory of Communicative Action*, volumes 1 and 2, trans. Thomas McCarthy (Boston: Beacon Press, 1987), vol. 1, pp. 286–344.

70. Alain-Gerard Slama, "Le remede dans le mal," *Le Figaro*, June 20, 2005, no. 18,934. Translated from the French.

71. Dewey, *The Public and Its Problems*, pp. 143–184.

72. Ethical views that emphasize the use of moral language to guide action, but deny its reportorial uses have a simpler conception of nature. See, for example, Mark Timmons, *Morality Without Foundations: A Defense of Ethical Contextualism* (Oxford: Oxford University Press, 1999), pp. 71–74, 77–94.

73. William James, "Pragmatism—What It Is," in *Pragmatism, the Classic Writings*, ed. H. S. Thayer (Indianapolis: Hackett, 1982), p. 133.

74. Friedrich Nietzsche, *Beyond Good and Evil*, trans. Walter Kaufmann (New York: Vintage Books, 1989), pp. 47–48.

75. Descartes, *Discourse on Method*, pp. 8–15; Hume, *A Treatise of Human Nature*, pp. 1–8.

76. Descartes, *Passions of the Soul*, pp. 337–338; Hume, *A Treatise of Human Nature*, pp. 470–476.

77. Aristotle, *Physics*, 194b16–195b3, pp. 240–242.

78. Plato, *Republic*, 327a–367e, pp. 576–614.

79. Aristotle, *Politics*, 1295b1–1296b11, pp. 1220–1222.

80. Spinoza, *Ethics*, p. 191.

81. Hobbes, *Leviathan*, pp. 90–96.

82. Hume, *A Treatise of Human Nature*, pp. 413–418.

83. Kant, *Critique of Practical Reason*, p. 87.

84. Kant, "Perpetual Peace," pp. 108–114.

85. Intuitionists believe that moral norms are known infallibly in the manner of Plato's Forms or Descartes' clear and distinct ideas. Their view is shared by religious fundamentalists and political ideologists.

86. Dewey, *The Public and Its Problems*, pp. 105–109, 149–151; Weissman, *Lost Souls*, pp. 163–169.

87. Hobbes, *Leviathan*, pp. 63–66.

88. Aristotle, *Politics*, 1252a–1274b, pp. 1127–1176.

89. Sigmund Freud, *The Ego and the Id*, trans. Joan Riviere, ed. James Strachey (New York: W.W. Norton, 1960), pp. 63–66.

90. Heinz Kohut, *The Restoration of the Self* (New York: International University Press, 1978), pp. 97, 178.

91. D. W. Winnicott, *Playing and Reality* (London: Routledge, 1971), pp. 139, 141.

92. John Stuart Mill, *Utilitarianism* (Indianapolis: Hackett, 1979), p. 7.

93. Friedrich Hayek, *The Road to Serfdom* (Chicago: University of Chicago Press, 1994), pp. 47–48.

94. Mill, *Utilitarianism*, p. 8.

95. Leibniz, *Monadology*, paras. 57–60, p. 157.

96. Kant, *Critique of Practical Reason*, p. 39.

97. Plato, *Meno*, in *Collected Dialogues*, 85c–86b, pp. 370–371; Descartes, *Meditations*, pp. 67–68, 80–82.

98. Alfred Jules Ayer, *Language, Truth, and Logic* (New York: Dover, 1936), p. 108.

99. Hume, *A Treatise of Human Nature*, p. 470.

100. Ibid., p. 471.

101. Ibid.

102. Jay Schulkin, *Bodily Sensibility: Intelligent Action* (Oxford: Oxford University Press, 2004), pp. 31–56.

103. Mill, *Utilitarianism*, p. 9.

Chapter Five. Aesthetic Norms

1. John Dewey, *Art as Experience* (New York: Perigee Books, 1980), p. 180.

2. Ibid., p. 182.

3. Plato, *Euthyphro*, in *Collected Dialogues*, 10c, p. 179.

4. "By common consent, the Parthenon is a great work of art. Yet, it has esthetic standing only as the work becomes an experience for a human being." Dewey, *Art as Experience*, p. 4.

5. Ibid., pp. 129–130.

6. Kant, *Critique of Judgment*, pp. 97–100.

7. Friedrich Nietzsche, *Thus Spake Zarathustra*, trans. Walter Kaufmann (New York: Modern Library, 1995), para. 6, p. 19.

8. Friedrich Nietzsche, *The Gay Science*, trans. Walter Kaufmann (New York: Vintage, 1974), paras. 108, 125, pp. 167, 181.

Chapter Six. Cultural Variation

1. Leibniz, *Monadology*, para. 2, p. 148.

2. See, for example, E. O. Wilson, *Consilience: The Unity of Knowledge* (New York: Vintage, 1998), pp. 160–162.

3. This rendering ignores the possibility that each determinable may have several or many possible expressions within a culture, and that some expressions for some determinables may not be connected in any way to others.

4. Aristotle, *Nichomachean Ethics*, 1155a1–1172a15, pp. 1058–1093.

5. Plato, *Republic*, 544a–e, pp. 773–774.

6. David Weissman, *Truth's Debt to Value* (New Haven: Yale University Press, 1993), pp. 315–329.

7. Aristotle, *Politics*, 1323a14–1337a8, pp. 1277–1305.

8. Friedrich Nietzsche, *Beyond Good and Evil*, trans. Walter Kaufmann (New York: Vintage, 1989), pp. 47–48.

Chapter Seven. Freedom

1. Leibniz, *Monadology*, para. 47, p. 155.

2. John Dewey, "The Reflex Arc in Psychology," *Psychological Review*, 3, 1896, pp. 357–370.

3. Robert Kane, "Two Kinds of Compatibilism," *Philosophy and Phenomenological Research*, vol. 50, no. 2, December 1989, p, 227.

4. Ibid., pp. 235–236.

5. David Weissman, *Hypothesis and the Spiral of Reflection* (Albany, N.Y.: State University of New York Press, 1989), pp. 187–189; and *A Social Ontology*, pp. 267–277.

6. Hobbes, *Leviathan*, pp. 87–90.

7. Kant, *Critique of Judgment*, n. 18, pp. 16–17.

8. James, "Will to Believe," pp. 720–721.

9. Peirce, "Fixation of Belief," in *Collected Papers*, vol. V, pp. 223–247; Dewey, *Experience and Nature*, pp. 1–36.

10. Michel Foucault, *Power/Knowledge*, ed. Colin Gordon (New York: Pantheon, 1977), p. 131.

11. Rorty, *Consequences of Pragmatism*, p. xlii–xliii.

12. Hilary Putnam, *Reason, Truth, and History*, p. 130.

13. Ibid., p. 201.

14. Hayek, *The Road to Serfdom*, pp. 77–78. Milton Friedman's introduction to this edition of Hayek's text assumes that "collectivist organization" is the single alternative to the individualism he prefers. This is the traditional, and mistaken, simplification of our political and social options: it ignores systems theory—communitarianism—hence the reality of associations and organizations that are sometimes mutually independent, but often nested and overlapping. Friedman wouldn't agree that positive freedom presupposes both textured contexts and the information, attitudes, and skills—acquired in systems—that qualify us to choose and act.

15. Adam Smith, *Wealth of Nations* (New York: Bantam, 2003).

16. Karl Marx, *Communist Manifesto* (New York: Bantam, 1992), pp. 33, 42–43.

17. Ibid., p. 38.

18. Weber, *Economy and Society*, volume 2, p. 1156.

19. Marx, *Communist Manifesto*, p. 43.

20. Quoted by Herbert Marcuse, "Some Social Implications of Modern Technology," in *The Essential Frankfurt School Reader*, eds. Andrew Arato and Eike Gebhardt (New York: Continuum, 1982), p. 142.

21. Ibid., pp. 156–157.

22. Amartya Sen, *Rationality and Freedom* (Cambridge: Harvard University Press, 2002), pp. 10–13.

23. Nietzsche, *Genealogy of Morals*, pp. 86–88.

24. "The intelligent mechanic engaged in his job, interested in doing well and finding satisfaction in his handiwork, caring for his materials and tools with genuine affection, is artistically engaged." Dewey, *Art as Experience* (New York: Perigee, 1980), p. 5.

25. "The liberty of choice allowed to the craftsman who worked by hand has almost vanished with the general use of the machine. Production of objects enjoyed in direct experience by those who possess, to some extent, the capacity to produce useful commodities expressing individual values, has become a specialized matter apart from the general run of production. This fact is probably the most important factor in the status of art in present civilization." Ibid., p. 341. " [A]rt itself is not secure under modern conditions until the mass of men and women who do the useful work of the world have the opportunity to be free in conducting the processes of production and are richly endowed in capacity for enjoying the fruits of collective work." Ibid., p. 344.

26. See Alasdair MacIntyre, *After Virtue* (Notre Dame, Ind.: Notre Dame University Press, 1984).

27. See Hayek's aversion to laissez-faire—unregulated—capitalism: *The Road to Serfdom*, p. 21.

28. Descartes, *Meditations*, p. 66.

Conclusion

1. Hume, *A Treatise of Human Nature*, p. 104.

2. Weissman, *Lost Souls*, pp. 5–26.

3. Ibid., pp. 118–122.

4. Descartes, *Meditations*, pp. 49–52.

5. Weissman, *Lost Souls*, pp. 97–172.

Index

Abduction: as conceptual exploration, 12
Absolute: as overarching system, 54
Absolutism, 158
Actions: voluntary, 237
Adaptability, 21
Aesthetic(s): experiences, 206–207, 210, 211;
 norms, 6, 201–219; values, 201–219
Affirmation: expression of dedication, 140
Altruism, 127; universalizing, 164
Appetite: cyclical, 68; normativities implied
 by, 68
Aristotle, 68, 95, 156, 238, 275n29; acknowledgment of efficient cause, 85; categorial
 form and, 9; on causality, 10, 67; on character, 94; cultural variables and, 226–228;
 description of friendship, 222; discerning
 norms in matters of fact, 186–187; emphasis on formal cause, 85; inference of relations of things and properties by, 47; on
 logic, 26; metaphysics of, 56, 67; notion of
 final cause, 182; systemic problems,
 226–228; *universalia in rebus* of, 41
Atomism/individualism, 15fig; autonomy and,
 96; conflict and, 90; cooperation and, 91;
 credibility of, 85; Democritean, 15; emphasis on self-sufficiency, 89; exemption from
 unsolicited duty in, 90; failure of, 235, 236;
 falsification of, 6; freedom and, 17, 233,
 234; freedom from constraint and, 85; generalization from favorable examples in,
 176; internalist version of, 96; logical, 42;
 markets and, 250; misrepresentation of

form of reality by, 176; morality and, 80,
 83–87; moral psychology of, 95, 96; narrow
 range of applications of, 85; notion of individuality in, 235; as ontological alternative,
 22; perceptions of conflict in, 90; possibility in, 17; public and, 170; reality and, 14,
 83, 84; responsibility and, 96; satisfaction
 of, 175; as secular version of Protestant
 conscience, 90; self-sufficiency and, 20; signature values of, 89–94; social, 83, 123,
 142; subversion by causality, 85
Attitude: boundaries established by, 99; determination of appraisal of circumstance and
 effect and, 146; habitual, 99; synthesis of,
 99
Augustine, 129; notion of individuality, 235
Autonomy: acquisition of, 22; atomism and,
 96; communitarianism and, 18; consolida-
 tion of, 133; derivation of *should* and *ought*
 from *is* and, 143–150; emergence with
 development, 240; of language games, 39,
 173; modularity of systems and, 62; moral,
 139, 143–150; in organizations, 62; practical conditions for, 76; psychic, 139; reduction of, 63; relative, 236; self-regulating, 84;
 socialization into, 277n9; in systems, 236
Averaging, 47
Awareness, 95

Beauty: conditions of, 210; contrasts and,
 214; creation of, 201, 202–219; emergence
 of, 209; exhilaration from, 214; experience

Beauty (*continued*)
   of, 72, 201, 207–208, 209, 210, 213; features of, 214; as function of material and formal properties of objects, 208; as function of sensibility enabling us to perceive, 208; indexical use of, 208; interaction of perceiver and perceived in, 208; judgment on, 211; natural, 213–215; objectivity and, 209; organizing idea of, 214; properties of, 210, 214; sites of, 210; space and time in, 215–217; subjectivity and, 211; visibility of, 203
Behavior: costs of, 127; creation of, 10; determinability of, 21; distorted, 22; interpersonal, 134; lawful, 139; morality and, 73; practical value in, 67; redirecting, 115; regulation of, 73, 160; social, 123, 145; stabilizing, 61; unreliable, 127
Being: cogito as ground for, 11; possibility as mode of, 31; in thought, 11
Bell's inequalities, 55
Berkeley, George, 2; *esse est percipi* of, 36, 46
Body: as attractor state, 181; as organic system, 178; stabilizable, 181; sustainability of, 178
Boundaries: breaching, 5; defining capabilities of, 5; defining spatial regions, 215, 216; established by attitudes, 99; of social systems, 62; topological, 45
Bridgman, Percy, 46
Butler, Bishop, 27, 29, 57

Calvinism, 96
Carnap, Rudolf, 175, 270n1
Categorial form: see Form, categorial
Causality: as energy transfer, 85; explanation for, 10; mechanical interpretation of, 274n25; natural laws and, 35–41; science and, 10–11
Cause: difference from, 85; efficient, 51, 67, 85; final, 67, 182; formal, 51, 67, 85; material, 67; natural, 68; need for appropriate for desired effect, 66; in systems, 51
Cause and effect, 70, 265; dependencies in, 44; expectation and, 2; human interest and, 66, 67; increasing magnitude in, 40; natural relation of, 64; perceptions and, 35; relation between, 38, 39; separability of, 38, 39
Cephalus, 186

Change, 228–229; acceptable, 228; accidental, 85; adjustments to, 1; in cause and effect interactions, 44; constraints on, 57; cultural, 228–229; in dispositions, 58; gradual, 1; in human interests, 66; identity and, 28; radical, 228; sameness as distinct from, 4; welcome, 228
Chaos, 49
Character: alteration of, 249; as basis for morality, 94; as cognitive-affective posture, 240; derivation of *should* and *ought* from *is* and, 141–143; determination of responses and, 141; emergence of, 20; formation, 78, 132; formed from learning cooperatively, 141–143; formed in core systems, 139; as foundation for duty, 141; moral, 93, 143; power as function of, 82; reduction of, 249; relation to systems, 142
Civility, 117
Cognition, 195; refinement of emotional experiences and, 213
Cohen, Morris, 26
Collaboration: long-term benefits of, 184
Communitarianism, 14, 15*fig*, 197–200; accuracy of, 22; autonomy and, 18; causal reciprocity of parts in, 16; confirmation of, 6; conflict and, 90; cooperation and, 91; corporate identity of, 88; duty and, 20; freedom and, 20, 233, 234; generation of *should* and *ought* from *is*, 176; idealization and, 191; moral psychology of, 96, 97; necessity and, 18; nested, overlapping systems and, 61; obligation in, 90; obscurity of, 88; perceptions of conflict in, 90; possibility and, 18; reality and, 22; reciprocity and, 18; resistance to, 88; satisfaction of, 175; signature values of, 89–94; systems in, 88; truth of confirmed, 176
Competition: alienation and, 136; promotion of, 247; for resources, 21; system, 127; as universal feature of life, 136
Conceivability, 57
Concepts: thick moral, 99–105
Conflict: acknowledgment of, 91; adjudication of, 158; alleviation of, 90; anticipating, 92; atomism/individualism and, 90; communitarianism and, 90; as curable distortion, 90; in duties of individual persons, 131–135; with early roles, 240; endemic, 90; holism and, 90; in law, 137–138;

between legal and other duties, 136–137; management of, 156; moral, 20, 126–138, 158; promotion by egoism, 154; in relations between persons, 135–136; resolution of, 162; social, 188; system relations to others, 126–131; in systems, 53

Conscience: demands of, 96

Consciousness: reduction of all processes to, 57

Constraints: of categorial form, 23; dissolution of traditional, 245; freedom and, 6; geometrical, 46; internal, 33; intrinsic, 59; of *is* on *ought*, 178; layered, 5, 52; limiting, 59; logical, 27; minimization of, 25; in nature, 58; in space and time, 217, 218; of systems, 87; verticality of, 51, 52, 53

Context(s): civil peace and, 242; conflict, 243; conventional laws, 243; cultural, 242–243; economic organization/productivity, 242; logical, natural laws, 243; nested, 5; overlapping, 5; personal health/illness, 241–242; personal/social history, 243; systems in which one participates, 241; technology and, 243; topography and climate, 242; variables, 241–243

Contextualism, 19

Contingency, 21

Contradictions, 74

Contraries, 27; disparate categorial forms as, 18; exclusion of, 59; as expressions of higher-order determinable, 27, 28; freedom and duty, 20; negation of legal *should/ ought*, 74; otherness of, 28

Cooperation, 104, 186; achieving, 162; atomism/individualism and, 91; communitarianism and, 91; competition and, 127; in core systems, 139; freedom and, 77; holism and, 91; learning, 92; normative context, 162, 163; as procedural value, 102; reciprocity and, 102; rules and, 157; systems and, 140; well-being and, 162

Creations: accessibility to human sensibility, 206–207; coherence, 203; complexity-with-economy and, 203; contrast and, 203; cultivation/idiosyncrasy of artist/perceiver, 207; ideas and, 203; innovation and, 205–206; materials of, 203; order and, 203; organizing schemas for, 203–204; proportion and, 203; resolution and, 205; rules for, 203–204; surprise and, 206

Critique of Judgment (Kant), 245

Cultural: change, 228–229; difference, 221–229; norms, 4, 6; relativism, 223

Darwin, Charles, 127

Darwinism: categorial form and, 9; social, 9

Deconstructionism, 25

Derrida, Jacques, 270n1

Descartes, René, 95, 153, 180, 263, 267; belief that natural necessity is geometrical, 60; conceptual analysis of, 265; on detachment from others, 119; on difference between mind and nature, 178; on effect of finite substances, 85; *esse est percipi* of, 36; geometrical hypotheses of, 49; on logic, 26; notion of individuality, 235; rules for reconstruction of confused ideas, 36; on self-love, 118, 129; on value of utilities, 65

Desire: appropriate to natures and situations, 187; manipulation of mind and, 66; transcendental, 266

Determinables: identity of, 222; idiosyncratic detail in, 222

Determinism: moral, 20; objections to, 25; pervasive, 236; soft, 239; strict, 238

Development: emergence of autonomy with, 240; moral, 93, 229; personal, 22

Dewey, John, 237, 246, 270n1; on cause and effect, 70; esthetic experience, 205; Great Community and, 170

Dispositions, 41–50; Aristotelian characterization of, 56; as basis for natural laws, 41; as basis for norms, 59; change in, 58; corporate, 53, 54; dynamically determined, 46–47; fixed by geometrical/topological properties of structures, 47; interactions and, 41; located in structures, 48; as nature's regulators, 40; particles and, 41; in physical structures, 42; as qualifications for dynamic relations, 56; as qualifications for relation, 48; as second-order properties, 43; as second-order properties of structures, 41; sustaining, 59; variation due to spacetime's structure, 48

Diversity, 159, 258; of moral theories, 190–197

Duty: allocation of, 113; ambiguity of, 78, 79, 124; communitarianism and, 20; conflicting, 127; contempt for, 112; to core systems, 79; distortions of, 78; and

Duty (*continued*)
  enforceability of contracts, 157; failures of,
  109; first-order, 115; formation of, 172;
  freedom and, 92; fulfilling, 80; fulfilling as
  complex achievement, 113; as habit, 176;
  holism and, 20; imposed, 156; to individuals, 114; instrumental, 155; interdependency and, 79–80; to law, 118, 122–125,
  137; learned, 101; legal, 80, 110, 156;
  legalistic context of, 78; legislated, 156;
  material considerations in, 83; moral, 124;
  natural, 77; obligation and, 83; obsessions
  with, 135; to others irrespective of shared
  systems, 114–118; *ought* of, 83; participation as, 168; to persons, 137; to preserve
  life, 114; priority of, 120; in relationships,
  77; respect as, 136; second-order, 115; to
  self, 118–121; self-referring, 120; situational, 155, 171; as state of affairs, 171; to
  strangers, 118; of system members to each
  other, 111–112; to systems, 80, 105–125; of
  systems to members, 108–111; of systems to
  nonmembers, 112–114; of systems to other
  systems, 112–114; vocational, 152, 153

Ego: Cartesian, 80
Egoism, 64, 129; promotion of conflict by,
  154; qualified, 64
Einstein, Albert, 20, 60, 275n35; geometrical
  hypotheses of, 49
Emotion: difficulty in disciplining, 212
Emotivism, 195–197
Empiricism, 39
Ends: achievable, 67; causal trajectory of, 67;
  ideal, 67; natural, 68; normativity of, 67;
  practical value of, 67
Entropy: and least energy principle, 68
Environmentalism, 1
Essence: accidental conjunctions and, 68;
  generative, 68
Essentialism: Aristotelian, 56
Ethics: contentiousness of, 73; discourse, 162;
  language of, 6; moral aim of, 73; ontology
  and, 6; principles of, 6; virtue, 191–193
Ethics (Aristotle), 94
Evolution: cause of interdependence, 76; cul-
  tural variables and, 227; map of categorial
  form and, 12; of religious thought, 95
Existence: of God, 11; as instrumental value,
  114; properties of, 27; self-love and, 129
Experience(s): aesthetic, 206–207, 210, 211;
  autonomous, 9; of beauty, 72, 201,

  207–208, 210, 213; behavior as part of, 10;
  cognitive, 210; fragmentary nature of, 13;
  of freedom, 232; moral, 74; ordinary, 207;
  organization of, 3, 25; perceptual, 206;
  practical, 7, 11, 74; provocative, 202; as
  reality, 13; *should* and *ought* in, 74, 75;
  thinkable, 3, 9
Experimentalism, 246

Factionalism, 186
Fairness, 151; as principal value, 152
Feedback: negative, 52, 127, 160, 181, 182;
  positive, 51, 160
Flourishing, 224, 225, 226
Form, categorial, 9–23; antecedent formulations and, 19; cogency of, 20; comprising
  features of all that is, 23; constraints of, 23;
  determinability of, 21; dialectic of alternatives, 14; disparate, 18; evidence of, 10–11;
  as framework of norms, 23; hierarchy of
  limits and; hypotheses, 14–19; implications
  for moral life, 20; information about, 12;
  Kantian objection to, 12–14; method for
  discovery of, 11–12; modalities of, 18;
  moral determinism of, 20; practical applications, 19–21; practical experiences of,
  10; of reality, 22; as regulative idea, 12,
  13–14; restriction and; theory of, 11
Forms: with freedom, 206; intrinsic, 1; of
  nature, 1; of reality, 175; resolving, 214;
  virtual, 215–217
Foucault, Michel, 246, 270n1
Freedom, 231–263; of action, 17; alternative
  ontologies of, 233–236; artistic, 218; atomism and, 17, 233, 234; to choose, 4; to
  choose system trajectories, 168; communitarianism and, 20, 233, 234; constraint
  and, 6; context of, 233; cooperation and,
  77; creation of sense of entitlement to,
  231–233; duty and, 92; experience of, 232;
  form with, 206; as good-in-itself, 263;
  holism and, 81–82, 233, 234; implications
  for, 6; limitations on, 123; maximization of,
  25; moral, 133; more ideal than real, 184;
  negative, 4, 5, 20, 231–233, 237, 258; as
  opportunity to satisfy one's place in whole,
  20; pathologies of, 245–262; as personal
  imperative, 232; positive, 4, 20, 231–233,
  236, 237, 240–245; power and, 82; practical value of, 263; praise for, 231; prudence
  and, 6; restricted, 17; situated, 180;
  to/from, 89, 90; as utility, 263

Games: constituted by rules, 32; differences in, 32; distinction of *is* and *ought* in, 58; language, 39, 173; possibility and, 31
Genealogy of Morals (Nietzsche), 145
Generalizations: inductive, 59
Glaucon, 185, 186
Globalization, 250
God: belief in, 231; as capstone for all Being, 11; as cause, 85; endowment of powers from, 235; existence of, 11; as surmise, 84
Goodness, 71; commitment to reason, 76; as highest form, 105; intrinsic, 71; novelty and, 71

Habermas, Jurgen, 162
Habit: as unreliable measure of morality, 149
Hayek, Friedrich, 247
Hegel, G.W.F., 78, 156, 167; communitarian views of, 88; on formation of laws, 123; on reason and law, 78; reason prevailing over social contingency and, 157; reduction of morality to respect for law, 80; on universal norms, 153, 154
Heidegger, Martin, 99, 270n1; reduction of practical value of things to their use, 101
Heisenberg indeterminacy, 45
Heraclitus, 4, 26
Hobbes, Thomas, 242; categorial form and, 9; on freedom, 21; on laws, 123; view of human character, 187
Holism, 14, 15*fig*; conflict and, 90; consequentialism in, 96; contentiousness of, 81; cooperation and, 91; denial of separable parts in, 15; emerging normativity and, 82; emphasis on affiliation and duty, 89, 90; emphasis on duty, 20; failure of, 235, 236; falsification of, 6; freedom and, 81–82, 233, 234; generalization from favorable examples in, 176; hierarchies and, 22; inversion of priorities in, 20; misrepresentation of form of reality by, 176; morality and, 81–87; moral psychology of, 96; necessity and, 17, 18; as ontological alternative, 22; organic metaphors in, 16; origin of, 81; perceptions of conflict in, 90; pervasive internal relations of, 84; possibility and, 18; possibility of different wholes in, 18; satisfaction of, 175; signature values of, 89–94; single particular in, 15
Homogenization, 257, 258, 260
Hume, David, 26, 33, 186, 196, 265; attack on natural norms, 34; on causality, 36, 38, 39, 80; on cause and effect, 36, 38, 39; conflation of causal and logical necessity by, 36–37; conflation of extra-mental states of affairs by, 36; describes *is* as *must*, 58; descriptions of nature by, 57; elimination of efficacy by, 85; emphasis on difference, 195; and God, 2; on gravity, 34; on internal constraints, 33; on *is* and *ought*, 22–23; notions of *must* and *ought*, 2; *ought* joined to *is* by psychological states, 180; reduction of morality to individual sentiments, 80; on structure of mind, 95; on successor events, 68; test for possibility of, 57; theory of cause, 85; on values of circumstances, 3

Idealization: communitarianism and, 191; contract theory and, 193; deontology and, 194; emotivism and, 195–197; intuitionism and, 194–195; preoccupations of, 191; principal, 191; utilitarianism and, 193–194; virtue ethics and, 191–193
Ideals: aesthetic objects and, 4; confounding, 177; instantiated, 177; rational, 150–160; social, 185; unachieved, 185
Ideas: extra-mental referents, 2; regulative, 21
Identity: change and, 28; content of, 133; corporate, 1, 88; of determinables, 222; factors critical to, 29; force of restriction of, 28; law of, 27, 28; material, 28; moral, 133, 168; nullification of, 28; personal, 77, 169, 232; principle of, 30; priority of, 29; psychic, 5
Ideology: individualist, 64
Imagination: figurative, 203; reality as product of, 175; unachievable objectives and, 178
Individualism. *See* Atomism/individualism
Induction: generalization from, 12; inference and, 12; perpetuation of norms and, 59
Inference: inductive, 12; probabilistic, 12; sufficient condition and, 12
Inhibition: as moral task, 95
Initiative: limits of, 6
Inquiry: point of, 13
Instrumentalism, 46
Interaction, 39; cause and effect, 44; character formation and, 132; differences due to velocity, 49; dispositions and, 41; morality and, 122; of particles, 46; recurring, 43; of same causes/same effects, 43; of structurally identical causes for same effects, 49; of structures, 49

Introspectionism, 96
Intuition, 194–195, 274n23
Irrealism, 173
Is: of affiliation, 78; constraints on *ought*,
178; and derivation of *ought*, 3; disparity
with *ought*, 183; limiting to *ought*, 23;
merging with *ought*, 179; to *must, should,*
and *ought*, 72; *ought* from, 174–186; prescriptive, 177; of self-discovery, 129; *should*
from, 174–186

James, William, 175, 178, 246
Judgment: affirmation of value and, 65; on
beauty, 211; informed, 211
Justice: as attractor state, 184; characterizations of, 185; distributive, 151, 152, 155;
extensions of, 152; imagined, 177; intelligent intervention and, 183

Kane, Robert, 238, 239
Kant, Immanuel, 153, 156, 175, 245, 266,
267; antinomies of, 19; argument for universalization, 188; on authority, 189; and
categorial form, 12, 13, 14, 23; categorical
imperative of, 76, 96, 114, 148, 187, 188;
categories of understanding and, 3; conflict
and, 149; on difference between mind and
nature, 178; distinguishing beauty from
sublime, 215; on duty, 107; emphasis on
rationality, 161; on features of nature, 2; on
goodness, 105; hypothetical imperative of,
75; intervention of will in material world
and, 191; and irrelevance of human inter-
ests/needs, 73; kingdom of ends of, 151; on
laws, 123; on morality, 187; moral testing,
149; moral theory of, 75, 76; objectivity
and, 104; pragmatic appeal to reason by,
76; priority ascribed to deontological *should*
and *ought*, 74, 75; reduction of morality to
respect for law, 80; on reflection, 153; on
structure of mind, 95; synthetic a priori
truths of, 6–7; transcendental necessity
and, 3; on universal norms, 153; validity
moral principles and, 146; on values, 3;
values and conceptualizations in thinkable
world, 100

Language: descriptive, 6, 171; ethical, 6;
games, 39, 173; local, 218; moral, 173; prescriptive, 171; reportorial uses of, 6; tribal,
13

Law of the excluded middle, 16, 27, 28, 31
Laws: accidental conjunctions and, 68; as
afterthought, 122; application to objects of
a domain, 26, 27; and basis for duty,
150–160; bridge, 40; causal, 37, 40, 41, 64;
conflicts in, 137–138; as constraints on
motion and change, 40; conventional, 243,
244; deference to, 114; duty in the absence
of, 114; duty to, 118, 122–125; efficacy in,
65; establishment of norms and, 123; expedient, 156; of identity, 27, 28; inherent, 68;
instrumental value of, 158; limiting freedom, 123; logical, 16, 26, 27, 34, 174, 217,
243; morality and, 78, 79, 157; of motion,
16, 33, 40; national, 54; natural, 243; need
for access to what applies, 40; with no
exceptions, 32; of non-contradiction, 28;
normativity and, 3, 65; ontological status
of, 11; pervasiveness of, 67; physical, 34,
218; place in nature, 11; of quanta, 40; reg-
ularization of practices and, 158; regularly
broken, 123; for regulation of relations
among persons and systems, 139; regulative
implications of, 11, 23; relations of variables in, 65; relation to local morality, 155;
respect for, 154; revisions of, 153; stability
of, 34; statistical, 37; status of, 11;
unbreachable, 32; universal applicability of
logical, 16; universalist aspirations of, 156;
violation of, 37
Laws, natural, 4, 11, 25, 32, 33; causality and,
35–41; contingency of, 34; material basis
for, 34–55; necessity of, 34; relation to phenomena regulated, 40; as signature laws,
34; spacetime and, 35; stability of, 34; variability in statistical character of, 37
Learning: acquiring and using skills in coordination with others, 135; collaborative, 131;
requirements for, 131
Leibniz, Gottfried Wilhelm, 56, 59, 235; communitarian views of, 88; on logic, 26
Leviathan (Hobbes), 242
Limits: challenges to, 5; deterrence by, 5;
fixed, 5
Locke, John, 21
Logic: controversy in, 16; excluded middle
and, 27; fuzzy, 30; identity and, 27; laws of,
16, 26, 27, 217; non-contradiction and, 27;
normativity and, 26–31; ontological implications in, 27
Loyalty: parochial, 155; self-concerned, 155

Luther, Martin, 15, 95, 96, 271n6
Lying, 75

Malebranche, Nicolas, 2
Marcuse, Herbert, 253, 255
Market(s): as appropriate organizational mode
  for vital social functions, 248–251; atomism and, 250; competition, 247; conflicts,
  252–253; costs and benefits, 256–261;
  economies, 247, 248, 251; effects, 248–262;
  efficiency of, 250; fellowship and, 249; free,
  249; globalization and, 250; as guarantor of
  social fluidity, 253–256; modes of production and, 255; norms in, 250; opportunism
  and, 249; transnational companies in,
  261–262; utility of, 252; values, 260
Marx, Karl, 252, 253, 254; categorial form
  and, 9
Mass, 10–11, 50
Materialism: Aristotelian primary substances
  and, 15; dialectical, 252
Matter: conservation of, 276n38; pervasiveness of, 67
McKeon, Richard, 19
Measurement: of momentum and position,
  45; sequential, 45
Mechanism, 19
Meditation (Descartes), 36, 263, 266
Mentalism, 11
Metaphysics: Aristotle's, 56, 67; categorial
  form and, 11; of nature, 18, 67; ontological
  status of laws and, 11
Mill, John Stuart, 196, 251; emphasis on
  autonomy, 22; emphasis on deliberation
  and choice, 85; exercise of power over
  individuals and, 89; on regions of liberty,
  260
Mind: as activity of physical system, 36, 66;
  awareness and, 95; Cartesian, 15; conscious
  of self, 17; controls action, 76; freedom to
  reflect on ideas and, 17; laying down of
  regulative principles for thinking by, 6;
  manipulation of, 66; mind itself known to,
  11; passivity in reception of sensory data, 3;
  rules in creation of thinkable experiences,
  3; structure and ideas of, 11, 95; value-
  bestowing intention of, 4; virtues of, 95
Modularity: consequential for freedom, 51;
  dissolution under pressure of nesting/over-
  lap, 63; emphasis on, 239; implications of,
  50; of systems, 62

Moral: action, 174; agency, 80, 131; aims, 73;
  ambiguities, 64; autonomy, 139, 143–150;
  character, 93, 143; choices, 96; concepts,
  99–105; conflict, 20, 126–138, 158; determinism, 20; development, 93, 229; discourse, 174; duty, 124; economy, 83;
  education, 131, 150; enlightenment, 167;
  experience, 74; flashpoints, 126–138; freedom, 133; habits, 107; identity, 133, 168;
  intuition, 101, 189; judgments, 95; justification, 96; language, 173; life, 20, 108;
  norms, 73–200; pathologies, 186; practice,
  79; principles, 146; psychology, 94–99;
  reflection, 73; responsibility, 239; scrutiny,
  95; selves, 22; sentiment, 187; tension,
  126; theory, 190–197; values, 105, 141;
  virtue, 105, 207; will, 82
Morality: action and, 97; as aspect of interpersonal behavior, 134; atomism/individu-
  alism and, 80, 83–87; based on laws, 157;
  based on reason's universalizing ideals, 157;
  and bases for duty, 150–160; behavior and,
  73; character as basis for, 94; conditions of,
  124; context of, 77–80; derivation from
  demands of system members on each other,
  117; as domain of utility, 79; duty and, 124;
  duty to systems and, 105–125; and
  economies of human social systems, 183;
  energy for, 158; flashpoints in, 126–138;
  folk, 190; freedom and, 124; generation of
  shoulds and oughts in, 139–150; of good
  intentions, 148; grounded in reason, 76;
  "herd," 149; holism and, 81–87; as imperative of rational nature, 23; interaction and,
  122; law and, 78, 79; learned in core systems, 132–133; least conditions for, 161;
  leverage of, 73; local, 157, 160; material
  basis of, 152, 173; measures of, 149; mind
  control of action and, 76; origins of, 105;
  partial perceptions of, 133; personal, 133;
  practical value of, 79; principal basis of, 78;
  of reason, 79; regulative implications of,
  23; requirements of, 89; respect and, 124;
  rights and, 165–166; socialization and, 92,
  93; for spectators, 148; trust and, 124
Moral practice: idealization and, 191; interpretation and, 191; practicality and, 191
Moral theory: idealization and, 190; interpretation and, 190; practicality and, 190
Motion, 50; accelerated on trajectories in
  curved spacetime, 49; categorial profile of,

Motion (*continued*)
19; inertial, 49; laws of, 16; pervasiveness of, 67; regulation of, 23; routed through reciprocity, 201

Must: behavior shaping by, 267; in constraining circumstances, 4; in context of *is*, 217–219; emergence without human intervention, 266; Hume and, 2; lack of place in nature for, 3; necessity as, 16; in thinking of states of affairs, 3

Nature, 25–60; absence of contradictions in, 30; as aggregate, 25; beauty in, 213–215; biological, 5; as blank slate, 178; compromises and contingencies in, 84; consistency in, 102; constraints in, 58; devoid of inherent aims, 68; elements of, 1; forms of, 1; human interests and, 65; laws of, 4; logical structure of, 30; metaphysics of, 18, 67; necessity and, 2; as network of systems, 54; normativity of, 56–57, 59; norms and, 6; obligation and, 2; rational, 23; self-differentiation of, 56; toleration by, 6; uniformities of, 48; as unitary system, 55

Necessity: causal, 36–37; communitarianism and, 18; essentialist, 17, 18; existential, 17, 18; geometrical, 60; holism and, 17, 18; local, 17, 34; logical, 18, 36–37, 58; minimization of, 17; *must as*, 16; natural, 4, 58, 59, 60; nature and, 2; of nature's laws, 34; negations of as contradictions, 33; obtaining in all possible worlds, 33; in ontological theory, 16, 17; parochial, 16, 17, 18, 33, 36, 37, 58; transcendental, 3; universal, 17, 33

Needs: biological, 222; culturally different means of satisfying, 222; determinate expressions of, 221–226; fulfilling, 126; generic, 221–226; as interests, 222; social, 222

Networks: breakdowns in, 127; freedom in, 82; negative feedback and, 127; of obligation, 20; of organized roles, 82; resource distribution in, 127; sustaining, 127; of systems, 127

Newton, Isaac, 20, 25, 89

Nietzsche, Friedrich, 26, 145, 175, 218, 246; cultural variables and, 226–228; on death of God, 219; emphasis on the will, 232; on herd morality, 149, 227; on maximization

of freedom, 25; nature as blank slate by, 178; systemic problems, 226–228

Nodes: accidents and, 69; attractor states and, 70; consequential states and, 69; human intervention and, 70; regulativity in, 69

Normativity: breakdown of, 25; confusions over, 58; constraint and, 34; as everyday feature, 65; external/internal, 53; as function of law, 131; in holism, 82; lateral, 51; in laws, 65; legal, 124; limit and, 34; logic and, 26–31; material bases for, 7; natural, 4, 7, 25, 26, 34, 48; as obstacle to positive freedom, 4; origin of, 3; principal implications of, 34–55; to regularly broken laws, 123; regulation and, 34; representations of, 25; rules or laws and, 3; signifying constant regulation over time, 34; stabilization of, 58

Norms: aesthetic, 6, 201–219; alteration of, 5; with basis in affiliative human relations, 178; categorical form as framework of, 23; in causal relationships, 4, 67; challenges to, 5; change in, 5; cultural variation in, 221–229; of culture, 4, 6; developmentally acquired, 118; discovery of, 4; dispositions as basis for, 59; enabling, 162; of everyday life, 65; exemption from, 4; failure and, 65; generic, 222; generic constraints on, 221–229; ideal, 180; identification of, 185; immanent, 228; inhibiting, 4; intrinsic, 59; intrinsic to systems regulated by, 6; legal, 123; logical, 26; making of, 4; market, 250; material, 1, 178, 201; maximal, 161; minimal, 161; natural, 48, 59, 118; nature and, 6; negation of, 156; origin and use of, 175; particularized by system's distinguishing task or style, 161–162; perpetuation of, 59; practical, 61–72; practical life and, 6; prescriptive, 162; procedural, 162–163; proscriptive, 162; reality and, 6; societal, 172; as states of affairs, 171; stipulated, 34, 171; subjectivity of, 3; of system formation, 161–165; universal, 153, 244; variable, 153

Norms, moral, 6, 73–200, 163–165; cognitive aspects of, 99–105; emotive aspects of, 99–105; justification for, 98; in material systems, 150–160; ontological assumptions on, 80–89; opposing perspectives on, 150–160; in rational ideals, 150–160; semantics of, 74–77; signature values and, 89–94

Objectivity, 104; beauty and, 209; experience of, 104

Obligation: nature and, 2

Ontological theories. *See also* Atomism/individualism; Communitarianism; Holism: accommodation in, 21; implications for status of norms and, 6; logic in, 26–31; supporting evidence for, 21–23

Operationalism, 46

Opportunism, 249

Opportunity: context, 241; as function of context, 244; reconciling interpretation and, 241; resources for, 241

Organicism, 19

Organization(s): as aggregates of mutual advantage, 22; of experience, 3, 25; modularity of members of, 62; reciprocities of parts in, 62; relative autonomy in, 62; of sensory data, 9

Ought: behavior shaping by, 267; categorical, 74; categorical-situational, 75, 76; in constraining circumstances, 4; in context of *is*, 217–219; deontological, 74, 76; derived from *is* of systems, 80; differences among, 177; disparity with *is*, 183; of duty, 83; emergence in engagement with others, 266; extraction from human relations, 3; Hume and, 2; indistinguishable from what is done, 218; from *is*, 174–186; lack of place in nature for, 3; legal, 74, 75; limited by *is*, 23; natural bases for, 177; and physiological *is*, 184; as practical value, 266; pragmatic, 74, 75, 76; of self concern, 129; in thinking of states of affairs, 3; underivable from *is*, 3; universal, 74

Paradoxes, 28

Parmenides, 28

Particles: indeterminacy of, 55; indeterminate, 46; joined by reciprocal causal relations, 56; spontaneity of, 55; uniformity among, 41; variant topological deformations in, 47

Peirce, Charles Sanders, 246; on logic, 26, 39

Pepper, Stephen, 19

"Perpetual Peace" (Kant), 76

Philosophy of Right (Hegel), 78

Plato, 60, 87, 96, 153, 180; on appetite, 68; categorial form and, 9; geometrical hypotheses of, 49; on goodness, 105; on

logic, 26; on moral character, 186; realization of goodness and, 90

Pleasure, 260

Polemarchus, 185, 186

Politics (Aristotle), 94

Possibility, 16; atomism and, 17; communitarianism and, 18; contradiction and, 31; eternal, 31; holism and, 18; logical, 31, 57, 58; material, 31, 33; as mode of being, 31; in ontological theory, 16, 17; qualitatively/quantitatively determinable, 32; signified, 31; for thought, 17

Pragmatism, 245

Principles: construction, 43; of distributive justice, 152; ethical, 6; least energy, 68; moral, 146; of plenitude, 31; regulative, 4, 7, 122, 150–160; of sufficient reason, 43, 236; sustaining, 84; universal, 76

Proclus, 49, 60

Properties: balance as, 37, 39, 44, 45; of beauty, 210, 214; constitutive, 28; corporate, 37, 39, 44, 45, 56; determinate, 44; dispositional, 56; geometric, 48; identity-fixing, 28; imagining, 31; local, 46; of logical laws, 34; magnitude of, 29; marks of, 29; mixing, 28; name, 29; quality of, 29; quantity of, 29; relation and, 29; structural, 41, 42, 43, 48, 50; topological, 48; values, 46

Prudence, 162, 163, 167; freedom and, 6

Public: benefits of, 169–170; formation of, 166; layered, 166–170; need for, 169; participation in, 168; self-analysis in, 167

Putnam, Hilary, 6, 7, 30, 103, 104

Pythagoras, 60

Quantum theory, 25, 44, 45, 46, 273n22, 274n25

Quiescence, 69

Quine, Willard van Orman, 175

Reality: as aggregate of self-sufficient entities, 85; as array of systems, 16, 21, 93; atomism and, 83, 84; atomistic affirmation of, 14; categorial form of, 9, 13, 22; communitarianism and, 22; comprehensiveness of, 276n40; corporate, 20; decided form of, 176; experience as, 133; formlessness of, 25; as function of ways of thinking, 100; human aims and, 100; imagination as

Reality (*continued*)
product of, 175; infinite, 187; local, 154;
material, 55; modes of, 31; necessity of,
187; norms and, 6; personal interests and,
246; self-sufficient particulars in, 14; social,
175; theories of, 14–19; of time, 84
Reason: commitment of goodness to, 76; consistency and, 23; constraining will, 76;
mechanics of, 76; morality of, 79; practical,
66; social contingency and, 157; sufficient,
43, 44; universality and, 23
Reciprocity, 124; binding systems, 113;
causal, 56, 62, 140, 201; communitarianism
and, 18; creating, 92; establishment of,
141; habit as basis for, 140; mechanical,
140; morally demanding, 113; routed
through motion, 201; stabilized by cooperation, 140; sustaining, 92; unbalanced, 171
Reflection, 94; aim expressed as unease, 156;
atomist, 99; contingency of roles and interests, 148; habit and, 147; incidental, 95;
individual rational, 96; objects of, 153
Regularity: bases for, 59
Regulation: contraries and, 58; systemic, 53
Relationships: causal, 44, 67; conflicting
among persons, 135–136; contractual, 79;
core, 139; due to structures, 47; duty in, 77;
dynamic, 47, 48; healthy, 185; of indeterminate particles, 46; limiting, 48; nested,
18; norms in, 67; reciprocal, 18, 186; reciprocal causal, 187; respect in mutual, 77;
social affective, 277n9; stability of, 70;
static, 47, 48; of subordinate systems, 113;
values and, 3; of variables, 37, 39, 44, 45;
in which beauty is perceived, 211; withering of, 249
Relativism: cultural, 223
Relativity: general, 46; theory, 55
Reliability: difficulty in, 134; mechanical,
142; as moral virtue, 105
Republic (Plato), 90, 96, 142, 186
Respect: generalized from self-esteem, 152; for
law, 154; morality and, 124; more ideal
than real, 184; mutual, 183; for partners,
134, 152; recognition of worth of others,
80; in relations with all persons, 136; for
role, 181; situated, 181; as universal duty,
136
Responsibility: acquisition of, 22; as burden,
249; of members to systems, 106–108;

moral, 239; to others, 249; to self, 134; ultimate, 238
Rights, 165–166; duties and, 166–170
Roles: accepted, 116; affirmed, 116; expectations in, 135; social, 5, 95; well-being and,
120
Rorty, Richard, 270n1
Rousseau, Jean-Jacques, 160, 245; and deference to general will, 22; emphasis on freedom, 22
Rules: cooperation and, 157; for created
works, 203–204; existence prior to formulation of, 31; necessity enforced by penalties
threatened, 32; with no exceptions, 32;
normativity and, 3, 32; unbreachable, 32;
universal, 76

Santayana, George: on logic, 26
Sartre, Jean-Paul, 246, 270n1; on existence,
114
Schrödinger equation, 37, 39, 44, 45, 46
Science: causality and, 10–11; empirical, 11;
imposition of order of theories, 25; indeter-
minist implications in, 25
Scientific management, 253
Self: duty to, 118–121; moral, 22
Self-consciousness, 95
Self-control, 186
Selfhood: acquisition of, 93; emergence from
participation in systems, 80; formation of,
119; inception of, 119; moral quality of, 20
Self-interest, 64
Self-love, 129
Self-regulation: corporate, 124
Self-sufficiency, 20, 21, 62, 80, 82
Self-understanding, 20
Should: behavior shaping by, 267; categorical,
74; in constraining circumstances, 4; in
context of *is*, 217–219; deontological, 74;
emergence in engagement with others,
266; indistinguishable from what is done,
218; from *is*, 174–186; lack of place in
nature for, 3; legal, 74; natural bases for,
177; as practical value, 266; pragmatic, 74;
in thinking of states of affairs, 3; universal,
74
Skepticism, 46
Smith, Adam, 250
Social: arrangements, 186; atomism, 83, 123,
142; behavior, 123, 145; cohesion, 188;

conflict, 188; contingency, 157; contract, 186; control, 124, 224; custom, 174; Darwinism, 9; flourishing, 224, 225; fluidity, 253; harmony, 76; health, 185; history, 243; homogenization, 257; ideals, 185; life, 4, 22, 85, 158; malleability, 176; needs, 222; order, 123; reality, 175; reciprocity, 187; relations, 175, 231; roles, 5, 95; stability, 5; systems, 62, 69, 113, 183; values, 105

Solecisms, 29

Space: in beauty, 215–217; categorial profile of, 19; contiguity in, 85; formlessness of, 215, 216; necessary for motion, 12; unbounded, 12

Spacetime, 10–11, 50; beauty and, 215–217; categorial form and, 18; change in, 60; dynamics of, 56, 60; effect of embedded particles, 45, 47; evolutionary route of, 59; evolution of universe from, 55; as formless receptacle, 216; form of, 56; gravity and, 54; natural laws and, 35; as necessary condition for freedom of material particulars, 17; as primary reality, 217; shape of, 215; structure of matter in, 41; system of, 16; toleration of inscription of some forms, 216; topology of, 60; as totalizing system, 87

Specialization, 126, 186

Spinoza, Baruch: categorial form and, 9, 60; emphasis on humility and courage, 187; values commended by, 187

States: attractor, 67–70

Stipulations: normativity and, 3

Structures: contrasting dispositions in identical contexts, 50; defining, 41; differing capacities of, 41; dispositions fixed in, 47, 48; diversity of interactions in, 49; elementary referents for, 45; physical, 42; relationships and, 47; responses to altered circumstances, 49

Subjectivity: in aesthetic objects, 207; beauty and, 211; of norms, 3; tolerance for conflicting artistic judgments, 207

Surprise, 206, 213

Sympathy, 151; generalization to unknown persons, 151; moral sentiment and, 187

Systems, 50–54; abusive, 147; acceptance of responsibilities to, 176; autonomy in, 236; behaving as individuals, 22; causal reciprocities of parts of, 50; causal relations in, 80; cause in, 51; choices of, 185; clustered, 84; competition and, 90, 127; complementarity of parts, 16, 50, 201; conceptual, 13–14; conflict in, 53; consequential value in, 70–72; constraints in, 50, 87; cooperation and, 140; core, 77, 78, 79, 90, 118, 126, 133, 139, 151, 154, 185, 277n9; corporate dispositions and, 53; corporate properties of, 126, 167; coupling, 68; creation by interaction of efficient causes, 51; dependence on members' work, 79; derivation of *should* and *ought* from *is* in, 139–141; differential regulation of members, 52; displaced by law, 78; dissolution of, 18; duties of members toward each other, 111–112; duties of toward members, 108–111; duties to, 78, 79, 80, 105–125; duties to nonmembers, 112–114; duties to other systems, 112–114; dynamic, 50, 68, 201; emergence and dissolution in, 69; emergence of persons from, 78; emergence of selfhood from participation in, 80; environmental alteration and, 62; equilibrium in, 68, 69; exchange of resources with other systems, 63; expectations in, 109; fairness and, 151; fit of parts in, 18; formation of, 61–63; gravity and, 51; healthy, 185; hierarchical organization, 18, 51, 54, 127; higher-order control of lower-order, 54; holistic behavior of, 16, 22; human, 237; independent, 16; instrumental value in, 70–72; internal economy of, 46–47, 50; least energy, 67–70; local, 167; material, 66; mechanical, 67–70; members' duty to, 106–108; membership in, 79; member's responses to norms in, 52; modularity of, 16, 22, 50, 62, 94, 236; moral economy of, 83; morality learned in, 132; moral tension and, 126–138; natural, 182; nature as network of, 54; need fulfillment and, 126; negative feedback and, 52; nested, 16, 22, 54, 60, 87, 94, 127; networks of, 127; nodes and, 70; obligation and, 90; organic, 178; overarching, 54; overlapping, 16, 22, 54, 60, 87, 127; participation in, 77, 176; physical, 36, 66; positive feedback and, 51; practical imperatives of, 63–67; reciprocal relations in, 62, 227; regulation in, 53; relations of parts of, 46–47; relations to circumstances in, 181; relations to other

Systems (*continued*)
members in, 16, 151; resources for, 83; respect to partners in, 134; responsibility to, 82; risk of exceeding range of viable behaviors, 61; roles in, 1; securing resources for maintenance, 63; self-equilibrating, 182; social, 62, 69, 113, 183; stabilizing mechanisms in, 61–63, 182, 186; stages in, 68; static, 50, 201; steady state, 68, 69; subsystems in, 52, 62; supply of services and resources, 63; survival of, 62; sustainability of reciprocal causal relations of members in, 181; sustaining, 50, 61; sustaining establishment reciprocities in, 63; teleology and, 67–70; totalizing, 22; unaggregated, 18; unitary, 55; utility value in, 70
Systems theory. *See* Communitarianism

Teleology: intrinsic to mechanical systems, 67–70
Testability, 55–57
Theology: rational, 11
Thought: Being in, 11; coherence of, 2; organization of, 1; practical, 245; reception of sensory data and, 3; regulative principles and, 7; religious, 95; in thinking of material and moral states of affairs, 3
Thrasymachus, 185, 186
Timaeus (Plato), 60
Time: in beauty, 215–217; categorial profile of, 19; contiguity in, 85; formlessness of, 215, 216; necessary for motion, 12; reality of, 84
Tolerance, 21, 247
Treatise of Human Nature (Hume), 36
Trust: abuse of, 75; as confidence in partners, 80; morality and, 124; mutual, 96
Truth, 246, 247; as accuracy of representation, 270n1; a priori, 6–7; conceptual, 6, 7; deflationary theory of, 173; engendering, 178; and error, 171–174; necessary, 37, 43; negations of, 7; practical value of, 75; restrictive; telling, 107, 156
Tyranny, 186

Universality, 23
Utilitarianism, 193–194, 260

Value(s): abiding, 63; aesthetic, 201–219; ascribed to material things, 65; belief in, 64; circumstances and, 3; consequential, 70–72; determinate, 45; embedded in fact, 105; enabling, 114; of ends, 67; enduring, 105; entanglement and, 99, 100; epistemic, 103; ethical, 103; fact and, 3, 105; fairness as, 152; inception of, 3; of inquiry, 105; instrumental, 63, 70–72, 114, 158; intrinsic, 63, 64, 70–72; market, 260; measured, 45; measured by effects on selves, 65; moral, 105, 141; organizing, 68; origin of, 141; practical, 61–72, 79, 101, 102, 140, 177, 190, 266; principal, 68, 152, 186–187; procedural, 102, 103–104; of properties, 46; ranking, 4; regulatory, 105; relationships and, 3; signature, 89–94; social, 105; of systems, 78
Variability: within limits, 23; restricted, 23
Veblen, Thorsten, 254, 255
Velocity, 49, 50
Verificationism, 215, 216
Volition, 237
Vulnerability: derivation of *should* and *ought* from *is* in, 139

Weber, Max, 253, 255
Whole, the, 55; inference of properties of, 56; properties of, 56; spacetime and, 55; unity of, 55
Whorf hypothesis, 13
Will: affirmation of value and, 65; choice of ideas to organize experience and, 25; constraint by reason on, 76; defining, 99; discipline of, 76; free, 231, 236–240; general, 22, 167; human, 25; moral, 82; purity of, 90; stubborn, 66, 227
Willing: absence of necessary condition and, 74; actions, 74
"Will to Believe, The," (James), 246
Wittgenstein, Ludwig, 39, 42, 173